VTOL

MILITARY RESEARCH

AIRCRAFT

VTOL
MILITARY RESEARCH
AIRCRAFT

MIKE ROGERS

ORION BOOKS

New York

Published in the United States in 1989 by Orion
Books, a division of Crown Publishers, Inc., 201 East
50th Street, New York, New York 10022

Originally published in 1989 in Great Britain by
Haynes Publishing Group

ORION and colophon are trademarks of Crown
Publishers, Inc.

Manufactured in England by J.H. Haynes & Co. Ltd

Library of Congress Cataloging-in-Publication Data

Rogers, Mike.
    VTOL military research aircraft.
    1. Vertically rising aircraft. 2. Airplanes,
Military, I. Title.
UG1242.V47R64   1990   358.4'183   89-23143
ISBN 0-517-57684-8

10 9 8 7 6 5 4 3 2 1
First American Edition

CONTENTS

PREFACE

VTOL is a fascinating subject. I have had great fun writing this book, and I hope it is as much fun to read. During the time spent researching the subject, I have been impressed by two things.

First, the very high degree of co-operation between aircraft manufacturers worldwide. There were, and still are, plentiful exchanges of ideas at frequent meetings, conferences and symposia. Test facilities were made available, hardware from one programme was often loaned or donated to another, and test pilots about to fly a new design would train on an existing experimental type belonging to another company, sometimes on the other side of the world.

Secondly, the kindness of companies, museums, and individuals. When I have asked them for information, drawings, and photos, they have always responded with tremendous enthusiasm and great generosity. Without their help this book could not have happened.

Mike Rogers
Bristol

Numerical data

In describing so many aircraft, it is not possible to give all relevant numerical data, nor to specify the exact conditions under which each piece of data is true.

Most of the aircraft in this book were experimental, and were modified to try out new configurations. Data may differ between similar prototypes or between updates of one particular aircraft.

At any one time, an aircraft would have many different weights: empty weight, maximum VTOL weight, maximum STOL weight and maximum conventional take-off weight. Each weight would vary greatly with airfield temperature and altitude. Similarly, an aircraft's engines could have several different power ratings: nominal rated power, maximum power, and emergency short-term maximum power. These again would change with temperature and altitude.

Figures quoted in the text are chosen as typical values which are of use when comparing similar aircraft. Quantities are specified in the units current during the years that the aircraft were flying, generally pounds, feet and inches, miles per hour, knots, and horse power. Conversions are given when relevant.

Source material

Wherever possible, material has been obtained from the manufacturer or responsible testing authority. Other material has come from a variety of sources, and every effort has been made to check accuracy.

It is difficult to establish copyright on material which may be thirty years old. Where possible, copyright has been traced and purchased.

Picture quality

The originals of the photos used in this book date from the fifties and sixties, and in some cases the quality has suffered over the years. In the selection of photos, historical content has taken precedence over quality.

All hovering aircraft, especially jets, kick up debris from the ground and recirculate it. Jets also create a lot of heat haze below the aircraft. These effects resemble photo defects but are in fact true representations of vertical flight.

8

1 INTRODUCTION

VTOL

The year was 1954. The piston engine, which had powered the world's aircraft for half a century, was giving way to the gas turbine. Civil airlines were flying the radial-engined Stratocruiser and Constellation, but would soon change to jets and turboprops. The giant B-36 bomber was still in service, with the eight-jet B-52 about to enter production as its replacement. Fighter aircraft were already jet-powered and the straight wing was being replaced by the swept wing. The aeroplane was evolving gradually to take advantage of the greater speed and range afforded by the new engines. Its shape was changing, becoming more smooth and sleek, but its overall layout of fuselage, wings, and tail remained unchanged. Each flight started with a long horizontal take-off run and ended with a horizontal landing.

In April and May of that year, in a sudden blaze of publicity, almost every newspaper and magazine carried pictures of the US Navy's new 'Vertical Riser' fighters, shown streaking skyward to intercept attacking enemy bombers. It appeared that the conventional fighter, capable only of horizontal take-off, horizontal flight, and laborious near-horizontal climb, had been superseded. The new Vertical Risers would take off vertically and climb vertically to their gaol. On completion of mission, they would land vertically, tail first. They needed no runways, they could be placed at short notice to defend any potential target, they could be sited in the middle of a city, or even on board a small ship. Here was a man-carrying interceptor fighter with most of the characteristics of a missile. The whole book of air defence had been rewritten overnight.

In reality the publicity was premature. The Vertical Risers ran into a succession of problems and were grounded in 1956. The Lockheed XFV-1 Salmon had cost $12 million and the Convair XFY-1 Pogo had cost $8 million. Both tabs were picked up by the US Navy. It is tempting to write off the whole exercise as an expensive failure, but this would not be fair. Lockheed and Convair had been probing the unknown, both had succeeded in building aircraft which flew both horizontally and vertically, one had demonstrated vertical take-off and landing, and both companies had learned many important lessons to be used in future VTOL exercises. The VTOL age had dawned, and everyone was aware of it.

Several other manufacturers were busy on their own experimental VTOL aircraft. In the years up to 1960 more than twenty different types of piloted VTOL aircraft flew successfully. The next decade saw a further

fifteen, but after 1970 interest waned and only three more new types flew. Overall, a total of over forty different types of piloted experimental VTOL aircraft were flown. Of all these types, only two entered production and became operational, and one more is still being developed. Three out of forty sounds a very poor success rate, but it is not as bad as it seems.

The conventional aeroplane was fifty years old, and had evolved a long way in that time. The helicopter was twenty years old

The Lockheed XFV-1 Salmon tailsitter poses in vertical take-off position. The XFV-1 was a contemporary of the B-47 Stratojet. (Lockheed)

and it too had evolved. Each was carefully designed and optimised to do its job. The VTOL aircraft was in competition with both. It had to take off and land like a helicopter yet fly as fast, safely, and efficiently as a conventional aircraft. It had to catch up all those years of development and be as good as both of its ancestors.

One might have expected the VTOL aircraft to evolve in the same way as the aeroplane or the helicopter, but at an accelerated rate. This did not happen. There are about fifteen different known ways to achieve VTOL, and each of these received attention. The VTOL aircraft resulted not from gradual evolution, but rather from trying every possibility in the hope of finding one which would work.

The great diversity of VTOL techniques is illustrated in the accompanying figure. The various techniques are divided into five major groups and some seventeen subgroups for convenience of discussion. Most of the configurations shown were made and achieved hovering flight. Also included are a number of STOL types, which qualify for inclusion because they supported a significant part of their weight on engine thrust.

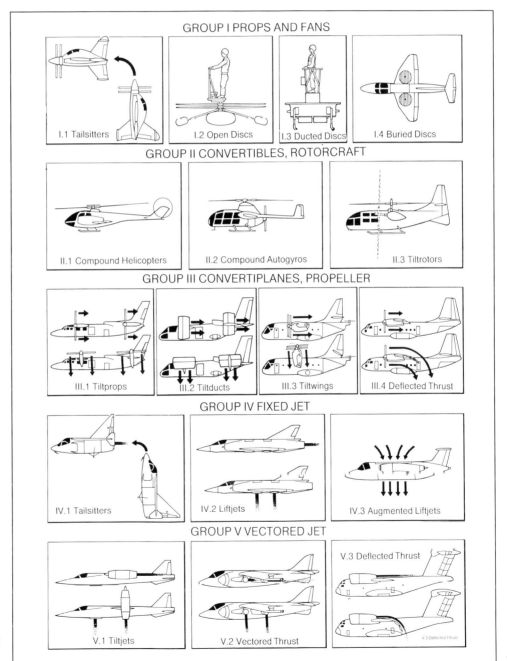

VTOL aircaft may be categorised into groups and sub-groups, as shown here. (Author)

VTOL

Group I includes the early disc-lifted aircraft. A lifting disc may be a rotor, a propeller, or a fan. These are divided into four subgroups:

I.1 Tailsitters — the glamorous XFV-1 and XFY-1 which ushered in the VTOL era.
I.2 Open discs
I.3 Ducted discs
I.4 Buried discs

The open and ducted discs were used to make small flying platforms intended for battlefield personal transportation and as observation platforms. As disc-lift techniques developed, it became possible to lift conventional aircraft using discs buried in the wings.

Group II includes those aircraft which are related to helicopters and use rotors for vertical lift. Helicopters take off vertically using engine power to generate lift, but they do not in general make use of aerodynamic lift in forward flight. The types included here are those which use the rotor for vertical take-off, but which are propelled and supported by other means when in cruising flight. There are three sub-groups:

II.1 Compound autogyros — rotorcraft with free-wheeling rotors and using aerodynamic lift.
II.2 Compound helicopters — rotorcraft with driven rotors, additional means of propulsion, and using aerodynamic lift.
II.3 Tiltrotors — rotorcraft with rotors which tilt to produce either lift for vertical flight or thrust for wing-supported flight.

In theory group II should include a fourth sub-group for rotors which fold, stop, stow, or otherwise dematerialise, but despite the existence of several projects, hardware has yet to fly.

A distinction must be made between the rotor and the propeller. The rotor is articulated by two hinges which allow it to flap and drag, and it has means of controlling both collective and cyclic pitch. Rigid rotors do not have hinges but are otherwise similar. Propellers have rigid blades without hinges, and may have collective but not cyclic pitch control.

Group III consists of propeller-driven craft where the thrust generated by the propellers is horizontal in forward flight and is directed downwards for vertical flight. There are four sub-groups:

III.1 Tiltprop — Thrust is directed by tilting the propellers only.
III.2 Tiltduct — The propellers are in ducts, and the propduct assemblies tilt to direct thrust. The ducts usually contain control surfaces.
III.3 Tiltwing — The whole wing tilts, taking engines and propellers with it.
III.4 Deflected thrust — The props stay where they are and their thrust is deflected by flaps.

The aircraft in sub-group III.4 were strictly STOL rather than VTOL, but they did support much of their weight by engine thrust alone.

Groups II and III were known as convertiplanes because they could convert from using rotor or prop lift in hovering flight to using aerodynamic lift in forward flight. Group II consists of aircraft which were basically helicopters and converted for forward flight, whereas group III aircraft were optimised for cruising flight and could convert to vertical flight.

Group IV includes all jet aircraft with fixed jets, that is jets which have fixed directions of thrust. There are three sub-groups:

IV.1 Tailsitters — Aircraft which take off and land with the nose pointing vertically upward. The same engine provides lift when vertical and thrust when horizontal.
IV.2 Liftjets — Aircraft with separate downward thrusting lift engines.
IV.3 Augmented jets — Liftjets with thrust augmented by some means.

Group V consists of those aircraft in which the jet thrust is progressively tilted to obtain a smooth transition from vertical thrust to forward thrust. There are three sub-groups:

V.1 Tiltjets — The engines may be tilted to point forward for horizontal flight or upward for vertical flight.
V.2 Vectored jets — The engines remain horizontal, but thrust may be directed rearward or downward by rotating nozzles.
V.3 Deflected thrust — Engine thrust may be directed downward by flaps.

Groups V.1 and V.2 include hybrid types which are primarily tiltjets or vectored jets, but which also use lift engines when in vertical flight. The aircraft in group V.3, like those in group III.4 are STOL rather than VTOL. They are included here because they support much of their weight on engine thrust.

These groupings are made purely for convenience of discussion. There are many different ways in which VTOL aircraft can and have been categorised, and each has its merits. None are perfect, and it is always possible to find an aircraft which is clearly VTOL-related but does not belong in any one category.

There are two aircraft which are difficult to categorise here. One is the Vought

The Hiller VZ-1 Pawnee flying platform was lifted by contra-rotating propellers within a duct. (Department of Defense)

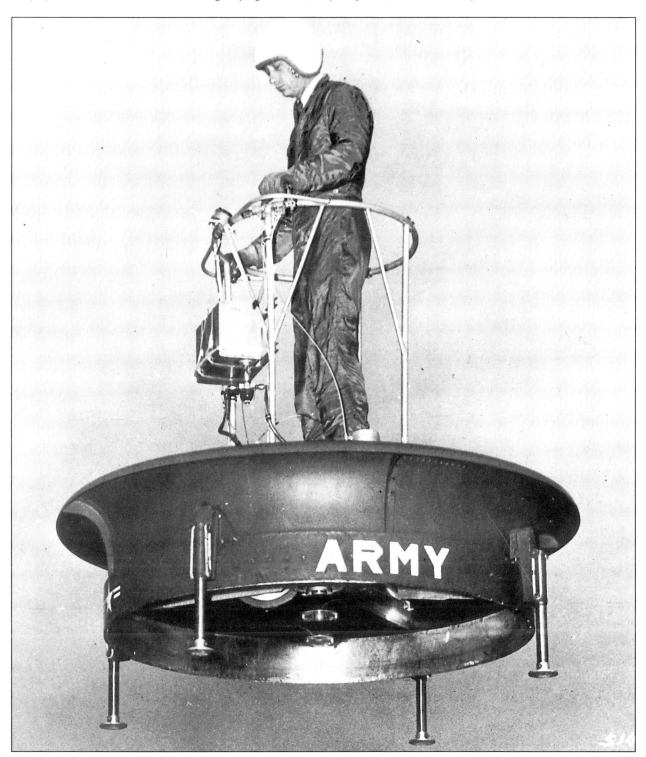

VTOL

XF5U-1 Flying Pancake, which was neither a tailsitter nor a flat riser, and had large propellers which were articulated like rotors. The XF5U-1 never flew, but the V-173, a smaller test vehicle, did. The other is the Hunting H126 research aircraft, which was used to investigate low-speed flight using exhaust-blown wings and control surfaces. It was not a VTOL aircraft, but it is of interest because it used a VTOL-type reaction control system.

Also difficult to categorise are the many test rigs. Some of these were for ground tests only, some flew tethered, and many flew in piloted free flight. Most test rigs were related to specific design programmes, and it is simplest to group them with the aircraft programme they supported.

Later in this book, the sequence is changed a little so that the types which were flying at the same time and which shared common problems are discussed together. The tailsitters, both propeller and jet appear in the same chapter. The disc-lifted platforms and fans are grouped together. The rotor-craft and the propeller craft each have a

chapter to themselves. Lift and tilt jets share a chapter, since they share common engine types. Vectored jets and deflected jets are similar in principle, and share a chapter. The final chapter describes those types which survived and went into production.

There was a lot of activity in all five major groups during the fifties and sixties. The accompanying figure shows the aircraft in each group and the years over which they were actively flying. Only one bar is shown for each aircraft type, and this may represent just one aircraft or several similar aircraft. The start of a bar indicates the date of the first flight, and its finish indicates the termination of test flying. This is only a rough indication of programme chronology. Each aircraft had several first flights: first vertical, first horizontal, first transition, and first complete vertical-horizontal-vertical. Most programmes were interrupted for redesign or wind-tunnel development, so the bars do not necessarily represent continuity of a flying programme.

In groups I.1, propeller tailsitters, and IV.1, jet tailsitters, flying began in the

This chart shows the progress made in the development of the various groups of disc-lift VTOL aircraft over the years 1950 to 1980. Disc-lift includes rotors, prop-rotors, and propellers. (Author)

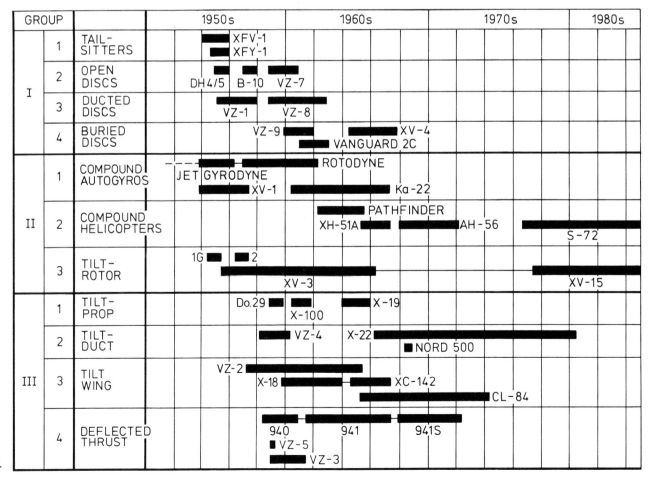

mid-fifties and ceased in 1959. The problems encountered were so fundamental that they could not be solved, and technology overtook them by making flat risers possible.

The fan-lifted platforms of groups I.2 and I.3 lasted almost a decade, in the search for simple lightweight military personnel transportation. They were superseded by troop-carrying helicopters, it being logistically easier to transport a platoon in a single helicopter than to give them a platform each. There was also a training problem. It is easier to expand military forces in times of crisis if hi-tech equipment can be used by low-tech personnel, and flying the platforms was never a low-tech task.

The jet-fans of group I.3 were flown during the sixties and were proposed as the ideal add-on to convert any aircraft, civil or military to VTOL by the addition of pods,

lumps, and bumps in various places. Work ceased by 1970, but the concept of the jet-fan was sound and was absorbed by the P.1127 programme to emerge as the fanjet engine.

In group II, work started on the auto-gyro convertiplanes of sub-group II.1 early after the Second World War, but was over by 1960. Slow progress had been made, performance was limited to helicopter speeds, and helicopter technology had caught up. There were a few attempts at compound helicopters in group II.2 during the sixties, but performance again was limited and did not warrant the additional weight, complexity, and cost of the additional wings and propulsion.

The tiltrotors of group II.3 were in theory able to overcome the helicopter speed barrier. Work began in the mid-fifties, re-

The British Fairey Rotodyne was a compound autogyro. It is seen here in its civil role as an urban transport. (Westland)

search flying continued through to the mid-sixties at relatively low speeds, and flying resumed in the late seventies with the more practical aircraft made possible by advances in technology. The group is still active, with series production imminent. The time elapsed from first design proposal to first production aircraft is some forty years. The original concept was fundamentally correct, but had to wait for the technology to make it practical.

Group III.1, tiltprops, included only two true VTOL aircraft, and these were two stages of the same programme. Flying started in 1960 and ceased in 1965. The tiltprop on its own was difficult to control, and gave way to the tiltducts of group III.2. Three tiltduct aircraft were built, and flying

in this group spanned the years 1958 to 1980. Although no tiltducts went into production, the research aircraft undertook many test programmes and provided useful data on flying characteristics, power requirements, stability, control, and instrumentation for use in other programmes.

Group III.3 included six tiltwing types, five of which flew and two of which were developed almost to production status. Early work started in the mid-fifties, flying and ground tests continued into the sixties, and evaluation of small production batches took place from 1964 to 1975. Both contenders for eventual production came very close to entering service, but neither was actually ordered.

In group III.4 the deflected thrust

The Bell XV-3 was used for many years to investigate tiltrotor technology.
(Bell Helicopter Textron)

Early tests on the VZ-4 Doak 16 proved the advantages of the tilt-duct over the tilt-prop and provided much useful test data to be used in later designs.
(Department of Defense)

aircraft were STOL rather than VTOL. Two small research aircraft were tried in the late fifties, but work on them was discontinued. Larger, more conventional transport aircraft were flown during the sixties, and a small production batch was made. These were assessed both for military and for civil use, but no orders were taken.

Group IV.1, jet tailsitters, had the same disadvantages as prop tailsitters, and were discontinued very early on to make way for the flat rising liftjets of group IV.2 and the augmented liftjets of group IV.3. True VTOL

liftjet flying went on from 1954 to 1966, and lift engines were used though to 1972, featuring in experimental STOL aircraft and to supplement the lift of vectored thrust types.

In group V.1, only two tiltjets were actually flown. The first of these was a very early test vehicle which never made full conversions, and flew in 1954. The second was a much later design which flew during 1964 and 1965. Although successful in proving that VTOL supersonic aircraft were possible, its test programme was not

The Ling-Temco-Vought XC-142 was the largest of the tilt-wings and nearly made it into production. (Vought Corp)

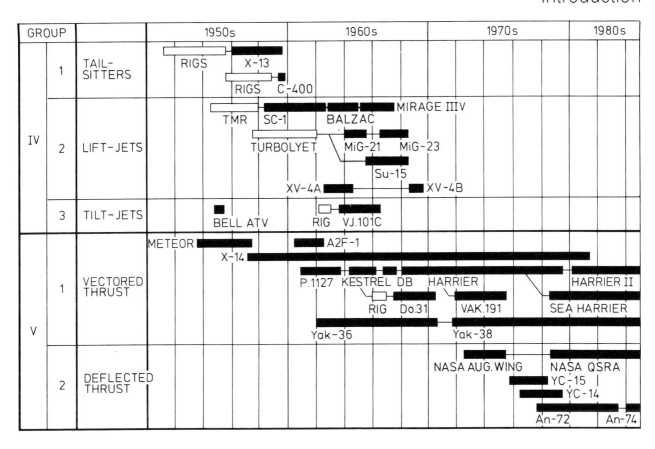

GROUP			1950s	1960s	1970s	1980s
IV	1	TAIL-SITTERS	RIGS X-13 RIGS C-400			
	2	LIFT-JETS	TMR SC-1 TURBOLYET	MIRAGE IIIV BALZAC MiG-21 MiG-23 Su-15 XV-4A XV-4B		
	3	TILT-JETS	BELL ATV	RIG VJ.101C		
V	1	VECTORED THRUST	METEOR X-14	A2F-1 P.1127 KESTREL DB HARRIER RIG Do.31 VAK.191 Yak-36 Yak-38	HARRIER II SEA HARRIER	
	2	DEFLECTED THRUST			NASA AUG. WING NASA QSRA YC-15 YC-14 An-72	An-74

Progress in the development of jet VTOL aircraft is charted here in the various groups, over the period 1950 to 1980. (Author)

Many programmes made use of test rigs. This is the SNECMA Atar Volant, which provided experience of VTOL for the Coléoptère programme. The C400 P1 was remotely controlled and the P2 was piloted. (Copyright reserved)

completed and development was not pursued.

Group V.2, vectored thrust, includes the VTOL fighter success stories. Work on vectored thrust during the late fifties led quickly to the P.1127 and its descendents, which dominate present-day VTOL fighter markets. Vectored thrust was also used in conjunction with liftjet engines in two other fighter aircraft and in a medium transport.

The final group, V.3, includes conventionally configured aircraft in which the jet exhausts can be deflected downward to support an appreciable part of the aircraft weight. Experiments were made as early as 1952, and deflecting tailpipes were included in one late fifties production design, but were later deleted. The late seventies brought a crop of medium-weight transports using thrust deflection over or under flaps. One of these types is in service as a STOL, and another is being used for QSTOL (quiet STOL) research.

Groups I, II, and III, the propeller and rotor type, were largely dominated by North American work, most of this being for transportation. Groups IV and V, the jets, were dominated by Europe and Russia, with emphasis on fighter aircraft. This may reflect some geographical influence on military thinking, the Americans perhaps stressing the need for transport to remote areas and to ships, while the Europeans needed dispersal of fighters in a small and crowded theatre of war.

The French Coléoptère was a
jet tailsitter which made use
of an annular wing.
(Rolls-Royce, Bristol)

The Bell X-14 was the first
aircraft to hover using
vectored thrust.
(Rolls-Royce, Bristol)

The Short SC-1 carried out
early liftjet research.
(Shorts)

Although many, if not most, projects were abandoned, they were not necessarily failures. Most of them succeeded in attaining their objectives as experimental or research aircraft. Very often the work done by a project in one group would benefit all groups, and each design team could draw on the results of all previous experiments. While the success of a particular group may be judged by the placing of orders for operational aircraft, the success of any individual project can only be assessed against programme objectives.

In the 1950s the first objective was to have a test rig lift a few feet off the ground, hover briefly, and descend gently back to the ground. If it did this without catching fire, falling over, or vanishing sideways at high velocity, then it was considered a success. It was no mean feat to devise a control system which would hold a VTOL vehicle in a stable attitude. The early rigs were as light as possible, consisting only of engines, fuel tanks, pilot's seat, controls, and supporting framework. Even so, endurance was usually only a few minutes.

As the art of VTOL developed, the objectives of each programme became progressively more complex. Greater weight had to be lifted for longer periods of time, so more powerful and more efficient engines had to be developed. Control methods and control systems had to be improved, to reduce the level of pilot skill and concentration required. Techniques had to be tried first on models, then on small experimental test vehicles, before applying the lessons learned to full-size prototype aircraft.

Most of this very expensive development work was funded by government agencies, and it was common for any one project to be funded by several different agencies as work progressed and as different applications were found. For example, the prop tailsitters were funded by the US Navy for shipboard convoy defence, the flying platforms were funded first by the US Army and later by the Navy, and the XV-4 by the Army and later by NASA. The X-19, X-22, and XC-142 all took part in a tri-service (Army, Navy, Air Force) evaluation programme. Programmes in other countries also were mainly government funded. One advantage of government funding was that it removed commercial barriers and made it easier to pool knowledge.

There were two notable exceptions where funding was private. The first was the Bell VTOL ATV, which was the first jet flat riser and contributed much via the X-14 to vectored jet programmes. The second was

VTOL

the P.1127, which in its early years was a joint venture between Bristols and Hawkers (both private venture), and the US Mutual Weapons Development Agency under Colonel Chapman. At that time there was no funding from its home government, and it is more by the perseverance of individuals than by government encouragement that this most successful design survived.

All aircraft in all groups have contributed to the better understanding of VTOL, its problems, and solutions. Many of the aircraft flew for extended test programmes, and were used as flying testbeds for the development of instrumentation and control systems. Several types got very near to production, but, for a variety of reasons, were not actually produced. To date, all production types come from group V, and include the Harrier and all its derivatives, the Yak-38 and the STOL An-72/74. Group II.3 should soon yield large-scale production of the V-22 Osprey.

Vectored thrust was used to good effect on the Hawker P.1127 Kestrel.
(British Aerospace)

The German Dornier Do 31 transport used both vectored jets and liftjets. It had the greatest lifting capability of any Western VTOL aircraft. (Rolls-Royce, Bristol)

23

2 VERTICAL FLIGHT

Theory of Vertical Flight

There are three ways of remaining suspended in mid-air. One is to displace enough air to equal your weight, so that you float. You are then a balloon. A second way is to throw parts of yourself downward, causing a net upward force. You are then a rocket, but not for long; on this planet, gravitation is too strong, you soon run out of disposable mass, and you cease to be self-supporting. The third way is to grab handfuls of air and throw them downward. If you grab enough air and throw it down fast enough, you can create an upward force equal to your weight. This is known as flying.

immediately above it. The same physical law holds: upward force is equal to the downward momentum imparted to the air. The more air the aircraft can grab, and the faster it can throw it downward, the greater the weight it can support.

An aircraft can support the same weight if it throws a little air down quickly or a lot of air down slowly, but it requires more power to throw a little quickly than it does to throw a lot slowly. The lift is mv (mass multiplied by velocity), but the power required is $\frac{1}{2}mv^2$ (half mass multiplied by velocity squared).

It follows that the most efficient hovering aircraft will be the one with the largest diameter rotor, because it has a large area

Right: The power required to lift a VTOL aircraft is a function of disc loading, as shown here. Downdraught velocity is directly related to power, and is shown on the same axis. Each dot represents the disc loading and power of a particular aircraft. The distance of each dot above the line indicates the power reserve of that aircraft. (Author)

In normal aerodynamic flight, the amount of air thrown down depends on the span of the wing, its shape, its angle of attack, and the speed at which it sweeps through the air. In theory, given its span, shape, angle, and speed, it should be possible to calculate the lift, but in practice it is usual and more convenient to talk in terms of lift and drag coefficients. It is still true to say that the wing lift is equal to the total downward momentum (mass multiplied by velocity) imparted to the air.

A hovering aircraft flies by exactly the same mechanism, but it can only grab the air

and can grab a lot of air. The more air it can grab, the slower it needs to throw it down, and the less power it uses. A propeller with its much smaller disc area can grab less air and must throw it down faster for the same lift, and the narrow exhaust stream of a jet engine has to move even faster and is less efficient again.

It is actually possible to calculate the power required to support any hovering aircraft, given its weight and total disc area (the total area swept by all rotors or propellers). In practice, rather more power is required so as to allow for rotor or propeller

There were several rocket-powered VTOL vehicles. This one is the Sud-Aviation 'Ludion' rocket-powered platform on French army trials at Melun-Villaroche. Rocket vehicles have severely limited endurance and are not considered to be aircraft for the purposes of this book. (Sud Aviation)

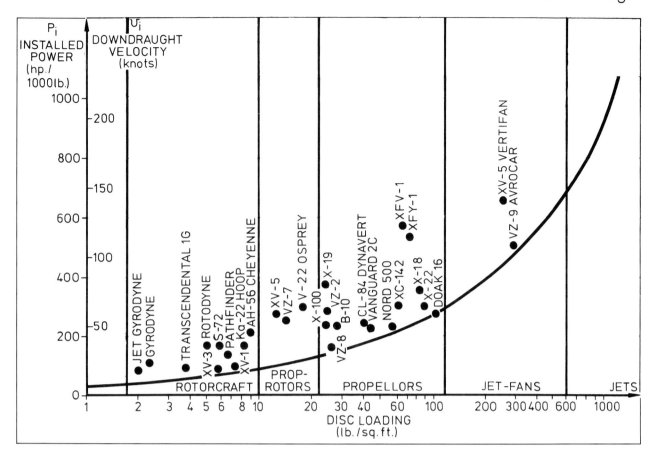

losses, and between 20 per cent and 50 per cent should be added to the theoretical figure.

It is also possible to present this calculation as a graph to cover all aircraft. The horizontal scale of the graph is graduated in

The Ryan YO-51 Dragonfly, made in 1940, shows how conventional aircraft may use full-span leading and trailing edge flaps to achieve extreme STOL. Many conventional aircraft have achieved impressive STOL performance by using aerodynamic aids. STOL aircraft are included in this book only if they are closely related to VTOL types or if they use VTOL techniques. (Ryan)

disc loading, pounds per square foot of rotor or propeller, and the vertical scale may be read in horse power required for every 1,000 pounds of weight. The vertical scale also gives the downdraught velocity.

This sort of graph is used in the early design stages to help predict aircraft performance. As the design progresses, this very simple approach will be replaced by much more detailed calculations based on the measured performance of rotors or props under simulated conditions.

It is also very useful when comparing different types of VTOL aircraft. The broad categories: rotorcraft, platforms, propeller craft, jetfans, augmented jets, fanjets, and jets may be compared in terms of disc loading, power requirement, and down draught velocity. It becomes clear that rotorcraft are the most efficient, and that both power requirement and downdraught velocity increase rapidly for other types with progressively higher disc loadings. As the power requirement per unit weight increases, so the engine is eating the fuel mass much faster. A helicopter can hover for typically twenty minutes on a tenth of its fuel load, a propeller-driven tiltwing will hover for five minutes, and a jet VTOL may burn a tenth of its fuel in thirty seconds.

Individual aircraft may be plotted on the graph, as points representing disc loading in pounds per square foot and available horsepower per thousand pounds of weight. Each aircraft should appear above the curve by an amount representing its power margin. It becomes easy to compare the power margins of aircraft, even if they are of very different types. It is useful to have a generous power margin, both for control and so that the aircraft can survive failure of one engine.

The graph as plotted represents conditions on a standard day at sea level. Flying in hotter conditions or at higher altitude requires more power, and the power margin of an aircraft is a direct indication of its likely performance under 'hot and high' conditions. For instance, a 16 per cent power margin should just allow an aircraft to hover at 10,000 feet.

The figures shown relate to hovering in free air, or out of ground effect (OGE). Rotorcraft hovering in ground effect (IGE), with the rotor less than one diameter above the ground, may experience up to double the OGE lift due to ground effect. Propeller craft tend not to have their props within one diameter of the ground, but both they and jet aircraft benefit from other ground effects, as the downward columns of air or gas hit the ground, spread out across the ground in sheets, collide with each other, and fountain upward again. If the upward fountain impinges on the underside of fuselage or wings, its pressure will support some of the aircraft weight. In many designs, flaps and strakes were added to make best use of this bonus, which sometimes amounted to one third of aircraft weight.

The actual lift obtained in any one design was not easy to predict with any accuracy, and it was usual to perform extensive wind-tunnel and rig tests, both on models and on full-size aircraft. The results of these tests would provide more accurate lift estimates as the design progressed, and also predicted the effects of ground air flow on stability.

Most ground effects tended to increase lift, since the ground prevents air from flowing downward, and tends to create a pressure cushion. Airflow out across the ground, however, can create a phenomenon known as suck-down which causes negative lift. Suck-down was experienced on low-wing aircraft such as the Bell X-14 on its original short undercarriage. It is not a problem when the wing is well clear of the ground.

Jet aircraft suffer from practical disadvantages due to ground effect. The hot exhaust gases tend to recirculate and become re-ingested by the engines, raising the intake temperatures and reducing engine thrust. Early VTOL aircraft were operated over louvred surfaces which diverted the hot exhaust gases away from the aircraft. The high velocity jet exhausts could cause surface erosion, and various types of temporary landing pads and mats were used to protect the surface of the ground. Any surface debris such as loose pieces of mud, stone, concrete, or grass could be kicked up by the exhausts and recirculated into the engine air intakes. Such effects were present only in a true vertical take-off or sustained hover, and could be avoided by letting the aircraft roll forward during take-off.

Control

An aircraft, in free flight, has six degrees of freedom. It can rotate in pitch, roll, or yaw, and it can translate (move) vertically, laterally, or fore-and-aft.

In normal aerodynamic flight, there is only forward motion, and the other five possible motions remain at zero. Usually the aircraft is designed so that it tends (when correctly trimmed) to keep these motions at zero, and if so it is said to be inherently stable. The function of the flight controls is to

Axis	Normal Flight	Hovering
Pitch	Stick to elevator	Stick to tail rotor active
Roll	Stick to flaps/ailerons	Stick to differential propeller pitch
Yaw	Pedals to rudder	Rudder pedals to flap/ailerons
Height	Power lever to engine	Power lever to engine and collective propeller pitch

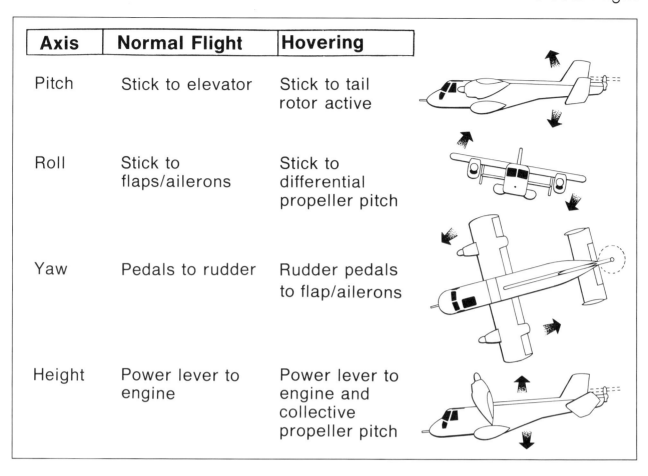

The pilot's controls must have the same apparent function in horizontal and vertical flight. In a tiltwing aircraft, the actual control functions have to change, as shown in this table. (Canadair)

deflect the aircraft away from its stable state, to make it turn or change altitude.

In hovering flight, all six motions should be zero, but there is no natural mechanism which provides inherent stability, and each motion must be continually controlled to hold it at zero. For instance, no matter how well the angle of pitch is set at zero, there will be a tendency for the nose to drift slowly either up or down, and this must be corrected. Like divergence will be experienced in roll and yaw. In addition, disturbances due to wind gusts must be corrected. The aircraft must have a control system which is capable of applying rotational forces (moments) to hold it stationary against likely disturbances.

When hovering, aircraft weight must be supported by a lift force vertically upward through its centre of gravity. Altitude may be controlled by changing the lift force. Excess lift force will cause upward acceleration until a rate of rise is attained at which drag equals excess force. Reduced lift force will similarly result in a steady rate of sink. Tilting the aircraft will tilt the lift force. The vertical component of lift will decrease, and engine power must be increased until vertical lift again equals weight. The horizontal component of the lift-force causes horizontal accel-

eration in the direction of tilt, and the aircraft accelerates horizontally to a velocity at which force equals drag.

In general, a hovering control system must hold the aircraft in an upright position at constant altitude, and must permit controlled deviations from this artificially stable state.

Any control system consists of sensors, intelligence, and controls. The sensors measure deviations from the required conditions, and the intelligence manipulates the control forces to attain, resume, or hold the required conditions in a smooth and acceptable manner.

In a hovering control system, the sensors might be gyros, radio altimeter and Doppler radar, or they might be the pilot's eyes and the seat of his pants. The intelligence might be electronic, mechanical, or cerebral. Usually in research aircraft the control system was a combination of electronic and human functions, but with varying apportionment of authority. In some VTOL research aircraft the pilot was in direct control, aided by an autostabiliser. In others the control system had full authority and was totally in control though accepting and implementing requests from the pilot.

VTOL

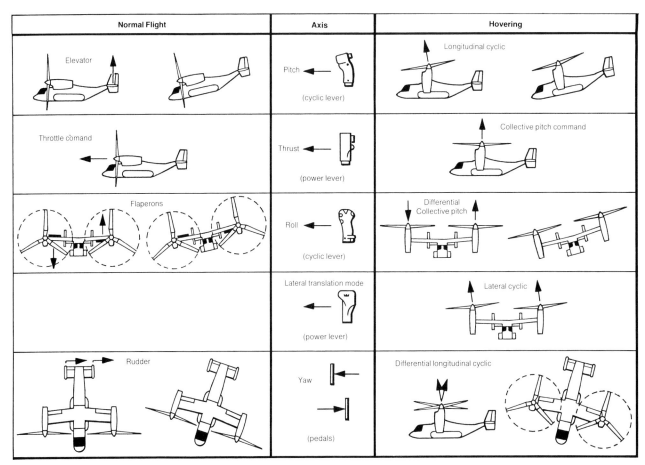

Normal Flight		Axis	Hovering	
Elevator		Pitch ← (cyclic lever)	Longitudinal cyclic	
Throttle command		Thrust ← (power lever)	Collective pitch command	
Flaperons		Roll ← (cyclic lever)	Differential Collective pitch	
		Lateral translation mode ← (power lever)	Lateral cyclic	
Rudder		Yaw ← (pedals)	Differential longitudinal cyclic	

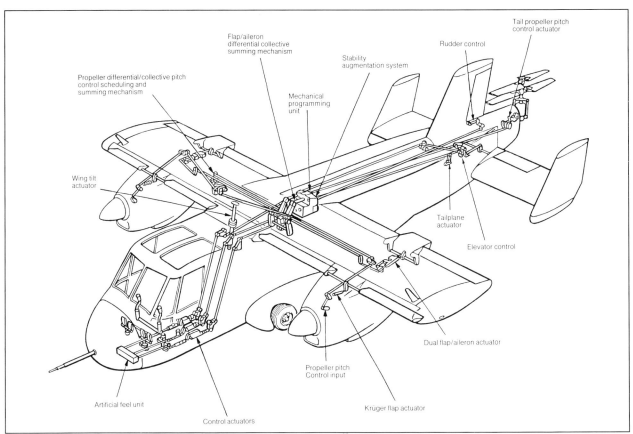

Tail propeller pitch control actuator

Rudder control

Flap/aileron differential collective summing mechanism

Stability augmentation system

Propeller differential/collective pitch control scheduling and summing mechanism

Mechanical programming unit

Wing tilt actuator

Tailplane actuator

Elevator control

Dual flap/aileron actuator

Propeller pitch Control input

Artificial feel unit

Control actuators

Krüger flap actuator

Much of the work done by VTOL research aircraft involved establishing the requirements of control systems, in terms of the necessary magnitude of control forces, the degree of pilot/autopilot sharing of authority, and the ways in which the autopilot should respond to pilot inputs. As always there were no ideally correct answers, since compromises had to be made. The control systems could not be made ideally effective, because the increase in response would result in overcorrection and oscillation. The pilot's controls should be low-geared to give him precision of control, but high-geared to give him large correction forces. The autopilot should have high authority so as to minimise the pilot's workload, but the pilot should have total authority in an emergency. These problems were approached in a variety of ways, and most VTOL research aircraft were provided with alternative systems to be compared and assessed by the pilot. In some cases the control system was arranged so that all parameters were continuously variable and could be adjusted by the pilot.

hover and in aerodynamic flight, and they also had to be controllable during transitions between horizontal and vertical flight in both directions. In some aircraft transitions were no problem, and the aerodynamic controls naturally took over from the hover controls (and vice-versa), but in others, especially in aircraft with tilting geometries, elaborate provision had to be made for the transfer of control between the two modes, whilst retaining all the requirements of control sensitivity and stability in all axes.

Many of the problems of control could be studied mathematically prior to the construction of an aircraft. The mathematical results would predict likely performance, but the real aircraft could have unexpected control couplings between the axes, or mechanical resonances necessitating control system readjustment or redesign. It would be hoped that the major problems would be discovered during ground runs and rig tests, before actual flights were attempted. Even after flying, many designs spent much time back in the wind tunnel trying ways of

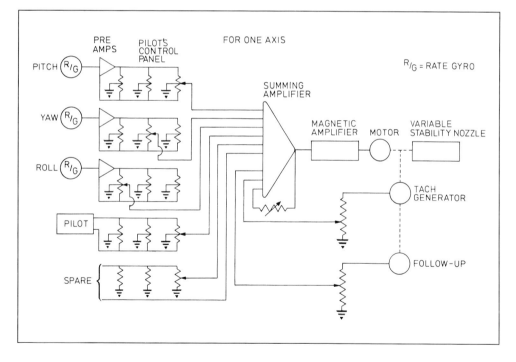

The actual method of applying control moments (rotational forces) depended very much on the way in which vertical lift was produced. In many cases the control forces were obtained by modifying the lifting devices. In others the control forces were separately generated, and in a few aircraft lift modification and separately generated forces were used in different axes.

VTOL aircraft had to be controllable in

solving stability problems before taking to the air once again.

The control channels for roll, pitch, and yaw were seldom independent. Gyroscopic effects due to rotating moving parts such as engines and propellers had the effect of converting a control moment in one axis to motion about a different axis. To obtain a movement in pitch and only pitch, it would be necessary to apply moments both in pitch (to

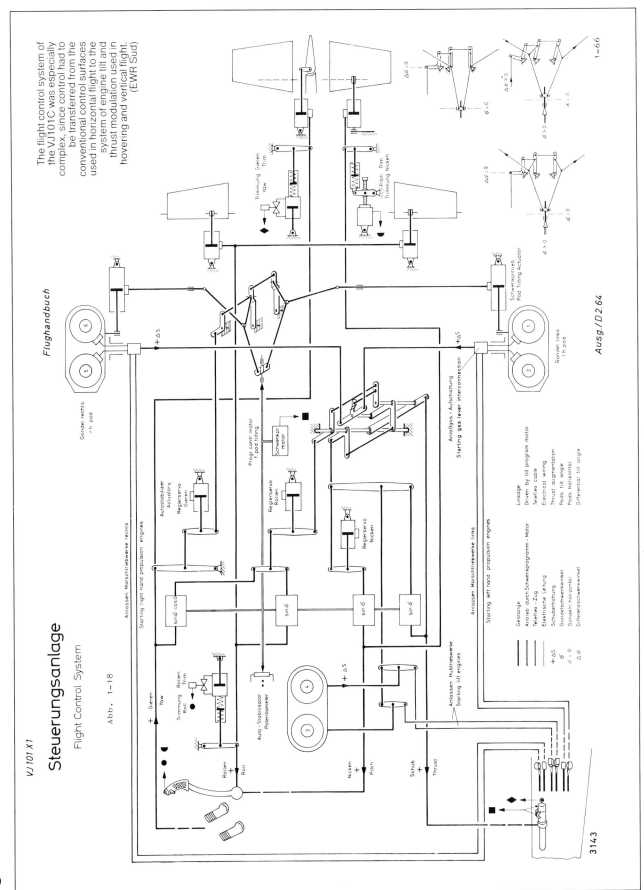

VJ 101 X1

Steuerungsanlage

Flight Control System

Abb. 1–18

Flughandbuch

The flight control system of the VJ101C was especially complex, since control had to be transferred from the conventional control surfaces used in horizontal flight to the system of engine tilt and thrust modulation used in hovering and vertical flight. (EWR Sud)

Ausg./D 2.64

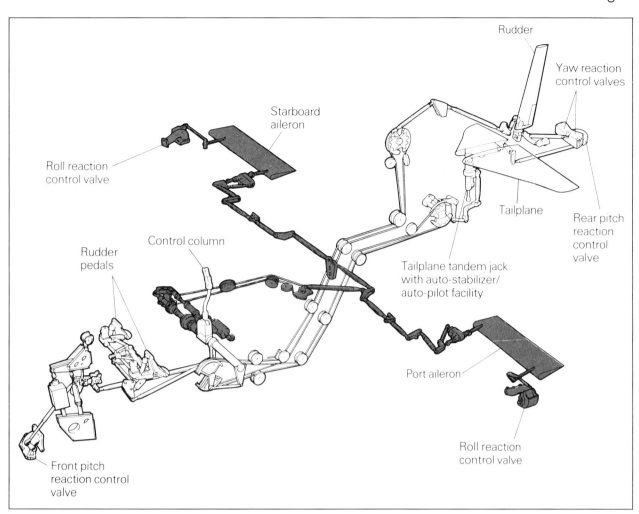

Rudder

Yaw reaction
control valves

Starboard
aileron

Roll reaction
control valve

Tailplane

Rear pitch
reaction
control
valve

Control column

Rudder
pedals

Tailplane tandem jack
with auto-stabilizer/
auto-pilot facility

Port aileron

Roll reaction
control valve

Front pitch
reaction control
valve

As always, the Harrier is the exception. Sir Sydney Camm's insistence on simplicity and battlefield survival produced a simple control system which could be flown either manually or with minimal autostabilisation. (British Aerospace)

move dead mass) and in yaw (to move in pitch engine parts which rotated about the roll axis). The control system would require cross-coupling between channels, and any one setting of parameters would be valid for only one engine speed. Even though the control system might be perfectly set up, it was possible to encounter gyroscopic effects so large that the control system, although trying to produce the appropriate correction, did not have sufficient power to hold the aircraft attitude. The control system would saturate at maximum — though still inadequate — power and the aircraft would be out of control. Aircraft which had contra-rotating propellers, rotors, or engine shafts did not suffer from gyroscopic effects, and were not so susceptible to control saturation problems.

Safety

Modern aircraft are designed to be failure-tolerant. The failure of any one component must not hazard life, and must not cause consequential failure of any other

component. This philosophy embraces all component parts of an aircraft, whether structural, mechanical, hydraulic, electrical, or electronic. Structural parts may fail slowly, in which case failure may be prevented by regular inspection. By contrast, other parts such as engines and electronics may fail without warning, and failure must be both expected and tolerated.

In normal aerodynamic flight at cruising altitude, most failures are non-catastrophic. At lower altitudes the consequences of failure become more severe, and the worst possible time for any failure is during take-off or landing when there is no time or space to recover from unplanned manoeuvres. Even so, during a conventional take-off or landing, it is possible to survive an engine failure.

Vertical flight is more hazardous than aerodynamic flight, since all lift comes directly from engine thrust and loss of an engine will result in immediate loss of lift, and may also result in an imbalance of lifting forces which causes a sudden high rate of roll or pitch.

A single-engined VTOL aircraft which

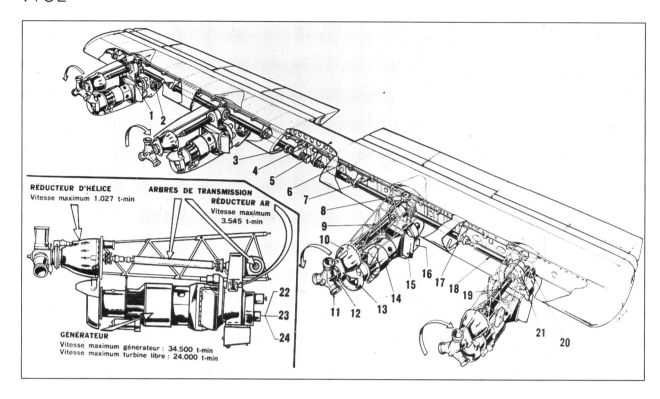

RÉDUCTEUR D'HÉLICE
Vitesse maximum 1.027 t-min

ARBRES DE TRANSMISSION
RÉDUCTEUR AR
Vitesse maximum 3.545 t-min

GÉNÉRATEUR
Vitesse maximum générateur : 34.500 t-min
Vitesse maximum turbine libre : 24.000 t-min

Most tiltwing and deflected-slipstream aircraft had interconnected mechanical power transmission systems for engine-out safety. This diagram shows how Breguet linked their transmissions. Note the sense of rotation of the airscrews for gyroscopic cancellation.
(Copyright reserved)

The power transmission shaft had to tolerate wing flexing. This Breguet rig tested the endurance of the shaft when rotating and transmitting power under flexure conditions.
(Copyright reserved)

lost all power whilst hovering at low level might survive the resultant heavy landing. It probably would not survive a loss of control at low level, or a loss of power during transition. In these cases the pilot must be able to eject and the aircraft must be left to its fate. Most small VTOL research aircraft were fitted with ejector seats, but the performance of early ejector seats at low speed and low level was not ideal. In the event of a control failure, the resultant powered pitch or roll could result in an unorthodox escape trajectory, as would ejection from a tailsitter, with or without the seat tilted. The X-14 was one of the few small aircraft not fitted with an ejector seat, and hovering flights were conducted only at very low altitude or at high altitude where recovery to normal flight would be possible.

Multi-engined multi-propeller VTOL craft generally had the engines driving via over-run clutches into a common mechanical power transmission system which in turn powered all the propellers. Loss of one engine was no problem, since the remaining engines could be run at an emergency rating and drive the propellers for a few minutes while the aircraft landed. The mechanical power transmission systems turned out to be more troublesome than expected, especially where power had to be transmitted through the aircraft wings. The flexure and vibration in the wing structure during full-power vertical flight did not make it a good environment for a highly stressed rotating shaft. While the mechanical power transmission system was a safety feature providing immunity from engine failure, a failure within the transmission itself could be catastrophic. Any mechanical failure of gearbox, shaft, hub, or propeller could instantly remove lift from one corner of the aircraft, producing very high moments in pitch and roll, and throwing it completely out of control. This might be tolerated as a necessary evil in a fighter aircraft where the pilot had an ejector seat, but would be intolerable in a personnel transport.

Rotorcraft have much greater safety margins in their ability to autorotate out of power failure situations. Multi-rotor craft are still dependent on mechanical linking of rotors, but less power need be transmitted, and mechanical stresses are lower. The great

Breguet tested the safety of their wing, flap and drive system under real conditions using this mobile rig. (Copyright reserved)

VTOL

The tilt-wing – here exemplified by the Canadair CL-84 – shared all the complications of the tilt-rotor but had the advantage that lift and control were enhanced by the propellers blowing air over the wing surfaces.

amount of kinetic energy stored in the rotors as flywheels allows the pilot greater time to respond to power loss.

Multi-engined jet aircraft usually relied on the automatic control system to compensate for engine failure, generally putting all engines near to the failed one on maximum emergency thrust and adjusting the others for balanced lift. With a large number of lifting engines and plenty of excess thrust over weight, sustained flight would be possible. With only a few lifting engines and a small excess of thrust over weight, the loss of one engine would reduce lift to a value less than aircraft weight, resulting in a controlled fast sink and a heavy landing.

Most VTOL aircraft had a high degree of autostabiliser authority, and a total failure of the autostabiliser could drive the aircraft into the ground with the pilot powerless to intervene. Usually the autostabiliser had three or more channels in each axis and would be arranged to monitor its own health by comparing the three channels. A single component failure should affect only one channel, which would then disagree with the other two. They would then outvote it, take over control, and alert the pilot of the malfunction. This voting type of system is successful in catching random component failures, but cannot correct for external failures which affect all channels equally.

Several aircraft had emergency revert-to-manual-control modes. In theory the pilot could switch to manual and override the autostabiliser. In practice things would happen very quickly and usually close to the ground. There was no guarantee that the part which had failed was in the autostabiliser and would not also disable the manual controls. The pilot would be a brave man indeed if he chose the manual override in preference to the ejector seat.

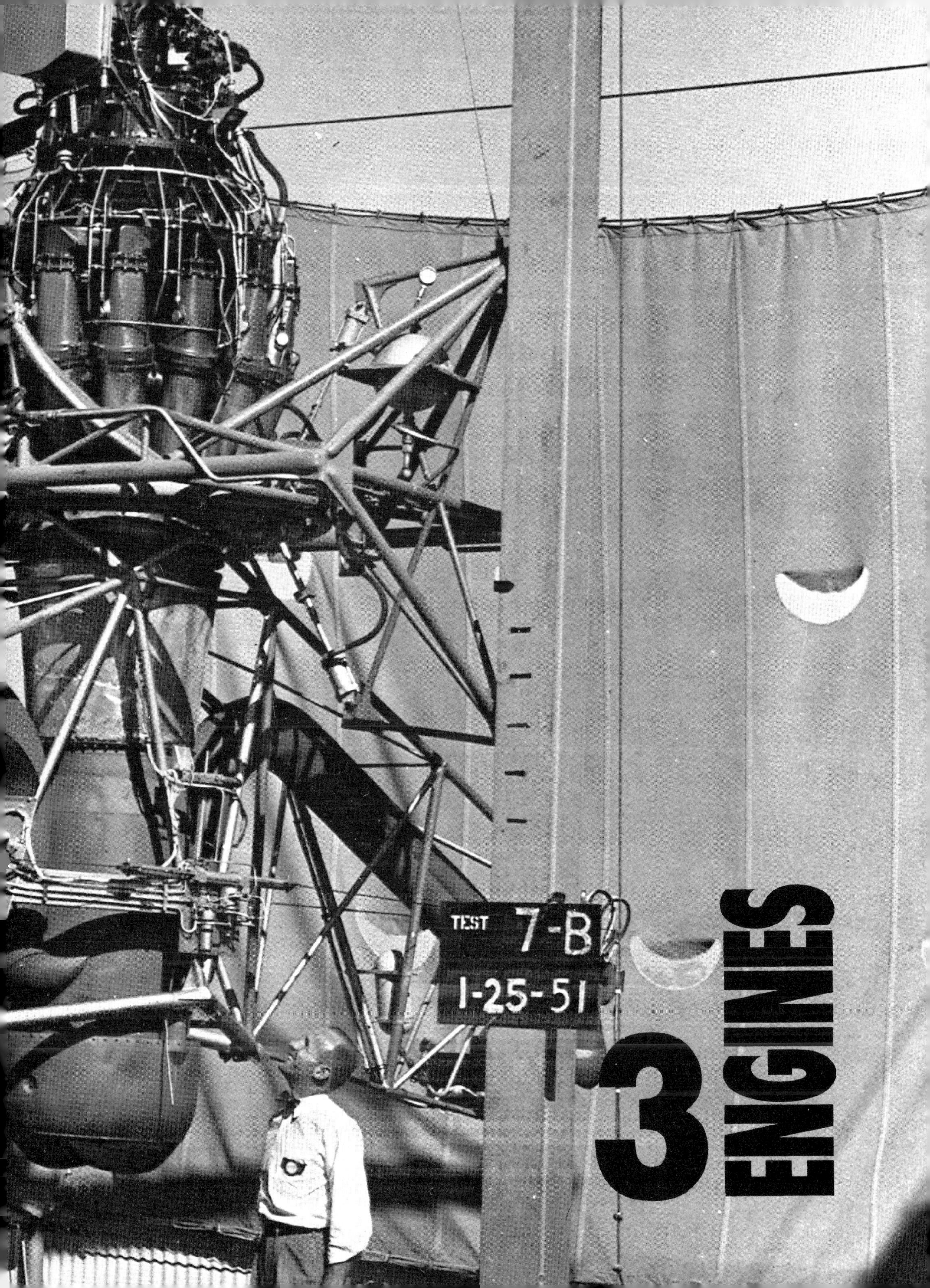

TEST 7-B
1-25-51

3 ENGINES

VTOL

All VTOL aircraft rely on engine power to get them into the air. In order to leave the ground, the total thrust of the propulsion devices must equal the aircraft weight. For disc-borne aircraft (where the disc may be a rotor, propeller, or fan), the disc loading in pounds weight per square foot of disc determines the number of horse power per thousand pounds of aircraft weight required to generate a thrust equal to weight. For jet aircraft, thrust must simply equal weight. In both cases, it is the availability of a sufficiently powerful engine that makes vertical flight possible.

Whilst it was necessary for the engines to lift the aircraft weight, they also had to provide additional thrust, usually an extra twenty per cent, for manoeuvring vertically, and they had to provide auxiliary thrust for manoeuvring in the other axes. In addition, multi-engined aircraft were required to be able to fly with one engine failed. This demanded still more thrust from the remaining engines. A typical value for total thrust with allowances for vertical acceleration, other controls, and engine out safety would be about 1.7 times aircraft gross weight.

As engine technology developed and more thrust became available, it became possible to build safe VTOL aircraft of modest lifting capacity. The same engines were available to the manufacturers of helicopters and conventional aeroplanes, who were able to increase the payload and range of their aircraft. The expectations of potential operators became greater, and VTOL aircraft had to follow suit with greater payload and range. Again, lighter, more powerful and more fuel-efficient engines were needed.

VTOL aircraft had a tremendous thirst for more and more engine power. They needed that power to be delivered smoothly and reliably, and, even at the highest power levels, they demanded fine vernier control with rapid response.

Thrust ratio was another problem. The thrust needed to get off the ground had to exceed aircraft weight, but the thrust required in cruising flight was only a fraction, a fifth or even a tenth of aircraft weight. The ratio of installed thrust to cruising thrust could be as great as fifteen to one. In a fighter aircraft this may be acceptable, since the excess thrust is of great value in high-speed manoeuvring and in attaining supersonic speeds. In transport aircraft the excess thrust is a great penalty, since payload must be reduced in order to carry the extra engine power.

In the early days of VTOL, just after the Second World War, high power at reasonable weight was just a dream. The piston engine could give thousands of horsepower, but weighed too much, and early jet engines had very little thrust. Helicopter and autogyro flight was just possible with piston engines, and the lightweight platforms could also get into the air on piston power. The other forms of VTOL flight had to wait for the development of better jet engines and for the gas turbine or turboshaft.

Piston engines

Two basic types of internal combustion engines were in common aeronautical use during the early VTOL era. These were the horizontally-opposed piston engine, common in light aircraft, and the radial piston engine, used in larger aircraft.

The Lycoming series of horizontally-opposed six-cylinder engines was popular for lighter VTOL aircraft. Transcendental used the O-290-A and the O-435-23 in their Model 1-G, Vanguard used the O-540-A1A in the Vanguard Omniplane 2C, and Dornier used the GO-480 in the Do 29.

The greater power of the radial engine found application in heavier VTOL types. Fairey used the Alvis Leonides in the Gyrodynes, McDonnell used a Continental R-975-19 in the XV-1, and Bell squeezed a Pratt & Whitney R-985 into the fuselage of the XV-3. All of these aircraft were desparately underpowered, but benefited from the tremendous reliability of their radial engines. Bell put reliability so far ahead of power that they retained the R-985 right up to 1960.

The earlier flying platforms also used piston engines. De Lackner used a Mercury outboard designed for marine use, Hiller chose Nelson engines for the Pawnee, and Bensen used a small McCulloch engine.

The Wankel rotary internal combustion engine came close to being used by Curtiss-Wright, who held a licence to build it, and proposed to use it the X-19, but they later opted for gas turbines.

Turboshaft engines

The early turboshaft engines were effectively simple jet engines with a power take-off. They had just one shaft, driven by the power turbine in the jet exhaust and driving both the compressor and the geared mechanical output. This simple design lacked flexibility. The engine rpm had to be kept high enough to prevent the compressor from stalling, and the engine could not be throttled back.

Two six-cylinder horizontally-opposed Lycoming GO-480 engines were used to power the Dornier Do 29. Similar engines were used in the Transcendental Model 1G and the Vanguard Model 2C. (Lycoming)

The Turbomeca Artouste was a small turboshaft engine used in the Curtiss-Wright VZ-7 and Piasecki VZ-8 flying platforms. (Rolls-Royce, Bristol)

The Allison T40 was made from two T38 single-shaft turbine engines geared together. When used in 1954 in the XFV-1 and XFY-1, the T40 had adequate power for vertical flight but could not be throttled back in horizontal flight. This proved to be a major embarrassment in horizontal to vertical transitions. On a much smaller scale, the French Turbomeca Artouste was a very simple single-shaft engine with a two-stage power turbine both driving a centrifugal compressor and providing the mechanical output. The

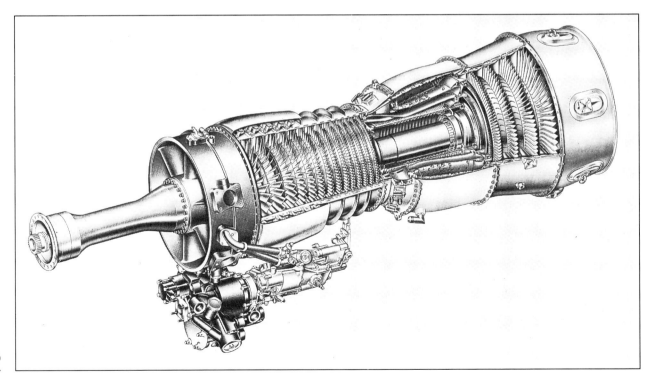

Artouste was used in 1958 in the Curtiss-Wright VZ-7 and the Piasecki VZ-8 Airgeep. Later gas turbine engines had two separate power turbines, one to drive the compressor, and one to drive the external mechanical load.

In Britain, the large and complex Napier Eland was used to power the Fairey Rotodyne. Two Elands were arranged so that they could either drive the propellers or blow compressed air to the rotor tipjets. The Eland gave 2,700 shp in 1957 and grew to 4,000 shp in 1961.

The two turboshaft engines most commonly used in American VTOL aircraft were the Lycoming T53 and the General Electric T58. The Lycoming T53 was used from 1957 when it produced 850 hp, for light experimental aircraft such as the Vertol 76,

Doak 16, and Ryan Vertiplane. It was also used in the Vanguard Omniplane and the Curtiss-Wright X-100. It continued to be fitted through to 1965 when it was rated at 1,450 shp and was used in the Canadair CL-84. It is still in service in the XV-15. The General Electric T58 series, designed by GE's Small Engines Department, was of similar power rating to the T53. In 1959 it was rated at 1,000 shp, and was used in the Fairchild Fledgling. It grew to 1,250 shp for use in the Bell X-22 in 1966, and to 1,500 shp for the S-72 in 1976. More powerful turboshaft engines became available in the early sixties. The 2,650 shp Lycoming T55 was used in 1963 for the X-19, and the 3,000 shp General Electric T64 was used in 1964 for the XC-142.

This cutaway view shows the simple internal construction of the Artouste. The reduction gearbox and auxiliary drives are almost as big as the power unit. (Rolls-Royce, Bristol)

The General Electric T64 used an external reduction gearbox to match the high turbine speed to the lower speed of the propeller shaft. (Rolls-Royce, Bristol)

This fine cutaway view shows the internal layout of the General Electric T64 turboshaft engine. The T64 was engineered for ease of maintenance. All castings could be split and individual turbine blades could be replaced. (Rolls-Royce, Bristol)

The T64 engines for the XC-142 tiltwing were tested on this rig to simulate engine operation in horizontal and vertical flight attitudes. (Rolls-Royce, Bristol)

Jet engines

The jet engine produces thrust by taking air in at the front and expelling it at the rear with increased rearward momentum. The forward thrust equals the increase in momentum, and the energy required to generate that thrust is the energy required to accelerate the air rearward. It works out that the jet engine is an efficient way of generating thrust at high speeds, but is inefficient at low speeds and when stationary.

Early jet engines were of two basic designs. The early British jet engines such as the Rolls-Royce Welland used centrifugal compressors. The Welland was developed in Britain to become the Rolls-Royce Nene, which was used in the deflected-thrust Meteor and the Flying Bedstead. It was also developed in the USA to become the Allison J33 used in the early Ryan rigs. The German BMW 003 used an axial-flow compressor, and this grew after the war into the French SNECMA Atar series of engines used as the Atar Volant and in the Coléoptère. In Britain and the USA, engine makers followed suit and replaced the simple centrifugal compressor with the smoother axial flow compressor.

Axial flow has the obvious advantage of cleaner airflow, but in early engines it was easy to get into a condition known as compressor stall, when the speed of the compressor was insufficient to maintain combustion chamber pressure. The result of

a compressor stall was that the contents of the combustion chamber would blow forward through the compressor to emerge at the intakes in dramatic and spectacular fashion, 'spitting flames from every orifice' as one test pilot put it.

Compressor stall was a very troublesome condition for VTOL aircraft. They were more likely to encounter it as they relied on rapid engine throttling for control, and they were especially vulnerable in the event of compressor stall and probable subsequent flame-out. Aircraft with very large air intakes designed to admit high mass flows for efficient hovering were even more likely to encounter stall due to interference between external and intake airflows.

The jet engine was difficult to apply to VTOL aircraft. The lift provided by jet engines had to act through the aircraft centre of gravity. Conventional aircraft have engines in mid-fuselage, and any attempt to direct their exhausts downward would result in a rapid nose-down pitch. One answer was to relocate the engines further forward. This was in conflict with the need to have the pilot and avionic equipment forward, and generally led to unsatisfactory compromises. The choice of VTOL configuration and engine mix was often driven by the need to centre the lift under the centre of gravity.

Jet engines used in the USA during the early days of VTOL included the 1,000 pound thrust Fairchild J44 used in the Bell ATV in 1954, and two British engines, the 10,000

The Rolls-Royce Nene was one of the more powerful centrifugal compressor jet engines. It was used in the deflected thrust Meteor and in the Flying Bedstead. (Rolls-Royce)

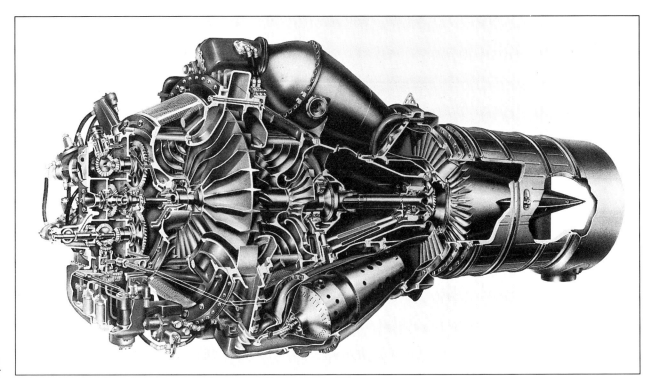

The Armstrong-Siddeley Viper ASV8 was a small lightweight turbojet of 1750 pounds thrust. It was used to power the Bell X-14. (Rolls-Royce, Bristol)

The Rolls-Royce Avon shows the clean lines inherent in axial flow jet engines. It was used in the Ryan X-13 Vertijet. (Rolls-Royce)

The Rolls-Royce Avon was one of the first British axial flow turbojets and its high thrust to weight ratio gained it

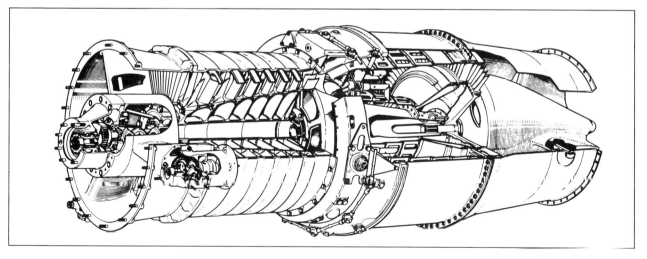

a place in the Ryan X-13 Vertijet. The only change made for the X-13 application was a modification of the lubrication system to enable it to work in vertical as well as horizontal attitudes. (Rolls-Royce, Bristol)

pound thrust Rolls-Royce Avon used in the Ryan X-13 in 1955, and the 1,750 pound thrust Armstrong-Siddeley Viper used in the Bell X-14 in 1957. The 3,400 pound thrust Westinghouse J34 appeared in the X-18 in 1959, but only to provide pitch control.

The Small Aircraft Engine Department of General Electric designed the lightweight

J85 jet engine to power the Quail missile. The J85 became a very successful engine. It weighed 700 pounds and produced 3,000 pounds of thrust dry or 5,000 pounds with reheat. The J85 replaced the Viper in the Bell X-14, and was used in the Ryan XV-5 Vertifan, the Lockheed XV-4B Hummingbird II and the Bell XF-109 tiltjet project.

VTOL

Liftjets

In Britain, Rolls-Royce had their lightweight Soar engine, intended for use in missiles. From this, Dr A. A. Griffiths developed a family of highly specialised axial-flow lift engines, starting with the RB108 and following on with the RB145 and the RB162. The lift engine was intended as an answer to the thrust ratio problem. It was optimised to produce maximum thrust for minimum weight, and for short duration only. In theory, the thrust needed for VTO could be had for very little weight penalty.

Liftjets were easy to incorporate in a new or existing design, the necessary control systems were proven, and transition did not present any problems. As such they were very attractive to manufacturers wishing to take their first steps into VTOL, and they were to influence much of European VTOL thinking for quite some time.

The RB108 in 1955 produced 2,130 pounds of thrust for only 270 pounds of weight, a ratio of almost 8 to 1. It was used in the SC-1 and Balzac, and in several flying test rigs. Subsequent development of the lift engine family led to thrust to weight ratios as high as 16 to 1. When used with separate propulsion engines, as in the Mirage IIIV, the lift engines turned out to be too much dead weight. They could, however, be used to good effect for both lift and propulsion in tiltjets such as the VJ101C, or to supplement

The Rolls-Royce RB108 was the first in their family of specialised lightweight lift engines. It powered the Short SC-1 and many hover rigs. (Rolls-Royce)

vectored thrust, as in the VAK191 and Do 31.

All of the Rolls-Royce lift engines are on display at Derby Industrial Museum.

Below: The Rolls-Royce RB145 lift engine was used to power the VJ101C both in vertical and in horizontal flight. Its thrust could be adjusted with a precision sufficient to control aircaft attitude, even when afterburning was in use. (EWR Sud)

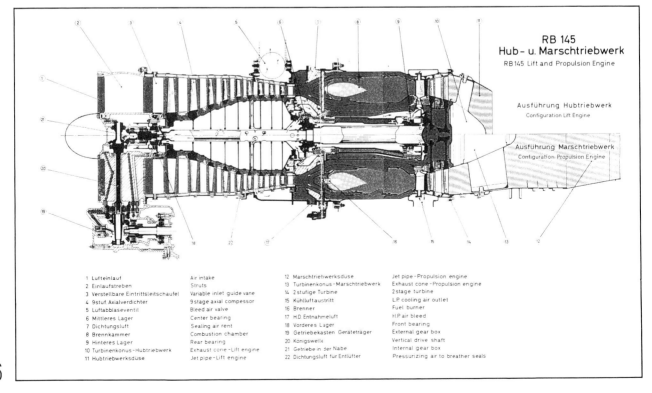

RB 145
Hub- u. Marschtriebwerk
RB 145 Lift and Propulsion Engine

Ausführung Hubtriebwerk
Configuration Lift Engine

Ausführung Marschtriebwerk
Configuration Propulsion Engine

1 Lufteinlauf	Air intake	12 Marschtriebwerksduse	Jet pipe - Propulsion engine
2 Einlaufstreben	Struts	13 Turbinenkonus - Marschtriebwerk	Exhaust cone - Propulsion engine
3 Verstellbare Eintrittsleitschaufel	Variable inlet guide vane	14 2stufige Turbine	2 stage turbine
4 9stuf. Axialverdichter	9 stage axial compressor	15 Kühlluftaustritt	L.P cooling air outlet
5 Luftabblaseventil	Bleed air valve	16 Brenner	Fuel burner
6 Mittleres Lager	Center bearing	17 H.D. Entnahmeluft	H.P air bleed
7 Dichtungsluft	Sealing air rent	18 Vorderes Lager	Front bearing
8 Brennkammer	Combustion chamber	19 Getriebekasten Geräteträger	External gear box
9 Hinteres Lager	Rear bearing	20 Königswelle	Vertical drive shaft
10 Turbinenkonus - Hubtriebwerk	Exhaust cone - Lift engine	21 Getriebe in der Nabe	Internal gear box
11 Hubtriebwerksduse	Jet pipe - Lift engine	22 Dichtungsluft fur Entlüfter	Pressurizing air to breather seals

The RB145 was designed to be used both for lift and for propulsion. It was used in the VJ101C tiltjet aircraft. (Rolls-Royce)

The Rolls-Royce RB162 used plastic parts to reduce weight to a minimum. It was used in the VFW VAK191 and in the Dornier Do 31. (Rolls-Royce)

Thrust Augmentation

The American approach to liftjets was to use conventional propulsion engines and to augment their thrust. The 3,300 pound thrust Pratt & Whitney JT12 was used in the Lockheed XV-4A Hummingbird in 1962 in a thrust augmentor system. The augmentation system was part of the airframe and is described along with the XV-4A. In its later XV-4B form, the Hummingbird used the 3,000 pound thrust General Electric J85 without augmentation.

Jetfans

Avro Canada introduced the jetfan in their Avrocar. Instead of using engine thrust directly, they used it to drive a power turbine around the periphery of a fan. This trans-

47

formed the low mass flow high-velocity energy in the jet exhaust to a high mass flow of air at low velocity. The result was increased lift for the same power.

General Electric took up the idea and used their J85 engines to drive turbine-fan units. These produced about a three to one increase in thrust, and were used in the Ryan XV-5. The jetfan was not developed further, but it lived on as part of the Pegasus and laid the foundations for efficient jet-powered flight.

The Orpheus

In 1952, Teddy Petter of Folland Aircraft approached Dr Stanley Hooker of Bristol Engines and asked him to design an engine to fit the proposed Folland Gnat lightweight fighter. Dr Hooker calculated that it would be

a large diameter thin-walled tube which was naturally very resistant to flexing. This one feature made other changes possible which eliminated much of the hardware of previous engines and made the Orpheus easier to assemble and service. It also had another advantage not appreciated at that time.

The Orpheus was a superb engine and was the ideal for the Gnat. The Gnat was an excellent lightweight fighter, but it was comprehensively ignored by the Royal Air Force who wanted conventional large, fast fighters equipped with all the latest avionics. Fortunately Captain Johnny Driscoll, USAF, head of the Mutual Weapons Development Programme (MWDP), was interested in light-weight fighters for the defence of European NATO countries. MWDP sponsored a competition for a NATO Light Strike Fighter. The Orpheus powered all serious contenders, and MWDP offered to provide 75 per cent of the

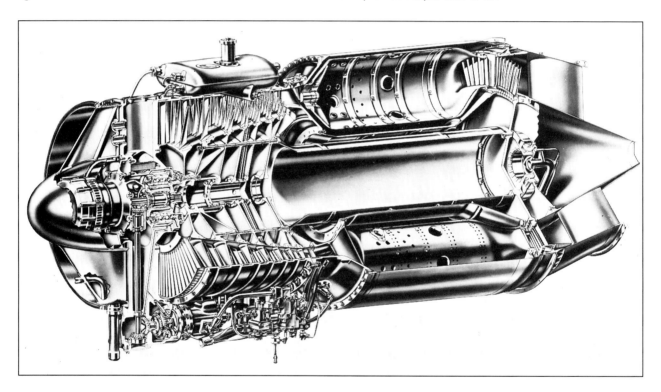

possible to make a small axial flow engine weighing 800 pounds and producing 5,000 pounds of thrust. The project became the BE26 Orpheus.

The design of the Orpheus was driven by the commitment to meet thrust and weight figures, and simpler, lighter methods of construction were developed. In most engines, it was usual for the drive shaft from the power turbine to the compressor to be supported in the middle by a third bearing to stop it from flexing. The Orpheus had no centre bearing and the shaft was replaced by

development funding for the Orpheus. Bristols accepted and put up the other 25 per cent themselves as a private venture, since the government showed no interest.

The Orpheus was very successful and was made both in Britain and under licence in Italy and Germany. It was used for propulsion in the Balzac V001, and to power the Hunting H126 blown-wing aircraft. The Orpheus was a very important stage in the development of vectored thrust, because it produced large thrust for little weight, and because it had a hollow central shaft which

The Bristol Orpheus was a simple, low-cost, light-weight engine with plenty of development potential. The hollow central shaft left plenty of room for the addition of a second spool. (Rolls-Royce, Bristol)

provided room for growth.

A complete Orpheus is on display at Bristol Industrial Museum. Another is at the Rolls-Royce Heritage Trust, Patchway, Bristol.

Vectored thrust

One of the problems facing VTOL aircraft designers was that of getting the lift force to act through aircraft centre of gravity without forcing the engines to inconvenient locations. Michel Wibault, veteran French aircraft designer, solved the lift centre problem with his design for the Gyroptère. He used a rear-mounted engine to drive four centrifugal compressors arranged in a square about the centre of gravity. The compressor casings could rotate to blow down, for lift, or rearward, for propulsion.

Once again government funding was denied. In a repeat of the Orpheus story, MWDP put up 75 per cent and Bristols put up the other 25 per cent.

The intention was to drive the axial compressor with a turboshaft, such as the Orion, but this was heavy. A lighter engine, such as the Orpheus, would be better. The internal layout of the Orpheus was especially convenient, since the central shaft was hollow. An extra power turbine stage was added, and this turned a second shaft which ran through to the front of the Orpheus and turned the additional compressor, two stages from an Olympus.

This design evolved into the BE53 Pegasus, and Hawkers designed the P.1127 aircraft around it. Hawkers contributed to the design of the Pegasus by suggesting the use of a bifurcated jetpipe and vectored rear as well as front nozzles, a configuration

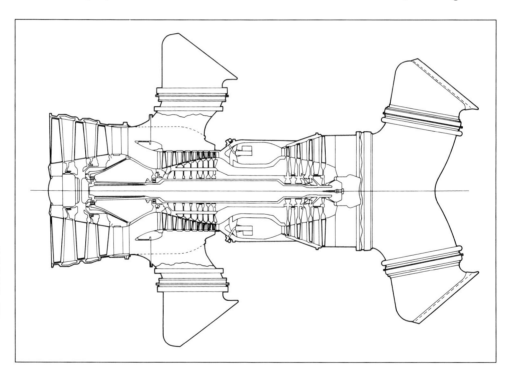

This simplified sectional view of the Pegasus shows clearly the three-stage low pressure front fan, eight-stage high pressure compressor, and four power turbine stages. (Rolls-Royce, Bristol)

Wibault could not get any support from the French or American governments, and he turned to to Captain Johnny Driscoll who still headed the MWDP. Driscoll liked the idea, and discussed it with von Karman, who christened it 'vectored thrust'. They called Dr Hooker of Bristols to Paris and got him interested in the concept. He put the idea to his staff back at Patchway, and Gordon Lewis came up with a proposal to replace the inefficient centrifugal compressors with a single axial compressor. This arrangement was patented in the joint names of Wibault and Lewis, British Patent 881,662.

anticipated in the Wibault/Lewis Patent, and by suggesting water injection to boost thrust.

After the experiences of their test pilots in the USA, Hawkers insisted that the two spools of the Pegasus should rotate in opposite senses, so as to cancel gyroscopic effects. Bristols complied, but were not happy about the cost of the additional tooling to make left-handed turbine and compressor blades. Gyroscopic cancellation turned out to be an important feature in making the P.1127 easier to fly.

The Pegasus at first had a thrust less than 10,000 pounds, and could only just lift

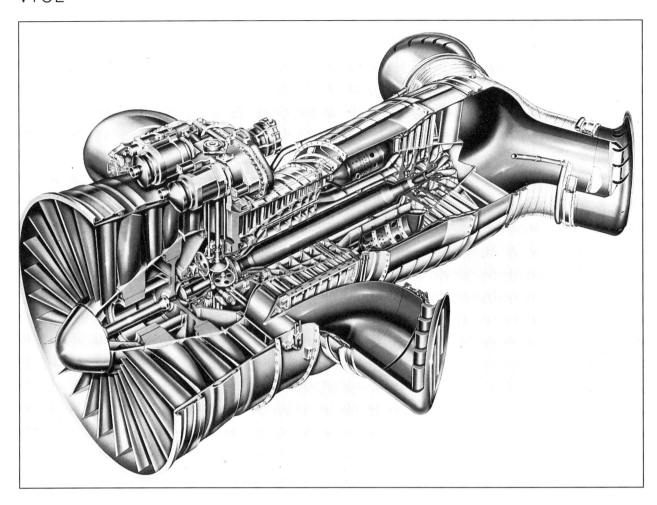

This cutaway view of the Pegasus gives a more detailed view of the complexity of construction. Note the pipe which takes 'cool' fan air at 100°C to the rear nozzle bearings. (Rolls-Royce, Bristol)

The Rolls-Royce RB193 was a vectored thrust jet engine based on the Spey. It was smaller and lighter than the Pegasus and was used in the VAK 191 along with the two RB162 lift engines. (Rolls-Royce)

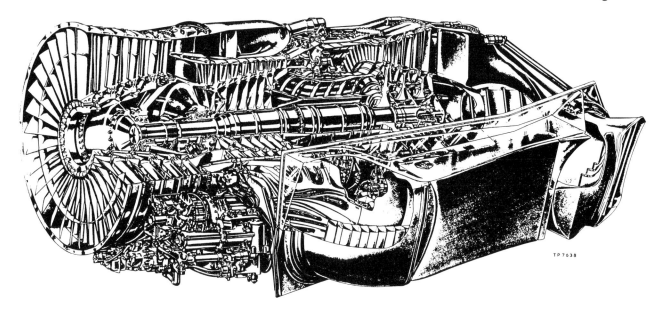

TP 7638

The Bristol Siddeley BS100 was intended for the Hawker P1154 and similar upersonic VTOL projects. The Plenum Chamber Burning system can be seen as a frond-like structure just inboard of the front nozzle, and the variable ramp is the external suface joining the front and rear nozzles.
(Rolls-Royce, Bristol)

the unladen P.1127 off the ground. The thrust of the Pegasus grew in stages to meet Hawkers' requirements as the P.1127 became the Kestrel and later the Harrier, which needed to carry a significant weapon and fuel load. The current thrust rating of the Pegasus is 21,500 pounds, more than double the original figure. This had to be achieved without any growth in size because the airframe fitted so closely around the engine.

A Pegasus is on display at Bristol Industrial Museum, Bristol Docks. This engine is shown in 'exploded' form, so that all internal components may be inspected. Visual comparison with nearby Orpheus and Olympus is possible.

The Pegasus made possible the Harrier, one of very few VTOL types to enter service. It also showed how a jet engine could be used to drive a fan, and laid the foundations for the new generation of high efficiency fanjet engines. It was the only vectored thrust engine to enter service in the Western world, but other vectored thrust engine designs were built in small quantities.

Rolls-Royce teamed up with the German company MAN (MTU) to build the RB193 for the VAK191. The RB193 was a smaller derivative of the Spey, and used scaled-down Pegasus nozzles built under licence from Bristols. An RB193 may be seen at Derby Industrial Museum.

Rolls-Royce also made a version of the Spey for the NASA Buffalo Augmentor Wing. Bypass air was bled to the wing and the engine hot exhaust was fed to Pegasus rear nozzles so that it could be vectored downward or to the rear. The Spey, in conventional form, may be seen at Derby.

During the mid-sixties, European in-terest in VTOL centred on the NATO NBMR3 supersonic fighter requirement. Hawkers designed their P1154 and Bristols produced the BS100 to power it. The BS100 was a larger version of the Pegasus, built around an Olympus core and with a large diameter front fan. The nozzles, instead of emerging horizontally from the sides of the engine and rotating about horizontal axes, were angled down and rotated about axes inclined below the horizontal.

The BS100 had a complex burner system located within the duct which fed cold air from the front fan to the front nozzles. This was known as PCB, or Plenum Chamber Burning. The front nozzles were each divided into two equal areas. When running dry, only the outboard halves were used. With PCB, inboard and outboard halves were used. The unused inboard halves were blanked off by a ramp when not in use. PCB was intended for use during vertical flight and for supersonic dash.

Dry thrust was about 24,000 pounds and was divided equally between front and rear nozzles. PCB doubled the thrust of the front nozzles, producing a total thrust of 36,000 pounds.

Six BS100 engines were made. Five were test run, and the sixth was assembled but not run. One is at the Rolls-Royce Heritage Centre, Patchway, Bristol, one is at the Science Museum, Wroughton, Wiltshire, and a third is at RAF Cosford. A Plenum Chamber Burner is on display at Bristol Industrial Museum, Bristol Docks. Also on display at the Docks is the Olympus, which provided the front fan for the first Pegasus and the core for the BS100.

4 TAILSITTERS

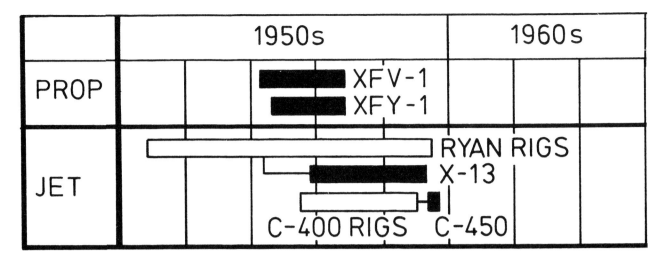

	1950s					1960s		
PROP			XFV-1					
			XFY-1					
JET				RYAN RIGS				
				X-13				
		C-400 RIGS		C-450				

The first VTOL projects to emerge in the mid-fifties were the tailsitters, or vertical risers. These were small almost-conventional aircraft in which the transition from horizontal to vertical flight consisted simply of pulling the nose up until the aircraft was hanging on its propeller, suspended on the thrust of its engine. The reverse transition, from hover to forward flight, was achieved by pushing the nose gently forward so that the aircraft accelerated to flying speed.

There were four tailsitters. Two were funded by the US Navy and used a powerful Allison turboprop engine driving contra-rotating propellers. These were the Lockheed XFV-1 Salmon and the Convair XFY-1 Pogo. The USAF funded the Ryan X-13 jet tailsitter, and the French engine company SNECMA made another jet tailsitter known as the Coléoptère.

Propeller-driven tailsitters

The US Navy was very concerned at the problems of convoy defence encountered during the Second World War. A great many Allied warships had been required to defend the covoys of merchant ships crossing the Atlantic with the supplies needed to defend Britain and invade Europe. The Navy proposed to free warships for other duties by equipping merchant ships with their own air defence system of midget vertical take-off fighters, and in 1950 they held a design competition.

Proposals were submitted by Convair, Lockheed, Martin, Goodyear, and Northrop. The Convair entry was judged to be outstanding, and also had the lowest quoted cost. Runners-up were Lockheed and Martin, and Lockheed were chosen because they

quoted a lower cost and because their geographical location was more favourable for co-ordination of effort between them and Convair.

The two aircraft were of similar size and weight. Both used the Allison YT-40-A-14 engine, which consisted of two T-38 gas turbines mounted side by side. Engine power was 5,500 eshp in normal use, with 7,100 eshp available as a short-term rating during take-off. In both aircraft the YT-40 drove a pair of 16 ft diameter three-bladed contra-rotating propellers. These were made by Curtiss-Wright, and incorporated electric control of blade pitch. Propeller static thrust was in excess of 10,000 pounds.

Lockheed were first with their XFV-1, designed by Clarence L. 'Kelly' Johnson. It was later named the Salmon, after test pilot Herman 'Fish' Salmon. The XFV-1 was very similar in appearance to conventional small propeller-driven aircraft. The fuselage was 37 ft long, and had a slender cigar shape, with the cockpit placed well forward. An ejection seat was provided, and this was arranged to tilt forward to give the pilot a more convenient position when the aircraft was in its tailsitting attitude. The straight, gently tapered wings were of 30 ft span and were set well back. Four stabiliser surfaces were provided in a cruciform arrangement at the rear of the fuselage, but at 45 degrees to the conventional positions. Each stabiliser had a full-width tabbed control surface. The separation between wing and stabilisers was much less than in conventional aircraft.

Control in hover was effected by using the stabiliser control surfaces to deflect the propeller slipstream. The 45 degree positions of the stabilisers reduced masking of the airstream by the wings, and the shortness of the rear fuselage brought the stabilisers forward and helped to keep them in the

Propeller and jet tailsitters were developed during the fifties. By 1960, they became obsolete as advances in engines and control systems made flat-risers possible. (Author)

The Lockheed XFV-1 Salmon poses in vertical take-off position. It never took off or landed vertically, but it did make transitions at altitude. (Lockheed)

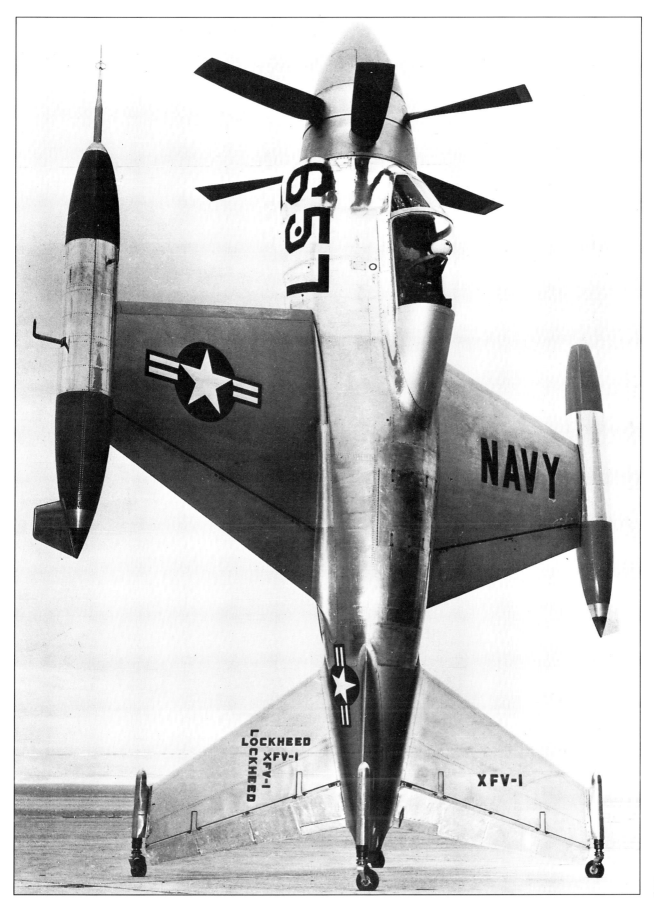

The XFV-1 Salmon on its handling trolley. The pilot got in with the aircraft horizontal and the trolley erected the Salmon, with pilot, to its vertical take-off attitude. (Lockheed)

airstream. Transition from hover to forward flight was initiated by tilting the nose forward and gathering horizontal speed until wing lift took over. The reverse transition involved pulling the nose up to lose horizontal speed until the aircraft was hovering.

The XFV-1 was provided with special ground handling equipment including a handling trolley which could transport it in a horizontal attitude, and swing it to the vertical for launch. When the aircraft was vertical, it stood on four castors and the trolley could be removed. The trolley used an ingenious combination of sliding and pivoting to keep the aircraft centre of gravity above the centre of the trolley during erection.

The XFV-1 was fitted with temporary conventional landing gear and made its first horizontal flight in March 1954. A total of 27 flights were made during the year, first exploring low-speed flight characteristics and then attempting partial transitions to vertical flight. Full transitions from horizontal to vertical and vertical to horizontal were made during Autumn 1954. The programme encountered several major problems. Transitions from horizontal to vertical flight in-

volved several hundred feet gain in altitude as the nose was pulled up and kinetic energy was converted to potential energy. Once vertical, there was very little control in hover, and the pilot had no visual reference to tell him how fast he was climbing or sinking. All low-speed and transitional flying was conducted at altitudes exceeding 1,000 ft, and no vertical take-offs or landings were attempted.

The XFV-1 was retired when it became clear that available engines and control systems would not be able to give it adequate VTOL performance. It was transferred to the San Diego Aerospace Museum, Balbao Park, San Diego. Although it never actually achieved vertical take-off and landing, it had provided much valuable information to be used in the design of future VTOL aircraft.

The Convair XFY-1 Pogo used the same Allison engine as the XFV-1 and was somewhat smaller in overall dimensions with a length of 31 ft and a 26 ft wingspan. Aerodynamically it was very different. Convair used a delta wing, which gave them more strength for less weight and had much better performance at low speed and high angles of

The Lockheed XFV-1 Salmon in horizontal flight with temporary wheeled landing gear.
(Lockheed)

The XFY-1 Pogo in vertical take-off position. Its squat shape produced better airflow over the control surfaces in vertical flight. Getting into the Pogo was a tricky business.
(Convair)

attack, an obvious advantage during transitions between vertical and horizontal flight. Large vertical stabilisers were provided above and below the rear fuselage, and these matched the delta shape of the wings. The lower stabiliser could be jettisoned in an emergency for a belly landing. Wings and stabilisers were equipped with control surfaces covering most of each trailing edge. The propeller slipstream was cut in four by wings and stabilisers, ensuring that all control surfaces had an airstream to act on when hovering. Even so, only small control forces were available during vertical flight and control must have been marginal.

Like the XFV-1, the XFY-1 had a ground handling trailer which transported it in a horizontal attitude and would tilt it to the vertical, leaving it standing on its tail. Early in the test programme the tip of the lower stabiliser was removed, probably to ease handling during trailer tilt. There was also a protective dome which opened like a clamshell on a vertical hinge. This could be wheeled up to the XFY-1 and closed around it. Platforms within the dome permitted the aircraft to be serviced under cover and while in its vertical attitude.

The large ventral stabiliser of the Pogo made impractical the addition of conventional landing gear for horizontal take-off. Convair chose instead to conduct tethered flight tests. These took place in the giant 200 ft high Naval airship hangar at Moffett Field, on the southern end of the San Francisco Bay. A tether line connected the nose of the Pogo to a drum in the roof of the hangar. As the Pogo rose off the ground, the drum operator reeled in the slack cable, but without supporting any of the aircraft weight. If the pilot got into difficulty he transmitted the message 'Catch me' and cut his engine. The drum operator would lock the reel and the Pogo would be left safely swinging in mid-hangar, to be lowered slowly to the floor.

Test pilot J. F. 'Skeets' Coleman started tethered tests in April 1954. In the confined space of the hangar, air blown downward by the hovering Pogo created several problems. The air in the hangar became turbulent, making control more difficult. Ambient temperature rose, and the engine became less efficient and lost thrust. Smoke, fumes and dust were circulated, and these, together with the noise of six or seven thousand horsepower in a confined space, contributed greatly to pilot fatigue. Whilst coping with all these problems, Coleman had to learn to hover. He was sitting at a 45 degree inclination towards the control panel with the aircraft nose pointed at the roof. He had no horizon and could only judge his attitude and altitude by staring fixedly back and down past his shoulder at the hangar floor.

After several months of tethered trials, the Pogo was moved outside and Coleman made the first free hovering flight on 1 August 1954. He found it easier without the tether, which had applied undesirable side-forces. Flight tests continued with further hovering flights and partial transitions. The first complete 'verticircuit' of vertical take-off, transition, horizontal flight, transition, and vertical landing was on 2 November 1954. This was the first ever true VTOL flight, and it won Coleman the Harmon Trophy.

Because the Pogo could only take off and land vertically, both of the transitions had to take place for the first time on the same flight. Coleman's comments on the horizontal to vertical transition make interesting reading. The Allison engine was so powerful that, even when throttled right back, it drove the Pogo at several hundred knots. Coleman had to approach the airfield in a series of sweeping turns to burn off speed before pulling up into a climb ending in a stall, at which point he had to balance thrust and weight so as to hover. Then came the worst part, a gentle backward descent to the ground.

VTOL flying techniques were in their infancy, and there was a certain amount of controversy over the 'right' way to fly and the amount of training required. Convair test pilot Johnny Knebel attempted to fly the Pogo early in 1955 after only training on a thrust balance rig and having a short briefing from Coleman. The flight involved some interesting unplanned manoeuvres. Both Knebel and Pogo survived the experience, but the point was well made that tethered training was essential for would-be VTOL pilots.

C. E. Myers Jr became the XFY-1 project pilot in April 1956. He trained both on the thrust balance rig and on the tethered Pogo. By now tethered flights took place outdoors under a tall gantry. Where Coleman had preferred to look down at the ground, Myers preferred to use the horizon, in combination with nearby tall objects of known height. This made it much easier to judge attitude, altitude, and, most important of all, sink rate, but the method was only effective at altitudes of 100 ft or less. The Pogo, like the Salmon, could only convert from horizontal to vertical flight by putting the nose up and gaining a few hundred feet of height. It then had to reverse gently tail-first to a vertical landing, and it was essential to control sink rate very

The Convair XFY-1 Pogo in vertical flight. Going up and converting to horizontal flight was a reasonably easy manoeuvre. Transition back to vertical flight and descent was more difficult. (Convair)

carefully. If the aircraft sank too fast, the control surfaces would cease to work, and even at full power it might be impossible to arrest the sink before arriving at zero height. There were no suitable instruments for measuring sink rate. Barometric devices lacked the sensitivity to measure slow rates, and would be upset by slipstream and vibration, while lightweight radio altimeters were not yet available. The pilot kept in radio contact with a member of the ground crew who measured altitude and sink rate visually by observing Pogo through a grid.

Throughout the programme there were continual problems with the engine and the electric propeller pitch change mechanism, neither of which was reliable enough for a VTOL project. These items of hardware contributed to the cancellation of both XFV-1 and XFY-1 programmes, and were put back on the shelf to emerge later in Hiller X-18.

The Convair XFY-1 Pogo ceased flying in November 1956 and was moved to the Smithsonian Institution in September 1957.

In hindsight, both the XFV-1 and XFY-1 were very ambitious projects. Both aircraft

had to hover by hanging on their propellers without the benefit of a separate contol system, without autostabilisation and with the pilot mostly out of visual contact with the ground. Despite all this, both aircraft made transitions and one made complete verticircuits. Several important precedents had been set. Lockheed had used temporary fixed landing gear to evaluate horizontal flight characteristics, and Convair had used both thrust balance rig and tethered testing for pilot training.

Jet tailsitters

While Lockheed and Convair had been working with US Navy funding on prop tailsitters, Ryan had a US Air Force contract for a jet tailsitter. Lockheed and Convair had been able to use the conventional control surfaces to deflect the propeller slipstream for control in hover, but Ryan had to devise a separate hover control system. They started with a thrust balance rig in which an Allison J33 jet engine supported its own weight. The rig allowed the engine to move up and down and to tilt. The control system regulated the throttle to control 'altitude', and controlled pitch and yaw by deflection of engine exhaust thrust in a two-axis rotating 'eyeball' jet nozzle. Roll about a vertical axis was controlled by two hot gas bleeds, one to each side of the main nozzle, each equipped with an eyeball nozzle. This rig made its first controlled 'hover' in 1950.

The next stage was a free-flying tethered rig. A similar engine was used, again equipped with a two-axis eyeball nozzle for pitch and yaw control. Delta-shaped wings were added to provide a realistic amount of damping in roll. The eye-ball roll control nozzles were replaced by simple right-angle bends which normally exhausted downward but which could be rotated about a spanwise axis to blow perpendicular to each wing so as to generate a roll moment. Hot exhaust gases were still used but with much smaller bleed pipes. This rig made the first ever jet-powered hover, loosely tethered under a gantry and under remote control, on 24 November 1951.

The rig was progressively developed, first by adding a pilot's seat on a platform above the engine, and later by adding a fuselage nose (actually a B-47 droptank) with pilot's cockpit. The roll control nozzles were moved outboard so they no longer blew hot gas over the wings, no longer suffered the splitting effect of the wings and had twice the leverage about the centreline. In its final

form, the rig was autostabilised and could be flown 'hands-off'.

Ryan's cautious approach to VTOL through three stages of tethered rig permitted the progressive development of controls and control systems. The rigs also proved valuable in pilot training both for Ryan's own test pilots and later for those from other companies. Rig design had commenced in 1947, tests were under way from 1950 and the rig was kept available through to the late fifties. It was known to Ryan personnel as 'The beast in the backyard'.

Following the success of the rig trials, the USAF awarded Ryan a contract in 1953 to proceed with the design of a VTOL jet aircraft. This followed the general shape of the rig, with a tiny fuselage just long enough at 24 ft to house the cockpit and a Rolls-Royce Avon jet engine. A small delta wing of only 21 ft span and equilateral in shape was mounted across the top of the fuselage. To this was added a large triangular fin and flat endplates. The control system of the rig was retained. Engine thrust was steered in pitch and yaw by an eyeball jet nozzle and roll was controlled by elbow pipes situated beyond

The Ryan test rig was modified by the addition of a simulated X-13 cockpit made from a B-47 fuel tank. (Ryan)

Below right: This sectioned view shows the compact internal layout of the X-13 Vertijet, with just enough room for cockpit and engine. The pilot's ejector seat tilts forward for vertical flight. The engine exhaust is vectored for control in pitch and yaw by two hydraulic rams which actuate the swivelling eyeball-type engine exhaust nozzle. (Ryan)

The Ryan test rig, known as 'the beast in the back yard' was capable of tethered hover under remote control. (Ryan)

the endplates where they could not interact with the wing. Fabrication of two prototypes began in 1954.

The first prototype, serial 41619, was fitted with temporary non-retractable wheeled landing gear for horizontal flight trials and made its first flight on 10 December 1955. On subsequent flights, still taking off and landing horizontally, it made transitions at altitude to and from vertical flight.

After proving its conventional flight characteristics and showing that transitions were feasible, 41619 was mounted in a vertical attitude in a framework on castors, known as the 'roller-skate'. It was stripped of all unnecessary weight, including control surfaces and cockpit cover, to compensate for the added weight of the support structure. In this guise 41619 carried out vertical take-off and landing trials. Test pilot Pete Girard also practised 'hook-on' manoeuvres using a wooden hook designed to break in case of mishap.

The second X-13, 41620, included detail improvements over '19. The most visible difference was the cockpit canopy. When '19 was vertical and the pilot's seat was tilted forward, the cockpit pillar seriously obscured pilot vision. On '20 the cockpit opened along the same line, but the pillar was split and additional glass panels were inserted, on the port side only.

1 Radio antenna
2 Control stick
3 Throttle control
4 Ratio changer
5 Telemetric antenna
6 Battery
7 CB containers
8 Oxygen cylinders
9 Fuel transfer pump
10 Fuel transfer tubes
11 Fuel booster pump
12 Fuel tank sump
13 Fuel tank vent tube
14 Rudder control cable
15 Yaw damper
16 Fuel tank vent
17 Anti-spin parachute container
18 Jet nozzle
19 Jet engine

20 Engine rear mount
21 Thrust velocity control actuator
22 Magnetic amplifiers
23 Lag rate integrators
24 Vertical gyro – manually operated
25 Mixer box assembly
26 Gyro plate
27 Anti-spin parachute release control
28 Pitch trim actuator

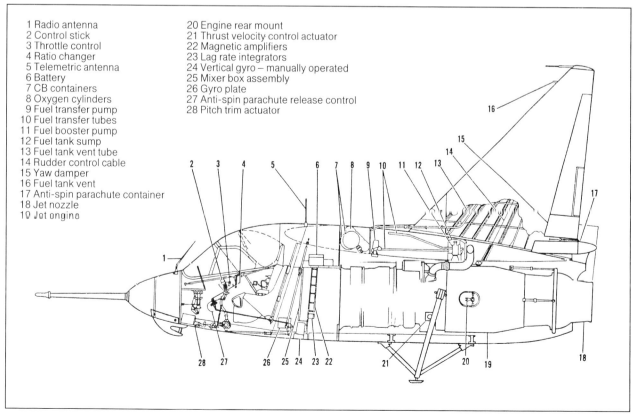

The first Ryan X-13 Vertijet, 41619, carried out horizontal flight trials using temporary wheeled landing gear. (Ryan)

The first Vertijet on its 'Roller Skate' framework practises hook-on manoeuvres. Test pilot Pete Girard had to hook the wire between the two striped pennants. For this test a fail-safe wooden hook was used. (Ryan)

The second X-13 with wheeled landing gear. The cockpit canopy design was revised on the port side to give the pilot a better field of view with the seat tilted forward in vertical flight. (Ryan)

Like '19, '20 also flew with wheeled landing gear before being fitted with a nosehook and two ventral pads. It was now fitted out as designed to take off from and land on its ground service trailer. For transportation, the trailer bed was horizontal and carried the X-13 Vertijet in a conventional horizontal attitude. For launch, the fuselage was anchored, the pilot climbed into the cockpit using a short ladder, and the trailer bed was elevated hydraulically to a vertical position taking the aircraft with it. The nose hook of the X-13 was already hooked onto a trapeze wire joining two arms on the trailer. These arms moved upward and away from the trailer bed, so that the X-13 hung from the wire just clear of the trailer.

Pete Girard opened the throttle until the Vertijet was just supporting its own weight, and, with guidance from the ground crew, backed away from the trailer and then performed a climbing transition to forward flight. Landing was the reverse operation, involving nose-up from horizontal flight into hover, gentle reverse to ground level, and a hovering 'walk' to the trapeze, again with the help of signals from ground crew and visual contact with a 'barbers pole'. 41620 completed this full cycle on 11 April 1957 and repeated it many times, including demonstrations in Washington on 28 and 29 July to mark the fiftieth anniversary of the US Air Force.

In May 1959, 41620 was transferred to the US Air Force Museum, Wright Patterson Air Force Base, Dayton, Ohio, where it may still be seen. 41619 was donated to the Smithsonian Institution and is on loan to San Diego Aerospace Museum, Balbao Park, San Diego.

The X-13 Vertijet programme demonstrated all that is good in programme planning and management. The overall goal of a lightweight jet VTOL fighter was approached in a progression of small steps forward, each step being safe in itself and providing further information required for the next step. The hardware, rigs and actual aircraft, were designed from the outset to make this step approach possible.

The overall concept of the Vertijet made use of VTOL to dispense with the weight, volume and complexity of retractable wheeled landing gear. It was therefore fully committed to a VTOL-only role with no prospect of operational use in STOL mode. As such, its maximum take-off weight was limited by available engine thrust and its payload and range were severely limited. It also suffered from the same drawbacks as the propeller tailsitters in the difficult hori-

zontal to vertical transition and poor pilot vision during landing. Although Ryan proposed a further project and an artist's impression showed an aircraft similar to an F-106 emerging vertically from a silo, the USAF declined to provide funding for further work.

SNECMA, the Société Nationale d'Etude et Construction de Moteurs d'Aviation, of Sèvres in France, also worked on jet tailsitters as part of a larger project. They proposed a manned ramjet interceptor fighter capable of fast response to high-altitude bomber threats. Under ramjet power this would behave more like a missile than an aircraft but at lower speeds it would fly aerodynamically using its annular ramjet casing as a wing and a jet engine for propulsion. It was to be trailer-transportable and would take off and land vertically.

The overall concept was very attractive and met the contemporary need for a transportable area-defence system. It also conveyed the same illusion as the XFV-1/XFY-1 concept that it would take off vertically and vanish skyward like a missile, whereas in practice it would have to make a transition to horizontal flight and fly for some time on jet power until it had accelerated to ramjet speed. The whole programme was very ambitious in combining the unknowns of VTOL, annular wing and ramjets. In retrospect any one of these appears difficult enough, and to attempt all three, with cross-compromises, in one aircraft design must have taken a whole lot of Gallic bravery.

SNECMA started work on the VTOL aspects of the project by flying a model on an indoor tethered rig. The model used a pulse-jet engine similar to that which powered the Second World War V1 flying bombs. The pulse-jet has no rotating parts and so has the advantage of having no gyroscopic effects, making control easier. The model flew successfully indoors by remote control during 1955 and 1956.

The next step was the full-size C400 P1 Atar Volant (Flying Atar). This consisted of an Atar D (developed BMW 003) jet engine, fuel tank and control system mounted vertically on a skeletal four-point landing gear. The control system included autostabilisation and worked by deflecting the jet thrust to create lateral forces and moments, whilst air jets were used to generate control moments in azimuth. The P1 was tethered beneath a tall outdoor overhead gantry and was remote-controlled from a desk in a cabin some 130 ft away. A joystick was used to control fore-and-aft and lateral tilt, and a knob on top of the stick steered the P1 in azimuth. A

Far left: Early SNECMA VTOL experiments included a pulse-jet powered model. The pulse-jet engine has no gyroscopic effects and makes control easier. The audience seem ill-equipped for the experience. (Copyright reserved)

The first SNECMA Atar Volant, the C-400 P1, was flown by remote control while tethered beneath the test gantry. (Copyright reserved)

The second Atar Volant was the C-400 P2. This had an ejector seat and pilot's controls. Here test pilot Auguste Morel boards C400 P2 with the aid of a man-powered gantry. (Copyright reserved)

separate lever controlled engine thrust. Over 250 successful tethered flights were made, starting in 1955 and concluding in February 1957. The Flying Atar and its control system proved very reliable and any 'incidents' which occurred were mostly attributed to the remote control system or to the lag in the pilots' perceptions at such a distance.

By March 1957 the C400 P2 was ready. This was similar to the P1 but had a pilot's ejector seat and control panel added on top of the Atar, some 15 ft above the ground. After tethered testing beneath the gantry during March and April, test pilot Auguste Morel made the first free flight on 14 May 1957. His account of flights on the P2 stress the need for delicate handling of throttle and tilt. He had 6,400 pounds of thrust available to support a machine of gross weight 5,700 pounds, which gave him only 0.1 g upward acceleration to arrest any sink rate. This meant that rates of descent had to be very slow, and the power lever had to be handled with great delicacy. The small excess of power also limited the amount of tilt which could be applied, since at angles beyond 25 degrees the downward component of thrust was insufficient to support the weight. So long as these limitations were observed the P2 proved to be a very controllable machine and it would hover 'hands-off' under the control of the autostabilisation system. The P2 scored greatly over other tailsitters in having the pilot seated right-way-up and in giving him an excellent unobstructed view of his environment, including the horizon.

The C400 P3 was similar to the P2 with

Auguste Morel flew C400 P2 on many occasions. Control was via an autostabilisation system, which made P2 reasonably easy to fly provided that fast sink rates and excessive tilt angles were avoided. (Copyright reserved)

the addition of an aircraft-type nose and cockpit, pointing vertically upward, as on earlier tailsitter aircraft. The P3 was intended as the next stage in the programme, but it did not fly and was used as a simulator for pilot training. Later it was mounted horizontally on the flat-bed of a railway train for dynamic simulation of airflow during a vertical landing. The P3 exhaust was pointed in the direction of motion and the train was slowly

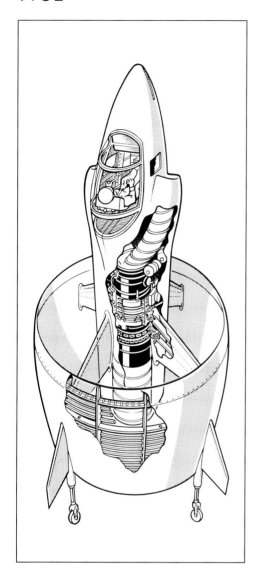

accelerated to find the speed at which the Atar began to have breathing problems and lose thrust.

The C450 Coléoptère was the next step in the programme, and was intended to achieve both VTOL and aerodynamic flight. The Coléoptère had a fuselage and cockpit similar to the C400 P3. The cockpit contained a tilting ejector seat as in other tailsitters, and the pilot was provided with additional windows in the fuselage floor and sides which afforded a much better field of view than in previous types. The engine air intakes each side of the cockpit were angled to provide the best compromise between breathing in forward flight and breathing at high angles of attack during transition. The rear fuselage was surrounded by an annular wing connected to the fuselage by four radial struts near to its leading periphery. The wing carried four small stabilisers at the rear, and the landing gear, consisting of four small

shock absorbers terminated in small castored wheels. The fuselage was 22 ft long and the annular wing was 10 ft 6 in diameter.

Control of the Coléoptère during vertical flight was by deflection of the jet exhaust. As in the C400, vanes protruding into the jetpipe were rotated to produce suitable deflections. This method of jet deflection was lighter and more compact than that of the Ryan X-13, where the whole exhaust nozzle moved. It also had lighter moving parts and could respond quicker to control demands. Where the C400 used air reaction jets to control roll about its axis, the C450 had no visible roll control mechanism. It is assumed that the exhaust vanes turned differentially to impart twist to the exhaust gases and produce roll moments. In normal forward flight, control was exercised by swivelling the four stabiliser fins. Two small strakes could be extended from the nose to assist in producing a pitch-up moment during hori-

The SNECMA C450 Coléoptère was road-portable on a special trailer. The trailer included a hydraulic jacking system to erect the Coléoptère to its vertical take-off attitude. (Copyright reserved)

Above left: This sectioned view shows how cockpit and annular wing were added to the Atar Volant to create the Coleoptere. (SNECMA)

Vanes in the Coléoptère's jet
exhaust deflected the thrust
of the Atar engine and
controlled the Coléoptère in
pitch and yaw.
(Copyright reserved)

zontal to vertical transition.

Only one Coléoptère was built, and this made a tethered hover lasting 14 minutes on 17 April 1959. The first free hovering flight lasted 3½ minutes and was made by test pilot Auguste Morel on 5 May 1959. Further flights followed and during his sixth flight Morel started to investigate transitional flight. On the seventh and eighth flights a small oscillation was encountered during the final descent.

The ninth flight took place on 25 July 1959. As in the previous flights, this would investigate partial transitions toward the horizontal and back to the vertical. The flight plan specified a vertical take-off and climb, a progressive tilt forward at 6 degrees per second for 6 seconds, constant attitude for 3 seconds, and tilt up again to the vertical, all whilst climbing. The climb was to finish with the aircraft hovering at 2,000 ft altitude from which it would descend vertically backwards at 7 metres per second (23 ft per second). The slow descent was intended to avoid the situation encountered on previous flights where at greater rates of descent the Coléoptère had lost control in roll and had developed minor instabilities in the other axes. Rate of descent would be measured by a helicopter anemometer graduated from 10 to 70 metres per second (33 to 230 ft per second)

Most of the flight took place just as planned. The Coléoptère took off vertically,

tilted, flew at constant attitude, tilted up again and climbed. At the top of the climb, it was higher than planned, at over 3000 ft, and it began to sink faster than planned, at an indicated 10 metres per second (33 ft per second), with a slow uncontrollable roll and small oscillations in the other two axes. The pilot of the chase helicopter advised Morel that he was descending too fast, but Morel was already using full throttle and still losing height. The Coléoptère sank faster and exceeded its stable vertical descent rate, at which point it tilted to an angle of 50 degrees. Morel ejected at 150 ft altitude but was badly hurt, partly because he did not have time to position himself properly in the seat and partly because, ejecting horizontally at low level, his parachute did not open fully and he hit the ground very hard. The Coléoptère retained its 50 degree attitude accelerating horizontally to nearly 200 mph and almost making a transition to horizontal flight before it crashed. The wing with its internal fuel tank burst into fire, but the fuselage broke free and slid clear, permitting the recording instruments to be recovered.

The Coléoptère was destroyed in the crash and not rebuilt. The Atar Volant C400 P2 was preserved and is on display at the Musée de l'Air, le Bourget, Paris.

The XFV-1, XFY-1, X-13 and Coléoptère all resulted from the early post-war burst of enthusiasm for tailsitter VTOL interceptor fighters. After this no more tailsitters were proposed. This is explained in part by the development of better early-warning systems

Pilot access to the Coléoptère required elaborate steps and gantry.

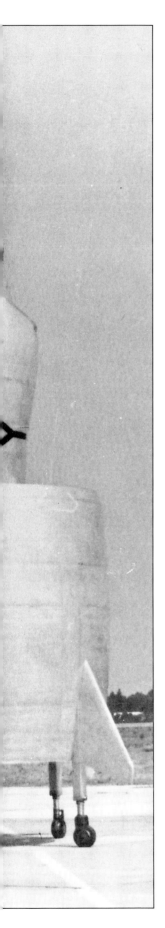

The SNECMA C450 Coléoptère made many successful flights including hovering and partial climbing transitions toward horizontal flight. In this picture the ground control man and radio link are visible.
(Copyright reserved)

and long-range surface-to-air missiles systems. Interceptor fighters were no longer required, and emphasis moved to air superiority, attack and, to a lesser extent, dispersal. The tailsitters, though too small for an air superiority role, had the attributes required for attack and dispersal. What they did not have was flyability and flexibility. They could carry only a small payload and had very limited endurance and range. Even under ideal conditions they were difficult to fly. Transition from horizontal to vertical flight was difficult and subsequent landing was near impossible. The tailsitters were superseded by flat riser designs which afforded better vision to pilots and provided the option of either VTOL with a small payload or STOL with a greater payload.

5 PLATFORMS & FANS

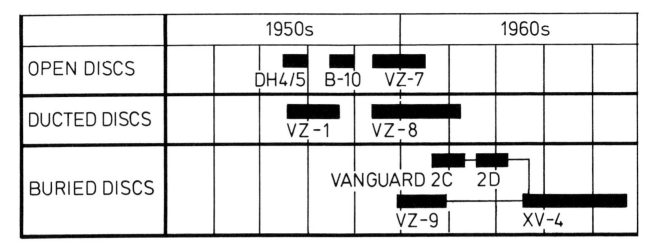

	1950s						1960s					
OPEN DISCS			DH4/5	B-10	VZ-7							
DUCTED DISCS			VZ-1		VZ-8							
BURIED DISCS					VANGUARD 2C 2D							
					VZ-9			XV-4				

Flying platforms

As early as 1946, Charles H. Zimmerman was experimenting with a small platform which had contra-rotating propellers for lift and could be controlled by a pilot standing upright on it. The pilot's natural instinct to remain upright was transmitted by his feet to the platform, which responded appropriately. These initial experiments produced promising results and in 1950 Zimmerman won the support of NACA for an extended programme aimed at producing simple and cheap one-man flying platforms for battlefield use.

Tests commenced at Langley Pilotless Aircraft Research Station in Virginia, chosen because it had a very large compressed air storage tank. It was the availability of compressed air in large quantities which made possible the world's simplest flying machine. This consisted of a plywood platform twenty inches by thirty inches in size and fitted with an air nozzle. The nozzle was fed with compressed air through two hoses attached at opposite ends of the platform. The use of two supply hoses cancelled any effects due to hose tension or to a tendency to straighten under pressure. The pilot stood on the platform, the compressed air was turned on, and the platform and pilot rose upward to hover a few feet above the ground. Altitude could be controlled by regulation of the pressure supplied to the air jet, since the platform would rise, picking up hose with it, until weight of pilot, platform and hose equalled air jet thrust. It was up to the pilot to control the pitch and roll, and hence fore-and-aft and lateral motion of the platform, by balancing. In practice it was found easier to control the platform by instinct. The less the pilot consciously tried to control the platform, the better he was able to maintain his balance. For safety, the pilot was connected by a harness and safety line to

an overhead gantry. This precaution proved its value on the occasions when the pilot, instead of looking at the horizon, glanced down at the platform or up at the gantry. As soon as he did this, all was lost. The platform would lurch violently and the whole gubbins – platform, pilot and hoses – would tip up and vanish sideways like a human rocket, saved only by the safety harness.

The theoreticians were surprised at the ease with which a human pilot could control the platform. They had expected all sorts of rotational coupling effects, but clearly the human brain, accustomed to controlling an unstable two-legged vehicle through all sorts of strange activities such as walking, running, jumping, cycling and so on, had long ago sorted out ways of handling the relatively trivial task of standing still.

The results of the airjet platform experiments were so encouraging that NACA decided to continue the work by testing a propeller-driven platform. To save weight, they again used compressed air as the source of power, this time using it to drive a 7 ft diameter propeller via airjets at its tips. The propeller bearings were attached rigidly to the pilot's footboard, which in turn was mounted resiliently to a steel platform 21 inches in diameter. The platform carried a tubular structure including propeller guards, landing feet, and pilot's handrail. Torque reaction was provided by airjets at waist height.

The platform was tested in various control modes. If the pilot did not hold the hand-rail, but simply controlled the platform by standing on it and flexing his feet, then satisfactory control was possible over a limited range of attitudes. Experienced pilots found it possible to fly when grasping the handrail. When the propeller was locked to the platform, disabling the resilient mounts, the platform became difficult to control, but

Platforms and fan-lifted aircraft were developed over the years 1955 to 1965. (Author)

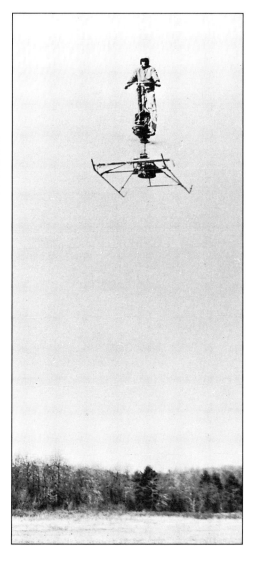

The de Lackner DH-5 Aerocycle was a flying platform which used open contra-rotating rotors driven by a marine outboard motor.

control. Below the rotor four horizontal struts ended in floats, permitting the Helivector to alight on land or on water. Altitude was controlled by the throttle twist-grip, and attitude by leaning. Performance was claimed to include horizontal speeds up to 65 mph, payload in addition to pilot of 120 pounds and endurance of one hour. The Helivector's rotors were large in area and quite dangerous, especially when landing on rough ground or in a confined space.

Hiller's flying platform resulted from work that Hiller was doing for the Office of Naval Research (ONR) on ducted fans. The ONR was interested in flying platform work and awarded Hiller a contract to develop a one-man VTOL vehicle with contra-rotating ducted propellers. The duct was intended to increase lift and would permit the use of a smaller diameter lifting disc. It would also protect personnel from injury and make for easier landing on rough ground.

Hiller designed a platform driven by two Nelson H-59 two-stroke piston engines rated at 44 hp each. The propellers rotated within an annular duct of 5 ft diameter, said to increase thrust by 20 per cent. The pilot stood on a platform above the propellers and controlled the vehicle by use of twistgrip throttle and by grasping a circular hand-rail and leaning to tilt the propellers. Extensive tethered trials were conducted with this

when it was attached via anti-teetering springs, control was satisfactory. Ground effect at low altitude tended to improve stability. The propeller platform was more stable than the airjet one in still air, but reacted worse to wind gusts.

Further test results were provided by a remote-controlled electrically-powered model, controlled by vanes in the propeller downdraught.

The test data were collated by NACA and were made available to the aircraft industry. Three companies, de Lackner, Hiller and Bensen responded with flying platform designs.

De Lackner's DH-4 'Helivector' and DH-5 'Aerocycle' used contra-rotating rotors of 15 ft diameter. The large disc area produced a very low disc loading and only a single 40 hp Kiekhaefer Mercury outboard motor was required. The pilot stood on a small platform above the rotors and held a handlebar assembly with twist-grip throttle

The Hiller VZ-1 Pawnee flying platform used contra-rotating propellers of 5 ft diameter. The props rotated within a duct to improve their thrust.

VTOL

version and the first free flight took place on 4 February 1955.

The platform was developed further to make it easier to control. The landing legs were lengthened to give more ground clearance and contol vanes were added in the propeller downdraught. Photos indicate that this developed version was sufficiently stable to allow the pilot to take his hands off the controls and aim a rifle.

A later version developed to a US Army contract for an observation platform was known as the VZ-1E Pawnee. This had three engines driving larger 8 ft diameter ducted propellers and was again controlled by vanes in the propeller downdraught. The larger propellers increased the disc area from 20 to 50 square feet and reduced the disc loading to less than half its former value. This increased payload and range while reducing downdraught velocity and noise.

A heavy-lift variant of the VZ-1 used a

When control vanes were added to the VZ-1, it could be flown hands-off. This enabled the pilot to snipe at the enemy while they politely held their fire.
(Copyright reserved)

Right: This later version of the Hiller Pawnee had larger, 8ft, diameter ducted propellers. Disc area was more than doubled, resulting in a much lower disc loading, improved efficiency and less noise.
(Copyright reserved)

Right: This three-view of the Bensen B-10 is a reconstruction which shows the approximate shape of the Bensen B-10 flying platform. The two fixed-pitch propellers were driven by separately throttled engines. Altitude was controlled partly by vanes and partly by engine throttles.
(Mike Keep)

much deeper duct. The greater depth of the duct reduced recirculation of the airflow and so enhanced propeller performance. The duct also increased the range of heights at which lift was assisted by ground effect.

Hiller Pawnee platforms may be seen at the Smithsonian Institution, and at the Hill Country Museum, Gilroy, California.

The third one-man platform was the Bensen B-10 Propcopter. This used a longitudinal beam as a basis for its structure. The pilot sat astride the centre of the beam, which was lifted by two 4 ft diameter propellers, one in front of the pilot and one behind him, both at waist height. The props were powered by two 72 hp McCulloch 4318E engines. Total weight, excluding pilot, was 650 pounds. The Propcopter was controlled by the engine throttles and by longitudinal and lateral vanes situated in the propeller downdraughts. Collective throttle controlled altitude, differential throttle controlled pitch and differential deflection of the longitudinal vanes controlled yaw. Station could be maintained forward and sideways by collective deflection of the lateral and longitudinal vanes, and these were also used for low-speed manoeuvring. Forward motion at higher speeds was attained by letting the B-10 pitch forward, so that the thrust vector had a component rearward, and adjusting the collective throttle to maintain altitude as the

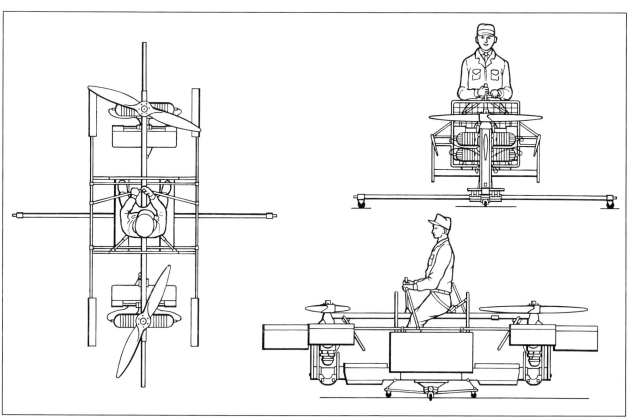

In this jumbo duct version of the VZ-1 lift was enhanced by lengthening the recirculation path. It could lift heavier loads and achieve greater forward speed. (Copyright reserved)

vertical component of thrust diminished slightly. Flying a complex machine like the B-10 without the assistance of an autostabiliser required intense concentration on the part of the pilot. The B-10 flew during 1959.

The one-man platforms relied on small lightweight piston engines for their power and carried a very small payload. When gas turbines became available, their much greater power-to-weight ratio made larger vehicles possible and the US Army became interested in 'flying jeeps' and 'flying trucks'. The US Army Transportation Research Command awarded contracts to Curtiss-Wright AeroPhysics and to Piasecki to develop vehicles in the one to two ton weight range.

The AeroPhysics Division of Curtiss-Wright at Santa Barbara were assigned the designation VZ-7AP for their flying truck. This had a box section beam as a fuselage.

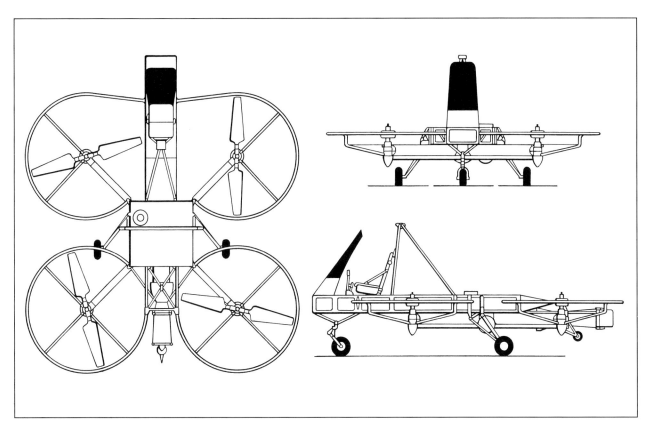

The Curtiss-Wright VZ-7 flying truck was lifted by four propellers and used their 'radial force' properties for propulsion. Control was effected via propeller pitch and by vanes in the Turbomeca Artouste exhaust.
(Author)

The control panel and pilot's seat were at the front of the vehicle and on top of the beam. Lift was generated by four horizontal propellers, one on each side of the fuselage front and rear, and attached by diagonal beams. The engine, a 425 hp Turbomeca Artouste IIB turboshaft, was slung under the centre of the beam and drove the propellers through a system of shafts and gearboxes. Conventional tricycle landing gear was used with a nose-wheel beneath the pilot's seat and main wheels each side of the central engine. The VZ-7 was 17 ft long, 16 ft wide and weighed approximately 1,700 pounds, including 550 pounds of payload.

The four propellers of the VZ-7 had variable collective pitch. Altitude was controlled by changing all four pitches together. Pitch and roll were controlled by applying pitch differentials between pairs of propellers, fore and aft for pitch and laterally for roll. The engine exhaust was piped to the rear of the fuselage beam and a rudder in the exhaust provided control in yaw. The VZ-7 had a stability augmentation system. Rate gyros sensed motion in pitch and yaw and the system applied appropriate control corrections.

The VZ-7 was tested during 1959 and 1960. The programme ended in 1961, and the VZ-7 was moved to the Army Aviation Museum at Fort Rucker, Alabama.

The other contender for the Transportation Research Command programme was the Piasecki 59 H Airgeep, known by the Army as the VZ-8P. The Airgeep was 26 ft long and 9 ft wide, most of this area being taken up by two horizontal ducted rotors, one at the front and one at the rear, with the pilot and passenger sat side-by-side amidships. The 8 ft diameter rotors each had three blades and rotated in opposite directions from one another to eliminate gyroscopic effects. They were driven by two 180 hp Lycoming O-360-A2A piston engines linked so that either could drive both rotors if the other failed.

Each rotor could be controlled in collective and in lateral cyclic pitch. In the ducts beneath the rotors, the downdraughts could be deflected by longitudinal and lateral vanes. Pitch was controlled by differential change of the two rotor collective pitches, roll by changing the lateral cyclic pitch of both rotors, and yaw by differential deflection of the longitudinal vanes beneath the rotors. Collective movement of the lateral and longitudinal vanes gave control of forward and lateral position. Forward motion at higher speed was attained by tilting the whole machine forward. Although the control mechanisms were similar to that of the Propcopter, the Airgeep would have been easier to control because the rotors were

The Piasecki VZ-8P Airgeep used ducted rotors. It was controlled by rotor collective and cyclic pitches and by vanes in the rotor downdraughts.
(Department of Defense)

The VZ-8P (B) was an improved version of the Airgeep with more power and better lifting capacity. The tilt of the rear rotor reduced drag and allowed it to fly at greater forward speeds.
(Copyright reserved)

relatively large and were close enough to the ground to obtain a cushion effect.

The Airgeep made its first flight on 12 October 1958. After a brief demonstration, it was returned to the workshops where the Lycoming piston engines were removed and replaced by a single 425 hp Turbomeca Artouste IIB gas turbine. It flew with the Artouste engine on 28 June 1959. In this form it weighed 2,500 pounds and could carry a payload of 1,200 pounds including pilot. The Artouste was later replaced in turn by the lighter and more powerful AiResearch 331-6. The Airgeep was evaluated both by the Army and by the Navy. For Navy trials, starting in June 1961, large floats were added so that the VZ-8, now known as the PA-59 N SeaGeep, could land on water.

Piasecki were still improving the 59 H and proposed an upgrade in the Model 59 K. The Army Transportation Research Command awarded them a further contract and the 59 K was designated VZ-8P (B) Airgeep II. The configuration of the Airgeep II was similar to that of the Airgeep I but with rotors and ducts tilted so that their airstreams diverged fore and aft, to reduce induced drag in forward flight. Two 400 hp Turbomeca Artouste IIC turbo shaft engines were installed, providing more than double the power available in the Lycoming-powered Airgeep I and increasing the maximum flying weight to 4,800 pounds. The outputs of the two engines were combined in a single gearbox so that either could drive both props to provide engine-out safety. One engine could also be connected through a hydrostatic transmission to the wheels of the landing gear to drive the 59 K at speeds up to 35 mph.

The Airgeep family of platforms had significant advantages over helicopters. They were smaller and more manoeuvrable, and could fly close to and even under obstacles. They made a better weapons platform, since the aircraft could remain behind cover and only the weapon need be exposed. The helicopter had advantages, however, in landing on rough ground and in its more convenient seating arrangements. The most significant difference was that of fuel consumption. The Airgeeps had very small disc areas compared with helicopters, and used a lot more fuel to lift the same payload.

The disc-lift technique was now a mature technology, capable of lifting substantial weights and it became feasible to consider combining the VTOL capability of disc lift with the aerodynamic flight capability of the aeroplane. It was not easy to combine the two technologies because the lifting discs were not easily accommodated in an aerodynamic vehicle.

Two former Piasecki engineers, Edward G. Vanderlip and John J. Schneider, founded the Vanguard Air and Marine Corporation with the express intention of building a VTOL executive aircraft. They intended to combine disc lift with aerodynamic lift by burying the discs in the aircraft wings. Their Vanguard Omniplane Model 2C used the 25 ft long fuselage of an Ercoupe light plane and the rotors and mechanical transmission from a previous Jacobs convertiplane project. The 6 ft diameter three-bladed rotors were buried inside cushion-shaped wings of 22 ft span. The rotors were driven via mechanical clutches so that they could be powered for take-off and landing and left stationary during horizontal aerodynamic flight. Covers over the tops of the rotors and louvres in the lower wing surface could be opened for hovering and closed flush with the wing surface in normal flight. Forward propulsion was provided by a 5 ft diameter ducted propeller in the tail. The elevator and rudder surfaces were directly behind the propeller duct and were intended to retain the power to control the aircraft in pitch and yaw during vertical take-off and landing. Roll was controlled by differential blade pitch at the two lifting propellers. The Model 2C was powered by a 265 hp Lycoming O-540-A1A piston engine. Total weight for a vertical take-off was to be 2,600 pounds.

The Omniplane in its Model 2C configuration was tested by NASA at Ames and they requested various modifications, particularly to the control system. Vanguard incorporated these modifications, updating the Omniplane to Model 2D during 1961. The Lycoming piston engine was replaced by a 600 hp Lycoming YT53-L-1 turboshaft and the nose was lengthened by 5 ft to house a third horizontal propeller. The function of the nose prop was to provide improved control in pitch and yaw during hover. In this form, roll was controlled by applying differential pitch to the wing props, pitch was controlled by applying appropriate blade pitch to the nose prop, and yaw was controlled by tilting longitudinal vanes in the nose prop downdraught.

The Model 2D completed tethered tests but suffered a mechanical transmission failure during subsequent wind-tunnel testing. Development was discontinued early in 1962. Although the Omniplane did not make free flights, the concept of a disc-in-wing aircraft had been converted into hardware and useful test results were accumulated to be used in later work.

The Avro VZ-9 Avrocar was an attempt to make an observation platform which would hover both in and out of ground effect and also be capable of aerodynamic flight. It proved to be too difficult to stabilise and flew only briefly in ground effect. (Department of Defense)

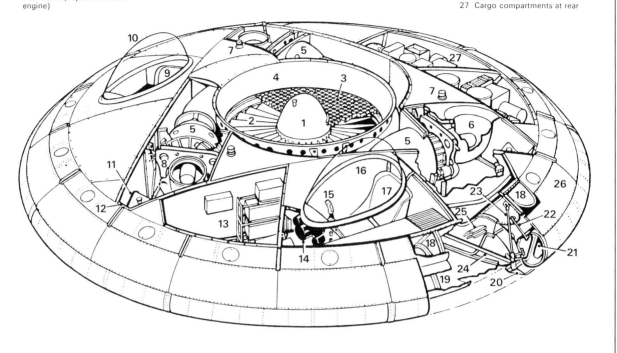

1 Turborotor hub fairing
2 Multi-blade turborotor, diameter 5 ft (1,52 m)
3 Anti-ingestion grille
4 Circular air-intake duct
5 Three J69 turbojets (tangentially mounted)
6 Engine air intakes
7 Fuel tanks (adjacent to each engine)
8 Engine bearing frame
9 Observer's seat
10 Observer's bubble canopy
11 Oil tanks (each engine)
12 Forward apex of triangular sub-frame assembly
13 Accessories compartment
14 Pilot's instrument panel
15 Control column
16 Pilot's bubble canopy
17 Pilot's seat
18 Upper section of inner rim
19 Lower section of inner rim
20 Adjustable 'focussing ring'
21 Section of outer rim
22 Outer rim supporting struts
23 Focussing ring supporting struts
24 Focussing ring control rods
25 Guide vanes for airflow to peripheral nozzle
26 Sealing plates between inner and outer rims
27 Cargo compartments at rear

At the Avro Canada plant in Malton, Toronto another team led by Englishman John Frost had also decided to combine disc lift with aerodynamic lift by burying the disc within a lifting surface. They produced a strange machine known as project Y or the Avrocar. This was perfectly circular in shape, and had no visible flight control surfaces.

Whilst the shape of the Avrocar was quite remarkable, its most significant feature was hidden inside. Avro Canada had harnessed the power of the jet engine without making it into a turboshaft, and they had done it at high efficiency. The high velocity exhaust of the jet engine was used to drive a turbine on the periphery of the fan. The turbine carried the fan with it, and the fan induced a larger mass flow at much lower velocity. The turbine and fan were taking energy from the high-velocity, low momentum jet exhaust and converting it into an airflow at low velocity and high momentum. Since lift is equal to momentum flow, the net effect was an increase in lift.

The Avrocar was intended to take off vertically, but to remain in ground effect whilst it accelerated to flying speed. It would then fly aerodynamically to the target area, where it would be able to hover at altitude or loiter in ground effect. The return flight would be aerodynamic, followed by a vertical landing. The use of ground effect for take-off would incease the fuel load which it could lift, and the use of ground effect during loiter would decrease its fuel consumption. This double use of ground effect would greatly extend the possible flying time.

The Avrocar was 18 ft in diameter and 3½ feet thick with flat underside and convex upper surface. In the middle of the upper surface there was a large air intake for the 5 ft diameter 31-blade fan. Other holes in the upper surface served as air intakes for the three jet engines. There were three fuelling points, one for each engine. Two cockpits with bubble canopies were situated well to each side and forward of centre, and the surface in front of them was painted matt black to prevent dazzle.

The internal structure was in the shape of an equilateral triangle. The fan took up most of the interior of the triangle. It was turned by the exhaust gases from three Continental J69 jet engines which, together with their fuel tanks, were mounted in the corners of the triangle. There were three

The Avrocar was built on a triangular frame, with fan and engines within the triangle and cockpits and equipment bay outside.
(Avro Canada)

segments of the disc outside the triangle. Two of these were used for the two cockpits and the third as a cargo compartment.

The air blown through the fan was mixed with the hot gas from the turbine and was used both to support the Avrocar in hovering flight and to provide propulsion. At low level, in ground effect, the engines were run at low power and the air was ducted out under the engines, cockpits and cargo bay to a peripheral nozzle which extended around the entire circumference of the airframe. This directed the airflow downward and inward to trap a cushion of high-pressure air, just as in a hovercraft. For flight at higher level, out of ground effect, the engines were run at full power and the fan air was blown straight down, as in flying platforms, though the power required was greater than that for a platform because of the smaller disc area. In forward flight, the air from the peripheral nozzle was directed backward to provide propulsion while the wing produced lift.

Because of its unorthodox shape and lack of conventional stabilisers, the Avrocar was unstable in forward flight. It therefore needed an autostabiliser for normal flight, as well as for cushion-borne hover and for full hover. The autostabiliser was very ingenious and used the fan both as a two-axis rate gyro and as a source of actuator power. The fan was resiliently mounted on springs. When the Avrocar tilted, the fan tended to remain in the same attitude, causing relative motion between fan and vehicle. The relative motion was transmitted by linkages to spoilers in the peripheral nozzle. These modified the nozzle airflow so as to produce moments in pitch and roll tending to restore the vehicle to the desired attitude. This was a very simple and reliable control system, but it made no provision for adjustment of control parameters, and it was not possible to change its parameters to suit the three modes of flight.

The Avrocar attracted the attention of the US Department of Defense, who awarded Avro a development contract in 1955 and gave it the designation VZ-9AV. The craft made its first tethered flight at Malton on 5 December 1959. After further tethered flights, it was moved to NASA Ames for wind tunnel tests. It was returned to Malton in 1961 and began forward flight trials on 17 May 1961. It made two trips down the runway a few feet above the ground and still in ground effect. It was not completely stable, a contemporary description reporting that it 'bobbled' down the runway.

Above a height of four feet off the ground, the Avrocar became unstable and for safety all further flights were tethered. The development contract ended in December 1961 and the project was discontinued. In retrospect it was audacious to expect a simple mechanical gyrostabiliser to be stable in the three separate flight regimes. Indeed, it would be difficult enough to stabilise such a vehicle even with modern technology.

Of two Avrocars made, one was scrapped and the other was presented to the Smithsonian Institution.

The most significant feature of the Avrocar was the jetfan. This made the jet engine more fuel-efficient in hovering flight. The US Army Transportation Research Command placed a contract with GE in November 1961 for two research aircraft which would combine the Vanguard Omniplane disc-in-wing concept with Avrocar-type jetfans. GE took responsibility for the engines and fans and subcontracted Ryan to design and build the airframes. The army designation for the aircraft was VZ-11, soon changed to XV-5A. Ryan followed their usual practice and gave it the in-house name Vertifan.

The design of the XV-5A was driven by the need to accommodate and power the fans. The wings were built around the two main lift fans, each wing having a small inboard sweep cranked to a greater outboard sweep and a straight trailing edge. The two engines were in mid-fuselage to permit the exhaust gases to be diverted either to the fans for lift or to the tailpipes for thrust. The single engine air intake was above the fuselage to minimise interaction with fan airflow. A long bulbous nose accommodated the third fan and its deflector vanes.

The fuselage was 44 ft long and had a T tail. The horizontal stabiliser angle was variable and was programmed to adjust pitch trim during transitions. Wingspan was 30 ft. As the wings were full of fan, the landing gear had to retract into the fuselage, resulting in a narrow track. The engines were two General Electric J85-GE-5 turbojets rated at 2,650 pounds static thrust each. They were cross-ducted so that either could drive all three fans in an emergency, though at reduced power. The wing fans were GE type X353-5B and the nose fan was a GE type X376. The total engine thrust of 5,300 pounds was multiplied by the turbine/fan units to produce a lift thrust of 16,000 pounds. Aircraft weight was 7,000 pounds empty and 12,200 pounds maximum for VTOL.

The nose fan was covered by flaps and the wing fans were covered by butterfly flaps above and transverse louvres below. In preparation for vertical flight, the flaps and louvres were opened and the engines were

VTOL

The Ryan XV-5A Vertifan was lifted by jet-driven fans in nose and wings. The clamshell doors over the wing fans are open and the nose fan air deflectors can just be seen each side of the nose.
(Ryan)

This cutaway view shows the internal details of the Ryan Vertifan. Engine air intakes are above the fuselage to the rear of the cockpit. Exhausts are fed either to the jetpipes or to power the three fans.
(Ryan)

run up to speed. A thrust spoiler system prevented the aircraft from being driven forward. When the engines reached full power, thrust was diverted to the fans for vertical take-off.

In vertical and hovering flight, roll was controlled by differential adjustment of wing fan thrusts, pitch by adjustment of nose fan thrust, and yaw by differential movement of the wing fan louvres. The louvres could also be used collectively to provide fore-and-aft propulsion.

Transition to forward flight was initiated by deflecting the wing louvres backward to generate forward thrust. At 120 knots airspeed, wing lift was sufficient to support aircraft weight, thrust was diverted to the jetpipes and the fan covers were closed.

In forward flight the XV-5 was controlled by the conventional control surfaces.

Transition from airborne flight to vertical flight started at 150 knots when the the fan covers were opened and the engine thrust was diverted to drive the fans. The engines were throttled for a sink rate of 3 to 4 ft per second and the aircraft descended gently to the ground.

Two XV-5A Vertifans were made. The first flight took place on 25 May 1964. Both aircraft flew and participated in the test programme. One was lost in an accident in April 1965. The second continued test flying until it too was damaged in October 1966. It was rebuilt in modified form as the XV-5B for use by NASA. Modifications included

1. Pitot mast
2. Fibre glass nose cone
3. X376 pitch fan
4. Nose-fan thrust control door
5. Nose-fan inlet closure doors
6. Windshield
7. Nose-fan supply duct
8. Rudder pedals
9. Instrument panel
10. Conventional control stick

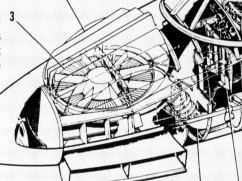

11. Observer's ejection seat
12. Nose landing gear
13. Throttle quadrant
14. Pilot's ejection seat
15. Collective lift stick
16. Hydraulic equipment compartment
17. Single split engine inlet duct
18. Electrical equipment compartment
19. Hydraulic pump
20. FWD main fuel tank
21. Generator
22. Right wing
23. J-85 gas generator

One Ryan XV-5A was converted to become the XV-5B shown here. The larger nose fan and wider fixed landing gear are clearly visible.
(Teledyne Ryan)

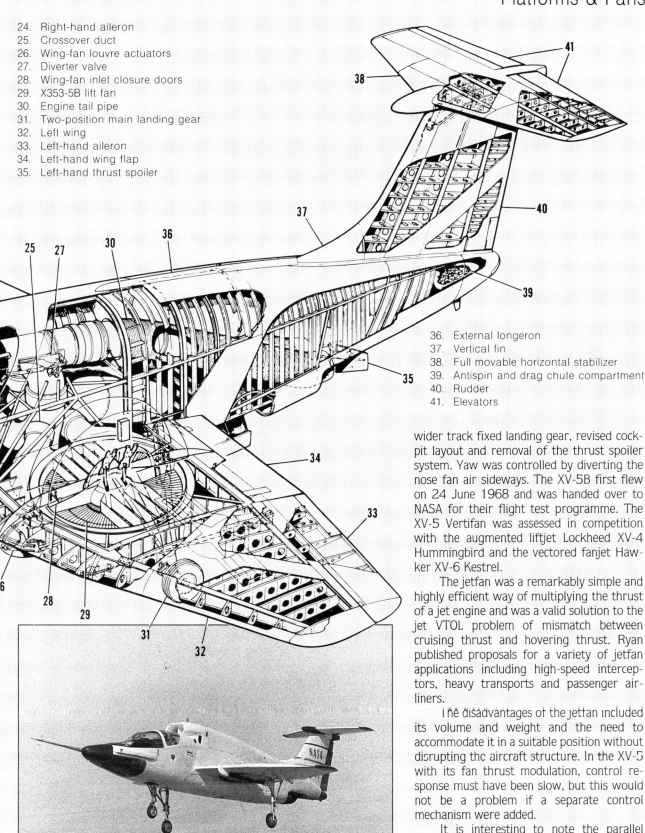

24. Right-hand aileron
25. Crossover duct
26. Wing-fan louvre actuators
27. Diverter valve
28. Wing-fan inlet closure doors
29. X353-5B lift fan
30. Engine tail pipe
31. Two-position main landing gear
32. Left wing
33. Left-hand aileron
34. Left-hand wing flap
35. Left-hand thrust spoiler

36. External longeron
37. Vertical fin
38. Full movable horizontal stabilizer
39. Antispin and drag chute compartment
40. Rudder
41. Elevators

wider track fixed landing gear, revised cockpit layout and removal of the thrust spoiler system. Yaw was controlled by diverting the nose fan air sideways. The XV-5B first flew on 24 June 1968 and was handed over to NASA for their flight test programme. The XV-5 Vertifan was assessed in competition with the augmented liftjet Lockheed XV-4 Hummingbird and the vectored fanjet Hawker XV-6 Kestrel.

The jetfan was a remarkably simple and highly efficient way of multiplying the thrust of a jet engine and was a valid solution to the jet VTOL problem of mismatch between cruising thrust and hovering thrust. Ryan published proposals for a variety of jetfan applications including high-speed interceptors, heavy transports and passenger airliners.

The disadvantages of the jetfan included its volume and weight and the need to accommodate it in a suitable position without disrupting the aircraft structure. In the XV-5 with its fan thrust modulation, control response must have been slow, but this would not be a problem if a separate control mechanism were added.

It is interesting to note the parallel between the turbine-powered fans used in the Avrocar and the Vertifan and the turbine-powered fan which drives the front nozzles of the Pegasus vectored thrust turbofan engine.

U. S. ARMY
4148

6 ROTORCRAFT

	1950s	1960s	1970s	1980s
COMPOUND AUTOGYROS	JET GYRODYNE ROTODYNE / XV-1	Ka-22		
COMPOUND HELICOPTERS		PATHFINDER / XH-51A AH-56	S-72 RSRA	
TILT ROTORS	1G — 2 / XV-3		XV-15	

The rotor is the most effective way of attaining vertical flight because its large area permits a very low disc loading, which minimises the power required to hover and also minimises the downwash to which objects below it are subjected. Of course, appreciable power is still required and downwash is still a significant effect, but much less so than in aircraft with smaller discs.

The conventional helicopter, which uses a large diameter rotor, is very efficient in vertical flight and should be the ideal VTOL aircraft. The rotor, however, which gives the helicopter such an advantage in vertical flight, presents severe limitations in forward flight because it can be used only at low forward speeds.

The conventional helicopter has a driven rotor, including both flapping hinges and drag hinges, collective and cyclic pitch controls and a tail rotor for yaw control. In forward flight, each rotor blade has to travel faster than the helicopter on one side and slower on the other, yet maintain the same lift on both sides. The flapping hinges allow the blades to rise and fall, and each blade naturally falls on the 'slow' side, increasing lift, and rises on the 'fast' side, decreasing lift. This is quite acceptable at low forward speeds, but creates problems at higher forward speeds. The speed of the forward-moving blade must not exceed its usable Mach number and the speed of the rearward-moving blade must not be so slow that it stalls and begins to flutter.

The situation is aggravated by the need to tilt the rotor forward to produce forward propulsion. As a result, the conventional helicopter is limited to a maximum forward speed of approximately 200 knots. Attempts to circumvent the speed limitations of the rotorborne helicopter led to a number of families of convertiplanes, which take off as a helicopter and convert in a variety of ways to aerodynamic flight.

The first two families were those which continued to use the rotor but which used separate forward thrust and additional aerodynamic lift. The forward thrust removed the need to tilt the rotor forward and the aerodynamic lift off-loaded the rotor and reduced the rise and fall of the blades. Both effects allowed the rotor to be flown faster. In theory a thin, rigid rotor can be flown at almost Mach 0.5, so that the advancing blade moves forward at a little less than Mach 1 and the retreating blade does not quite move backward. In practice, it was very difficult to meet all of the conditions for optimum speed, but the addition of thrust and aerodynamic lift did enable higher speeds to be attained

The addition of separate thrust and aerodynamic lift to helicopters created the compound helicopter family of convertiplanes. A compound helicopter has a driven rotor, thrust and lift. There was a second very similar convertiplane family in which the rotor, although driven during take-off, was not driven in forward flight. These were compound autogyros and had undriven rotor, thrust and lift. Because they used rotors, these two types of convertiplane – compound helicopter and compound autogyro – were still limited in speed by their horizontal rotors. Speed limitations ranged from 200 knots for a loaded rotor to around 280 knots for a completely offloaded rotor under ideal conditions.

In theory there was a third family of convertiplanes where the rotor was stopped and the aircraft flew by aerodynamic means alone. Several ways of making stopped rotor convertiplanes were proposed, but none are known to have flown.

A fourth family of convertiplanes was that in which the rotor was tilted forward through 90 degrees. It ceased to be a rotor, and became a propeller, both providing forward propulsion and circumventing the forward speed limitations of the rotor. Lift in forward flight was provided by conventional aerodynamic wings. The tiltrotor family of convertiplanes had all the advantages of the helicopter in vertical flight and all those of an aeroplane in forward flight.

Because rotorcraft required less power,

Rotor convertiplane development spans the years from 1950 to the present. Compound autogyros lasted to the mid-sixties, and compound helicopters to the early seventies. Tiltrotor work continues. (Author)

it was natural that the rotor convertiplanes should be the first of the early VTOL designs. It was possible to make piston-engined rotorcraft, but all other VTOL aircraft (except lightweight platforms) had to wait for the lighter and more powerful gas turbine.

This chapter describes VTOL rotor convertiplanes. The conventional helicopter and autogyro are not included, since they do not convert to aerodynamic flight. Both are well-documented elsewhere.

Compound autogyros

A conventional autogyro has a free-wheeling rotor and a means of forward propulsion. As the autogyro is propelled forward through the air, the periphery of the rotor is driven by the airflow causing the rotor to autorotate; the inner area of the rotor then creates lift. Because the weight of the aircraft is supported by only part of the rotor, disc loading is greater than that for a helicopter of the same weight and rotor diameter. The autogyro is therefore less efficient than the helicopter.

A pure autogyro would have an unpowered rotor and would not be able to take off vertically. It was however, usual to provide a low-power coupling from engine to rotor which, though incapable of providing enough drive for helicopter flight, was able to spin the feathered rotor up to design speed. A sudden increase in blade pitch would then cause the machine to jump into the air as the flywheel energy of the rotor was converted to potential energy. At the same time the propeller accelerated the machine to forward flying speed. This hazardous manoeuvre does little to enhance passenger comfort and confidence and the simple autogyro has been used mainly for small sports craft.

A compound autogyro has the means to transmit full power to the rotor for helicopter take-off, and it also has wings to off-load the rotor in forward flight. In theory it combines the best features of all types of aircraft. For take-off and landing it is a helicopter, providing vertical flight with low disc loading. In transition it becomes an autogyro and during forward flight it becomes an aeroplane with the rotor providing only a small part of the lift, the very low disc loading then permitting faster forward flight.

Compound autogyros were built by McDonnell, Fairey and Kamov. The McDonnell XV-1 took part in the competition for US Army Transportation in the mid-fifties, Fairey conducted an extended programme comprising the Gyrodyne, Jet Gyrodyne, and Rotodyne from 1947 to 1962 and Kamov

The McDonnell XV-1 compound autogyro lifts off the ground. The rotor is driven by tipjets and the pusher propeller is stationary. (Department of Defense)

produced the Ka-22 which flew from 1960 to 1966.

The McDonnell XV-1 was developed jointly by McDonnell Aircraft Corporation, the US Army Transportation Corps and the USAF Wright Air Development Center. It was originally designated the L-25 (liaison) but was transferred to the USAF helicopter series and became the H-35. In 1952 it became the first of the V series as the XV-1.

The XV-1 had a short fat fuselage with plexiglass helicopter-style nose and tandem two-seat cockpit. The engine was in mid-fuselage and drove a pusher propeller. Landing gear consisted of two skids beneath the fuselage. Wings of 26 ft span were shoulder mounted and two tail-booms carried the horizontal stabiliser between them and one vertical stabiliser each. A faired·pylon above the fuselage carried the 31 ft diameter rotor. Overall length was 50 ft. Weight was 4,300 pounds empty and 5,500 pounds loaded.

The engine was a Continental R-975-19 seven-cylinder radial piston engine of 550 hp. This could be coupled to the 6 ft diameter two blade pusher propeller, for forward flight, or to two air compressors, which fed air to the burners of pressure jets at the rotor tips, for take-off. The pressure jets can be thought of as jet engines without moving parts. Instead of extracting energy from the jet exhaust and using it to compress the incoming air, the tipjet was fed with compressed air from the compressors on the engine. Fuel was added to this and burnt in the tipjets to generate thrust which turned the rotor directly.

The first prototype started tethered hover tests early in 1954 and first flew on 11 February. The second prototype first flew on 14 July but was damaged in autorotation trials during December 1954. First transition to horizontal flight was made on 29 April 1955 and during trials on 10 October 1956 a speed of 200 mph was recorded. The XV-1 was the first rotorcraft ever to reach this speed.

The XV-1 might have been the precursor of a larger family of autogyros, but advanced helicopters were catching up fast and the programme was abandoned in 1957.

The British Fairey compay were also trying to find a compromise between the helicopter, the autogyro and aerodynamic lift. Between 1945 and 1947 they had created the Gyrodyne, a small compound helicopter.

The Gyrodyne fuselage was 25 ft long. The two pilots sat side by side in the nose and there was room for two or three passengers behind them. The engine was housed in the middle of the fuselage which tapered to a pointed tail on which was mounted a tailplane with two endplate vertical stabilisers. The 17 ft span stub wings were mid-mounted. The landing gear was of tricycle type with one wheel under the nose and one under each wing.

Above the fuselage a small faired pylon

This rare photo shows the two XV-1 convertiplanes flying together. (Photo Deutsches Museum Munich)

The Fairey Gyrodyne was a compound helicopter. Power from the Alvis Leonides engine drove both rotor and single offset propeller. (Westland)

carried the 52 ft diameter rotor. A single two-blade airscrew was mounted at the tip of the starboard wing. The airscrew provided both torque reaction and forward thrust. The rotor was only required to provide lift. This reduced the loading on the rotor and increased its safety margin.

The Gyrodyne was powered by a 520 hp Alvis Leonides nine-cylinder radial engine. This, together with a complicated system of gearboxes and clutches, accounted for half the aircraft weight, which was 3,600 pounds empty and 4,800 pounds loaded.

The rotor lift was controlled by a throttle lever and collective pitch changed automatically as power was applied. The cyclic control tilted the rotor blade paths relative to the hub and the pedals operated both airscrew pitch and rudders. The first prototype Gyrodyne was completed in September 1947 and first flew on 7 December 1947. On 28 June 1948 it gained the International Helicopter Class G Speed Record for outright speed in a straight line. The average speed for the two opposing runs was 124.3 mph. The next year an attempt was made on the closed-circuit record, but the Gyrodyne crashed killing both crew members. The cause of the crash was diagnosed as a fatigue failure in the rotor head and the second prototype was grounded until a full investigation and fatigue testing had been completed.

The second prototype Gyrodyne was rebuilt as the Jet Gyrodyne. This retained its fuselage, wings, and engine, but gained a new rotor, pusher airscrews and mechanical power transmission system. The rotor auto-rotated in forward flight, and in vertical flight was driven by tipjets similar to those on the McDonnell XV-1.

There were two variable-pitch pusher propellers, one on each wingtip, driven by gear drives from the engine. Differential pitch was applied to provide directional control. There was no torque reaction, so the propellers had only to generate a very small torque to overcome rotorhead friction.

Rotor diameter had grown from 52 ft to 60 ft, giving a useful 25 per cent reduction in disc loading. The longer lever arm was also useful in giving 12 per cent more torque for the same tipjet thrust. Aircraft weight, however, had grown from 4,800 pounds to 6,000 pounds.

Tethered trials began in January 1954 and the first free flight was made later in the same month. The Jet Gyrodyne was under-powered and had great difficulty getting off the ground, even with the Leonides at full boost. The first complete transitions were made in March 1955 but there was insufficient power to maintain level autorotative flight. Transition from horizontal flight to vertical descent was especially hazardous since engine power had to be diverted to the compressors before the tipjets could be lit. With no drive to the airscrews, the Jet Gyrodyne was in unpowered autorotation during the transition and failure to light the burners would force an autorotative landing. Despite these problems the Jet Gyrodyne made many flights and completed some 200 transitions by late 1956. It is now on display at the Aerospace Museum, RAF Cosford, England.

research conducted by Fairey at Hayes into tipjet propulsion systems. The tipjets were scheduled to be tested on the Jet Gyrodyne.

The design grew steadily in size, from the original 15-seat Leonides powered proposal, through Armstrong Siddeley Mamba and Rolls-Royce Dart turboprop versions to a design for a 40 seat passenger transport powered by two 2,800 shp Napier Eland turboprops. This design was built as the

Once again the point was well made that the reciprocating engine did not have the power-to-weight ratio necessary for safe VTOL flight. The information gained from the Jet Gyrodyne test programme contibuted greatly to the design of its successor, the much larger turbine-powered Rotodyne.

The Fairey Rotodyne was intended as a medium capacity VTOL transport for both civil and military use. Preliminary design studies from 1947 to 1949 resulted in a formal proposal for a 15 seat convertiplane with wing-mounted Alvis Leonides engines driving propellers in forward flight and a four-blade rotor with tipjets in vertical and hovering flight. This design was based on data from the Gyrodyne programme and on

prototype, or Model Y, version of the Rotodyne.

The prototype Rotodyne had a box-shaped fuselage with an overall length of 59 ft and internal load space 7 ft wide by 6 ft high by 50 ft long. At the front there was a two seat helicopter-style cockpit affording good vision forward and downward. The box fuselage section was carried back to the tail where it ended in clamshell loading doors. High-mounted straight wings of 46 ft span carried engines and main landing gear in large nacelles at mid span. A high-set horizontal stabiliser carried vertical stabilisers at its tips and a third central vertical stabiliser was fitted during subsequent development. Above the centre of the fuselage a tall faired

One of the Gyrodynes was modified to become the Jet Gyrodyne compound autogyro. The Leonides engine was used to compress air for the rotor tipjets in vertical flight and drive the two pusher propellers in horizontal flight. (Westland)

pylon carried the 60 ft diameter four blade rotor. The rotor was made of stainless steel and incorporated air ducting and fuel pipes to feed the tipjets.

During forward flight the Rotodyne was driven by the propellers and the rotor autorotated. About half of the weight was supported by the aerodynamic lift of the wings and the rest was supported by the rotor, so as to keep it positively loaded and so that it could be used for control. In vertical flight the propellers were feathered and the tipjets were used to turn the rotor.

The rotor was semi-rigid, having flapping hinges but no drag hinges. The flapping hinges allowed the blades to rise and fall in conventional helicopter fashion so as to equalise lift between advancing and retreating blades. Drag hinges were not required because the blades were self-driven. There were plans for powered folding of two opposed blades to minimise parking area. Each blade included three air ducts, fuel feed and igniter circuits for the tipjets. The main structure of the rotor was made from stainless steel to withstand the high tempera-

The Rotodyne, like the Jet Gyrodyne, was powered by tipjets for take-off and by propellers in forward flight. (Westland)

The Napier Eland 7 turboprop engines drove the propellers directly and could be coupled to additional compressors by means of hydraulic clutches. With the clutches engaged, most of the engine power went to compressing air which was fed through the rotor to the tipjets. Each engine supplied air to one opposed pair of rotor blades to ensure balanced operation in the event of an engine failure. Fuel was pumped out to the tipjets by the centrifugal action of the rotor. Fuel and compressed air were combined and burnt in the Fairey designed tipjets producing thrust which turned the rotor.

ture of the compressed air and the aluminium trailing edge was segmented to avoid stresses due to differential expansion.

Control was similar to that of the Jet Gyrodyne. Yaw was controlled by applying differential pitch to the two propellers, while pitch and roll were controlled by cyclic rotor pitch. These controls were used in both vertical and horizontal flight, permitting the control system to be very simple compared with other convertiplanes. In forward flight, rudder movement provided additional yaw control. At first the elevators were used only to trim pitch in forward flight, so controlling

This photo of the Fairey Rotodyne being refuelled gives a good view of one of the tipjets. Tipjet noise was a great problem. (Westland)

incidence and wing lift. This was not satisfactory and pitch control was later modified to use cyclic pitch in hover and elevator control in cruising flight. At a later stage ailerons were added to provide roll control at higher speeds. Thus the control system progressed from helicopter type in both flight modes to being helicopter type in vertical flight and aeroplane type in horizontal flight. This was logical, since the Rotodyne would spend most of its time in horizontal flight and it was only reasonable to provide the pilot with comfortable and stable horizontal flight controls.

The Rotodyne underwent a protracted test and development programme. Critical system components were ground tested during 1956 and 1957 and the tipjets were air tested on the Jet Gyrodyne. The prototype Rotodyne made its first helicopter flight on 6 November 1957. On further helicopter flights it reached speeds up to 150 mph and altitudes up to 7,000 ft. By 10 April 1958 sufficient experience had been gained to try transitions to and from autogyro flight mode. These were approached with some caution and in gradual stages. Problems were encountered relighting the jets at altitude and changes were made both to compressor hardware and flight procedures. It was October before transitions could be carried out with complete confidence.

One problem which was to plague the Rotodyne was that of noise from the tipjets. The jets were small and with their low mass flow they could only generate the required thrust by using very high jet velocities. This produced a lot of noise which became very unpleasant as the motion of the rotor caused it to appear at any one location as a series of sharp pulses. The answer was to use a larger mass flow at lower velocity, and it was planned that separate air compressors should be used and that the tipjets should be extended along the outer part of the rotor trailing edge.

Late in 1958 the Rotodyne was flown over a closed 100 km course at an average speed of 191 mph, some 50 mph faster than the existing helicopter record.

Despite its long development programme, the Rotodyne showed itself to be a very strong competitor for the short-range medium payload VTOL transport market. Both civil and military options were proposed in the Type Z, which was basically the same aircraft but would have longer wings, more powerful Rolls-Royce Tyne turbo props and separate Rolls-Royce RB176 turbines to drive the air compressors. Interest was shown by the British government for military use, by British European Airways for civil use and by overseas manufacturers and operators.

With all this interest, development should have proceeded as fast as possible. Fairey, however, was taken over by Westland, development dragged on and potential customers lost interest. In 1962 the British government withdrew all support for military applications, leaving the programme in the civil sector. The Rotodyne was flown in and out of London to demonstrate that VTOL transports could operate between city centres, but the excessive noise of the tipjets proved intolerable in an urban environment. In other applications the Rotodyne could not compete with more modern transport aircraft and helicopters.

The Rotodyne was cut up for scrap, but parts of it survived and may be seen at the International Helicopter Museum, The Airport, Weston-super-Mare, Avon, England. There is a small section of fuselage, a test rotor with tipjet, an engine with sectioned compressor and the complete rotor head assembly. The rotor head is of great interest, since it includes a concentric combination of rotor controls, the two separate compressed air feeds, the fuel feed and the tipjet igniter circuits.

The Kamov Ka-22 Vintokrulya, NATO codename Hoop, was first made public in 1961 and was a close contemporary of the Rotodyne. It had a 75 ft long box-shaped fuselage with a rounded glazed nose and a conventional upswept aircraft tail with loading ramp. High-mounted straight wings of 67 ft span terminated in nacelles housing 5,600 eshp TB-2 shaft turbines. Each turbine drove a propeller at the front of the nacelle and a rotor on a faired pylon above the nacelle via a system of gears and clutches. It is presumed that the two nacelles were linked by a cross-shaft so that either engine could drive both rotors if the other failed.

The Ka-22 broke the Rotodyne's speed record of 191 mph by recording a speed of 221 mph. It also established a number of payload to altitude records, including one in which it lifted 36,000 pounds to a height of 8,500 ft. This was more than the loaded weight of most VTOL aircraft.

All of the autogyro convertiplanes broke records and established new standards of performance but none of them resulted in production designs. Perhaps the single greatest reason was that, while they were being developed, slowly overcoming various

The Kamov Ka-22 Vintokrulya was a large compound autogyro. Rotors were mechanically driven for take-off and landing. (Westland)

teething problems, engine technology was making great strides forward. Where previously only the compound autogyro could approach the helicopter speed limit of 200 knots, it was becoming possible for the helicopter, with the more powerful and lighter turboshaft engine, also to go as fast. On the economic side, the convertiplanes were prototypes which did not earn money, whereas each successive helicopter development generated income which could be used to finance further development.

Compound helicopters

As helicopters developed and engines became more powerful there was continual pressure to increase forward speed. Various ways were tried, the most successful being the rigid rotor. In order to reach higher speeds, attempts were made to off-load the rotor by adding forward thrust and aerodynamic lift. This created the compound helicopter, a helicopter with wings and either propeller or jet engine.

Just as the compound autogyro was going faster by off-loading its rotor and flying more as a conventional aeroplane, so the compound helicopter was doing the same. The difference was that the compound helicopter rotor was lightly loaded and driven, whereas the compound autogyro rotor was lightly loaded and autorotating.

There were several high-speed compound helicopters. Piasecki made the 16H-1 Pathfinder, and Lockheed built a compound version of the the XH-51A followed by the AH-56 Cheyenne high-speed attack helicopter. Sikorsky made the S-72 Rotor Systems Research Aircraft (RSRA) for NASA. This was compound, as a necessary part of its rotor systems work.

The Piasecki 16H-1 Pathfinder was an early attempt to make a high-speed compound helicopter. It was 37 ft long, weighed 11,000 pounds maximum and used a 44 ft diameter rotor in conjunction with a 5ft 6in diameter ducted tail propeller and 20 ft span wings. The engine was a 550 shp Pratt & Whitney PT6B-2 turboshaft, later replaced by a 1,250 shp General Electric T58 and later still by a 1,500 shp T58-GE-5.

For take-off, power was fed mainly to the rotor and the tail rotor was used only to provide torque reaction by means of vertical vanes in the duct. As forward speed was gathered, more power was diverted to the tail propeller and wing lift took over from

rotor lift, permitting higher speeds to be obtained.

The Pathfinder first flew in February 1962 and attained speeds up to 150 knots. After extensive modification in 1964 speeds up to 195 knots were achieved. The Pathfinder was strictly a research programme and did not lead to further designs. The programme was terminated in 1965.

The Lockheed XH-51 high-speed research helicopter was a conventional helicopter which used a rigid rotor to provide improved control and higher performance. The US Army's Aviation Material Laboratories sponsored a version of the XH-51 which had wings and a jet engine and was known as the XH-51A Compound.

The basic XH-51 had a 31 ft long fuselage designed and constructed to minimise drag. It was of streamlined shape from steeply raked front screen to tapered tail, the rotor mechanism was covered by a streamlined fairing, the skids retracted flush with the underside and even the rivet heads were flush with the skin. The rigid rotor was 35 ft in diameter and was powered by a 500 shp Pratt & Whitney T74 turboshaft.

The XH-51A Compound had wings of 17 ft span and a 2,600 pound static thrust Pratt & Whitney J60-P-2 turbojet fitted on the port wing where its thrust would help to counter torque reaction. Only one Compound was made. This first flew as a helicopter on 21 September 1964 and was flown in compound form during May 1965. It was used for research into high speed helicopter flight.

The XH-51A Compound set an unofficial helicopter speed record of 302.6 mph. This was a tremendous increase over previous speed records and proved that a thin, rigid, off-loaded rotor could be flown at speeds approaching Mach 0.5, which is the limiting speed if the rotor blades are not to exceed Mach 1 and not to go backwards.

Both the XH-51A and the XH-51A Compound may be seen at the US Army Aviation Museum at Fort Rucker, Alabama.

Lockheed followed up the XH-51 with the AH-56A Cheyenne compound helicopter, designed for use by the US Army. The Cheyenne had a slender 55 ft long fuselage. Width was minimised by seating the two crew in tandem. It had a 50 ft diameter rotor and 27 ft span wings. There were two tail rotors, one conventional anti-torque rotor and one pusher propeller. The engine was a 3,435 shp General Electric T64-GE-16 turboshaft.

The Cheyenne had an advanced third-generation mechanical control system, in

The Lockheed XH-51A Compound Helicopter had wings and a single offset jet engine. It flew at more than 300 mph. (Lockheed)

This view of the XH-51A Compound from below shows the wings, horizontal stabiliser and offset engine. (Lockheed)

which the mechanical gyro stabiliser was removed from above the rotor blades and located lower down within the fuselage.

The Cheyenne was large by attack helicopter standards. Empty weight was 12,000 pounds, gross VTOL 17,000 pounds normal or 22,000 pounds maximum, and in STOL it had an amazing 28,000 pounds maximum take-off weight.

It flew for the first time on 21 September 1967, and ten prototypes had been produced by mid-1968. A maximum speed of 253 mph (220 knots) was expected, but the rotor system became dangerously unstable above 200 mph and the third prototype crashed on 12 March 1969 when the rotor hit the rear fuselage.

The Cheyenne was very manoeuvrable and was a stable weapons platform, but it was too expensive and the development contract was terminated during budgetary cutbacks in 1972. One example is on display at the US Army Aviation Museum, Fort Rucker, Alabama.

The Sikorsky S-72 is a compound helicopter, but for a different reason. The S-72 was built for NASA as the RSRA or Rotor Systems Research Aircraft. It was designed to be able to air-test any type of rotor and was required to survive rotor failure. In an emergency, the rotor blades can be removed explosively and the S-72 then reverts to aerodynamic flight on small wings, powered by two jet engines. The lift of the wings also makes it possible to test rotors too small to support the 18,000 pound weight of the S-72.

The S-72 RSRA has a 71 ft long fuselage with helicopter-type nose and a cockpit accommodating three crew. The fuselage tapers to the tail which consists of tail rotor and swept vertical stabiliser. The two main wheels and tail wheel retract into the fuselage. The standard rotor is 62 ft in diameter and is powered by two 1,500 shp General Electric T58-GE-5 turboshaft engines.

The optional extras supplied with the S-72 include low wings of 45 ft span, two General Electric TF34-GE-2 turbofans for mounting on outriggers just ahead of the rotor bearings, a horizontal stabiliser and a rudder.

The S-72 was designed specifically for its RSRA role, and carries comprehensive instrumentation to measure and record rotor performance. Provision is made for the testing of bearingless, variable geometry, hingeless, reverse velocity, and jet flap rotors.

Two S-72's were built, the first flight being on 12 October 1976. Both were

The Cheyenne in flight with both tail rotors visible. Rotor stability problems prevented the Cheyenne from attaining its design maximum speed. (Lockheed)

Lockheed made the AH-56 Cheyenne to US Army requirements. It had wings for lift at high forward speeds and a second tail rotor for propulsion. (Lockheed)

delivered to NASA in 1978 and one was subsequently modified, starting in 1982, into X-wing form.

The compound autogyros and helicopters did much to increase rotorcraft performance. They were later caught up by conventional helicopters as engine power to weight ratios improved. The articulated rotor com-

pounds, even with off-loaded rotors, still did not exceed 200 knots (230 mph). The rigid-rotor XH-51A Compound research aircraft flew at more than 300 mph, but this was under specially controlled conditions and could not be repeated in the subsequent production AH-56 Cheyenne.

The Sikorsky S-72 Rotor Systems Research Aircraft can be flown as a helicopter compound helicopter or fixed wing aeroplane. In compound mode it can test rotors too small to carry its full weight. (NASA)

Stopped rotors

Various attempts have been made to stop the rotor in flight. The first of these was the Sikorsky S-57 project of 1952. This was given the designation XV-2 and would have competed with the McDonnell XV-1 and Bell XV-3 to meet the Army requirement for a small fast battlefield transport. It had an aircraft fuselage, cockpit similar to that of the later Grumman A-6 and high-mounted swept wings. The single-blade rotor was counterbalanced by a short opposing arm and mass. After a vertical rotor-borne take-off and acceleration to flying speed, the rotor was to be feathered, stopped in an aft-pointing direction, and retracted to be covered by hatches. Design studies were conducted but the project was abandoned as being impractical.

Another proposal for stopping the rotor in flight was the gas rotor. Each rotor was a long tube of symmetrical cross-section. In rotor-borne flight a sheet of gas would be blown out through slots in the tube to give it lift. For horizontal flight the gas supply would be removed and the symmetrical section of the tubular rotors would permit them to be stopped and stowed.

A further stopped rotor system is the X-wing. This is to be tested on a Sikorsky S-72 RSRA modified to accept a rotor with four blades of symmetrical cross-section. The rotor acts as a normal helicopter rotor when driven and when stopped provides aerodynamic lift. The ability of the RSRA to support its own weight will be useful in making a gradual approach to assessment of rotor characteristics.

Tiltrotors

A further approach to the rotor problem lay in recognising that the 200 knot speed limitation applied only when the rotor axis was vertical. If the rotor was tilted forward so that it became, in effect, a large airscrew, then much higher foward speeds should be possible. Two types of tiltrotor aircraft, the Transcendental T1G and the Bell XV-3, were built during the fifties, using reciprocating engines of low power. It was two decades later that Bell followed the XV-3 with the XV-15, which eventually led to the current Bell-Boeing V-22 joint project.

The first tiltrotor to fly was the Transcendental Model 1-G. Transcendental Aircraft was a company founded by of Mario Guerrieri and Robert Lichten in 1945. They enlisted the part-time help of engineers from other companies to design and build the Model 1-G and started ground tests in 1951. The design had major dynamic problems and

This artists impression shows how one RSRA will look when converted into the stopped rotor X-wing. (US Navy)

the craft was badly damaged in an accident during testing. The problems were recognised to be fundamental to tiltrotor design and Transcendental won a contract from the US Air Force to do further work. They spent 1952 and 1953 investigating the behaviour of rotors during transition, with gyroscopic effects and large angles of oblique airflow.

Model 1G had a short fuselage containing a well-glazed cockpit and a 160 hp Lycoming O-290-A piston reciprocating engine. A tailboom, carrying vertical and horizontal stabilisers, made the length up to 26 ft. The 21 ft span wing was high-mounted and carried a 17 ft diameter rotor at each tip. Inside each wing, a drive shaft supplied mechanical power to the rotor and three concentric tubes around the shaft controlled rotor tilt, collective pitch and cyclic pitch. The engine ran at 3,000 rpm, its output being stepped down to 633 rpm when the rotors were used as airscrews and 240 rpm when they were working as helicopter rotors.

The Model 1G first flew as a helicopter on 6 July 1954, and made its first transition, taking three minutes, in December 1954. It made more than a hundred flights and accumulated over twenty hours of flying time. It was lost in an accident on 20 July 1955 when a mechanical failure in the rotor controls caused it to crash in the River Delaware.

Transcendental later made the Model 2 with 250 hp reciprocating engine and almost 4,000 pounds gross weight. This flew in 1956 but was unable to compete with the Bell XV-3 and the programme was terminated in 1957. The proposed Model 3 with turboshaft engine was not made.

Robert Lichten had parted company with Transcendental and moved to Bell where he led the design of the Bell XV-3.

The Bell XV-3 was the third competitor for approval by the US Army Transportation Command. The McDonnell XV-1 Compound Autogyro had flown for only two years and the Sikorsky XV-2 Stowed Rotor had not been made. The XV-3 was a tiltrotor and therefore was free from the speed restrictions of fixed rotor types. The fundamental advantages of the tiltrotor concept were recognised by NASA and the XV-3 underwent an extended test programme, the project remaining alive for fifteen years and contributing useful information to subsequent programmes.

The XV-3 had a rounded well-glazed nose which accommodated pilot and co-pilot in tandem. The intended production version would have accommodated one pilot and three passengers. The engine, a 450hp Pratt and Whitney R-985 radial piston type, was installed in mid-fuselage behind the cockpit. From there back the fuselage tapered upward to a conventional aircraft tail comprising large single vertical stabiliser with rudder, and horizontal stabilisers with elevators. Two long skids were attached to the underside of the fuselage via fluid-type energy absorbers. The skids included small wheels to permit rolling take-off from firm surfaces.

The fuselage was 30 ft long and carried slender 31 ft span wings at shoulder height. At each wingtip a pod housed the rotor bearings, control linkgages and rotor tilt mechanism. The original rotors were 23 ft in diameter, had three blades and were fully articulated, having both flapping and drag hinges. The rotor axes were tilted by electric motors, one for each rotor, mounted in the wing tip pods. The motors were capable of driving a full 90 degree transition in 10 seconds and could be stopped in intermediate positions to provide a slower stepwise transition.

Less obvious features included a two-speed epicyclic gearbox which permitted engine speed to be reduced in horizontal flight and two ranges of rotor pitch control, one for helicopter and one for propeller operation.

The XV-3 was controlled by the pilot through conventional rudder pedals and control column and a helicopter-type collective pitch lever with twist-grip throttle. Rotor tilt was controlled by a switch on the control column, and two further switches selected rotor pitch range and engine gear ratio.

The control stick and rudder pedals operated ailerons, rudder and elevators at all times, though of course with no effect at low speeds and during hover. During conversion and hovering flight, the stick and rudder pedals also controlled the rotors. Lateral stick caused pitch differentials between the rotors and, hence, roll. Fore and aft stick controlled longditudinal cyclic pitch and, hence, aircraft pitch. The rudder pedals were used to create a differential between the longitudinal cyclic pitches of the two rotors, hence controlling yaw. These helicopter-type control functions were progressively engaged and disengaged during transitions. The transition mechanism also adjusted the collective pitch.

The original contract for the XV-3 was awarded in 1951. During the following five years, the various parts of the aircraft were designed, built and individually tested. Wind-tunnel tests of a quarter-scale model proved the efficiency of the standard rotor design in both hovering and forward flight modes. Airframe components were load-tested and strengthened where necessary, transmission components were run for an extended period and rotor assemblies were tested on a whirl stand.

The first XV-3 was completed and unveiled to the US Army on 8 February 1955. Fitted with the original three-blade fully-articulated rotor it flew as a helicopter during August 1955 and made conversions as far as 15 degrees forward rotor tilt before being damaged in a heavy landing on 25 October 1956.

The second XV-3 was subjected to a protracted programme of tests both in the wind tunnel and on test rigs. As a result of these tests a number of modifications were made. The original three-blade fully articulated rotors were found to suffer from a marginal flutter condition and were replaced by a 24ft diameter two-blade semi-rigid type with overslung pitch control. The rotor rigidity would also help it to resist gyroscopic effects during transition. At the same time, the rotor controls were stiffened and the very slender wing was braced with struts. The trailing 25 per cent of the wing was arranged to droop during hover, both to reduce the masking of rotor air down flow and to reduce the stalling speed of the wing to 85 knots, making transitions possible at lower forward speeds.

The power loading of the XV-3 was more than ten pounds of aircraft weight per engine bhp. Bell stated a preference for five pounds per bhp in future designs. The R-985 engine was retained since, despite its limited power, it had a very good record of reliability. Engine coooling in forward flight was improved by the addition of a forward-facing duct above the fuselage.

While the XV-3 was in the wind-tunnel, pilots were able to practise conversion procedures and gear changes. Conversion was found to be quite straightforward, both as a

This historic photo shows first Bell XV-3, 4147, in early hovering trials with the original three-blade rotors and before wing bracing. (Westland)

The second XV-3, 4148, was subjected to extensive wind tunnel testing to evaluate the stability of the semi-rigid two-blade rotors during transitions. (Bell Helicopter Textron)

continuous operation and if done step by step. It was the engine speed gear shift which caused problems. Considerable manipulation of both pitch and throttle controls was required and gear changes took twenty seconds to make in either direction.

XV-3 flying resumed on 12 December 1958 with flights in helicopter configuration, including an autorotation test which showed an optimum rate of descent of 1600 feet per minute at a forward speed of 50 knots. Helicopter characteristics were good, especially in high speed forward flight and vibration and stress levels were lower than previously.

On 17 December, a conversion to 30 degrees was made followed by one to 70 degrees on 18 December. After a minor rigging correction a second flight was made on 18 December with a full conversion to 90 degrees. The conversion was made in steps, starting at 90 knots in helicopter mode and finishing at 115 knots in full aerodynamic flight. A second full conversion was made the next day and held for three minutes. Conver-

sion and aerodynamic flight were smooth throughout, but directional stability was marginal. It was improved by adding more fin area below the rear fuselage.

Forward speed in level flight was initially limited by engine rpm to 105 knots. On 14 April 1959 the first in-flight gear change was made and a forward speed of 120 knots was maintained at much lower engine rpm and with a low level of vibration.

A temporary wheeled undercarriage was added for short take-off tests. The XV-3 took off at two thirds power in less than 200 feet, indicating that with full power it would take off at 50 per cent overload. Short take-off was performed in the helicopter mode of flight, with an optimum rotor mast tilt ten degrees forward of vertical and a forward speed of 30 knots.

XV-3 testing was a joint effort by Bell, NASA and the US Air Force. Wind tunnel testing of the second XV-3 was performed by NASA at Ames, flight tests to April 1959 by Bell, followed by seven weeks of flight tests by the USAF at Edwards Air Force Base. It

The second Bell XV-3 in its earliest flight configuration demonstrates hovering flight. The wing brace stiffness could be changed in flight. (Bell Helicopter Textron)

Above right: The second XV-3, 4148, partially converted to horizontal flight. The cowling over mid-fuselage was added to duct cooling air to the engine in forward flight. (Bell Helicopter Textron)

Bell XV-3 with additional stabiliser below tail. Detail of the overslung rotors is clearly visible. (Bell Helicopter Textron)

was then transferred once again to NASA's Ames Research Center at Moffatt Field, where it continued flight trials through to 1961.

From 1962 to 1965, Bell engineers worked on improvements to high speed stability and control under a NASA contract. The necessary modifications were made to the XV-3 and it completed a number of wind-tunnel trials before being damaged when a pylon mounting failed.

The XV-3 had made over 250 test flights including 110 full conversions by nine different test pilots. It had demonstrated that the tiltrotor could fly safely both as a helicopter and an aeroplane with smooth transitions in both directions and could take off either vertically or, with greater load, after a short ground run. Although it did not achieve any great forward speed, it proved that the rotor could be tilted out of the horizontal plane and therefore freed from the helicopter speed restriction. The XV-3 programme had spanned fifteen years, from 1951 to 1966, and had laid the foundations for further work on tilt rotors.

Bell Helicopter continued to work on the tiltrotor concept and produced proposals for the Model 266 tiltrotor intended both to meet the US Army's light tactical transport requirement and to serve as a 30 seat short-haul civil aircraft. Overall weight would be 21,000 pounds, disc loading 10 pounds per square foot, engines two 2850 shp General Electric T64s and power loading 3.8 pounds per horsepower. These parameters would have resulted in a hovering ceiling, out of ground effect, of 7,000 feet, a forward speed of 350 knots and a range of 400 miles with 8000 pounds of payload.

Where the XV-3 had been limited in performance by the use of existing available helicopter rotor blades, the D266 was to use blades developed specifically for use as tiltrotors, optimised for best performance both in the helicopter rotor mode and in the propeller mode. The conflicting requirements were those of small twist for the fine pitch helicopter mode and large twist for the very coarse pitch high-speed cruising propeller mode. These conflicting requirements would be met by using a high rate of twist to satisfy

The second Bell XV-3, 4148, was used by NASA for flight trials from 1959 to 1961. It is seen here in NASA colours with test instrumentation boom added to its nose. It is fully converted to horizontal flight.
(Bell Helicopter Textron)

the propeller application from the hub to forty per cent radius, and switching to a lower rate of twist from there to rotor tip to satisfy the helicopter rotor application. This 'dual twist' rotor design should have permitted efficient operation both in hover and up to 300 knots forward speed.

The D266 was a very ambitious project and it was decided that a smaller research tiltrotor should be built to test the technology. On 13 April 1973, Bell were awarded a contract from NASA Ames and the US Army Air Mobility research and Development Laboratory to build two of their Model 301 Research Tiltrotor aircraft, under the military designation XV-15, over a four year programme.

The XV-15 had an aircraft-style fuselage 42 ft long with two side-by-side pilots seats in a cockpit which would have looked equally suitable in a helicopter or light aircraft. The landing gear was of tricycle layout, the nosewheel retracting into a bay forward of the cockpit and the main wheels into Hercules-style pods each side of the lower fuselage. The main wheels came from the Canadair CL-84 tilt-wing. The tail surfaces consisted of a high-mounted horizontal stabiliser with two end-plate vertical surfaces. The wings, of 35ft span, were high-mounted and were swept forward seven degrees to maintain centre of gravity. The engines, mounted one at each wingtip, were Avco Lycoming LTC1K-4Ks each rated at 1,550 shp continuous or 1,800 shp for two minutes. Each engine drove a 25ft diameter three-blade semi-rigid rotor, the engines swivelling with the rotors as they tilted from vertical to horizontal. The rotor gearboxes were linked by a cross-shaft through the wings with centre constant-velocity joint so that both rotors could be driven by one engine if the other failed.

The rotor blades were made of stainless steel and were of high-twist design. They had no flapping hinges and so were rigidly confined to the plane of rotation. They were gimballed to provide compliance in drag and were restrained by elastomeric spring-dampers.

The XV-15 design take-off weight was 13,000 pounds at a rotor disc loading of 13 pounds per square foot, and 4.2 pounds per bhp of engine power. Estimated performance included a maximum level speed of 330 knots, a service ceiling of 29,000 ft and a range of 500 miles.

The first XV-15 was in final assembly in October 1975 and was rolled out at Arlington Flight Research Center on 22 October 1976. Carrying the serial N702, it made its first hovering flight at Arlington on 3 May 1977. In March of 1978 it was shipped to NASA Ames for extensive wind tunnel tests. XV-15 number two, N703, commenced ground run tests in August 1978 at Arlington and made a hovering flight on 23 April 1979. On July 24 it made the first conversion from helicopter to aerodynamic flight, for which pilots Ron Erhart and Dorman Cannon received the Frederick L. Feinberg Award from the American Helicopter Society for the most outstanding piloting achievements of the year.

On 17 June 1980 the XV-15 set an unofficial world speed record for rotorcraft of 301 knots (346 mph) at Arlington, Texas.

On 13 August 1980 aircraft number two was shipped to NASA's Dryden Flight Research Center for further trials. During October Erhart and Cannon were named Test Pilots of the Year by the Society of Experimental Test Pilots. The XV-15 went on to complete seaboard trials on the USS *Tripoli* in August 1982 and a demonstration tour of the Eastern US in August 1984.

The two XV-15s by 1986 had accumulated 530 flight hours, had made 1,500 conversions, reached 26,000 feet of altitude and speeds in the dive of 397 mph. Further tests are planned using Boeing graphite-Nomex glass-fibre rotor blades which have a 43 degree twist and are designed to increase gross weight from 13,400 to 15,000 pounds, and level speed from 300 to 322 knots.

During the XV-15 programme, Bell joined forces with Boeing Vertol to submit a tiltrotor design in the Joint Services Advanced Vertical Lift Aircraft (JVX) programme. Bell's continuous involvement in tiltrotors from 1951 and Boeing's experience with the Vertol 76 tiltwing and many heavy helicopters won them a contract from the Naval Air Systems Command in April 1983. Their tiltrotor design became known as the V-22 Osprey during 1986 with an incentive award from the Navy in May and Department of Defense approval of a full-scale development programme in December.

The V-22 Osprey is due to fly during 1989 and is due to enter service in 1991. It will be the first practical application of Bell's forty years of continuous tiltrotor research and development. It is designed to meet the needs of the US Army, Air Force, Navy and Marines for a VTOL transport capable of fast horizontal flight, current production requirements call for 900 to 1200 machines.

The tiltrotor is seen by Bell as one way of implementing a stopped-rotor design. After transition to forward flight, the rotor

The Bell XV-15 in a conversion sequence from aeroplane mode through transition to helicopter mode. Take-off and landing are performed in helicopter mode. STOL is possible with small tilt angles and rolling take-off.
(NASA)

would be feathered, stopped and folded backwards. The aircraft could then accelerate to even higher speeds under jet power. Such a design would combine the low disc loading and efficient hover of a rotorcraft with the efficient high-speed cruise of a jet aircraft.

Priority is being given to developing the basic tiltrotor before this advanced variant is attempted. It is interesting to note that the Osprey will have powered self-folding rotors for on-deck stowage.

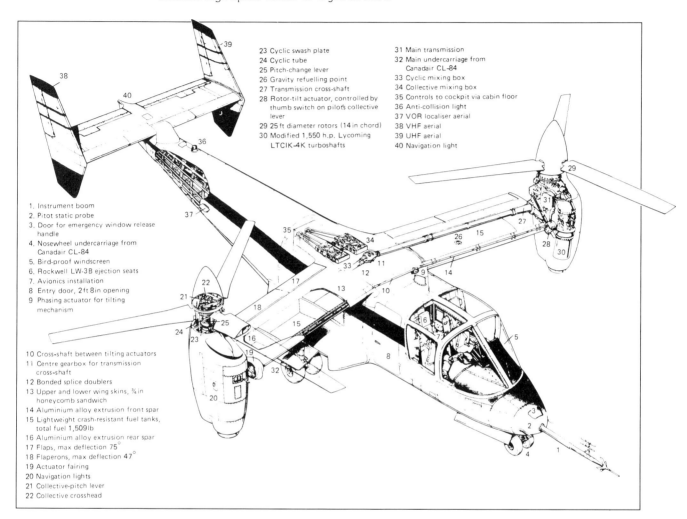

1. Instrument boom
2. Pitot static probe
3. Door for emergency window release handle
4. Nosewheel undercarriage from Canadair CL-84
5. Bird-proof windscreen
6. Rockwell LW-3B ejection seats
7. Avionics installation
8. Entry door, 2ft 8in opening
9. Phasing actuator for tilting mechanism
10. Cross-shaft between tilting actuators
11. Centre gearbox for transmission cross-shaft
12. Bonded splice doublers
13. Upper and lower wing skins, ¾in honeycomb sandwich
14. Aluminium alloy extrusion front spar
15. Lightweight crash-resistant fuel tanks, total fuel 1,509lb
16. Aluminium alloy extrusion rear spar
17. Flaps, max deflection 75°
18. Flaperons, max deflection 47°
19. Actuator fairing
20. Navigation lights
21. Collective-pitch lever
22. Collective crosshead
23. Cyclic swash plate
24. Cyclic tube
25. Pitch-change lever
26. Gravity refuelling point
27. Transmission cross-shaft
28. Rotor-tilt actuator, controlled by thumb switch on pilot's collective lever
29. 25ft diameter rotors (14in chord)
30. Modified 1,550 h.p. Lycoming LTCIK-4K turboshafts
31. Main transmission
32. Main undercarriage from Canadair CL-84
33. Cyclic mixing box
34. Collective mixing box
35. Controls to cockpit via cabin floor
36. Anti-collision light
37. VOR localiser aerial
38. VHF aerial
39. UHF aerial
40. Navigation light

This cutaway view of the Bell XV-15 shows the features needed to make a tiltrotor aircraft work. The two mixing boxes progressively transfer control functions from horizontal to vertical requirements as the rotors tilt. For safety, nacelle tilt actuators are synchronised and engine outputs are cross-connected. (Bell Helicopter Textron)

The XV-15 makes a vertical take-off during seagoing trials aboard the amphibious assault ship USS Tripoli. (US Navy)

Rotorcraft Summary

Rotorcraft, with their low disc loading, have always been the most efficient hovering aircraft. In the days of reciprocating engines, only rotorcraft were able to fly. With the development of the gas turbine and turboshaft, rotorcraft have always been able to make better use of increases in power to lift greater loads to higher altitudes and to provide safety in the event of engine failure. The forward speed limitation of the horizontal rotor has been overcome by tiltrotor technology, but it has taken four decades of continuous research and development to progress from the first design work to actual service aircraft.

The XV-15 runs up its engines while chained to the deck during sea trials aboard USS *Tripoli*. (US Navy)

The Sikorsky S-72 NASA RSRA compound helicopter was built for NASA as the Rotor Systems Research Aircraft. (Sikorsky)

Left: The Ryan X-13 Vertijet sits on its trailer in the horizontal road transportation attitude. The jetpipe eyeball nozzle, here seen deflected, was used for control in pitch and yaw. (USAF Museum)

With trailer erected to the vertical, the Ryan X-13 Vertijet lifts off its trailer for its first full verticircuit. (USAF Museum)

The Ryan XV-5 Vertifan had one fan in each wing under butterfly doors and one in the nose. (Ryan)

The Ryan XV-5 Vertifan had two jet engines which drove three fans in vertical and hovering flight. (Ryan)

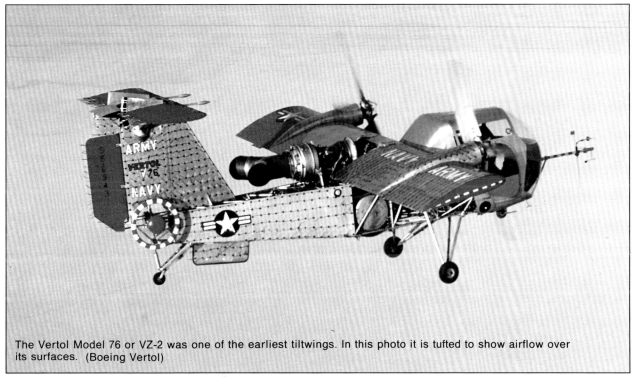

The Vertol Model 76 or VZ-2 was one of the earliest tiltwings. In this photo it is tufted to show airflow over its surfaces. (Boeing Vertol)

The Ryan VZ-3 Vertiplane, with flaps full down, flies very slowly over the NASA Ames wind-tunnel. Route 101 and the beginnings of Silicon Valley can be seen in the distance. (Ryan)

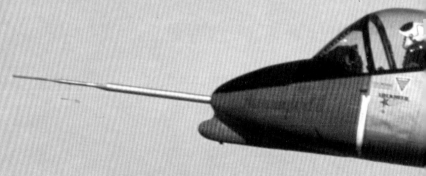

The Lockheed XV-4A Hummingbird hovered in a nose-up attitude because exhaust was vectored backward to assist acceleration to forward flight. (Lockheed)

The Lockheed XV-4B Hummingbird II
had four extra liftjets and an improved
fly-by-wire control system.
(Lockheed)

The Bell XV-15 is seen in horizontal flight with rotors used for propulsion.
(Bell Helicopter Textron)

The engine pods and rotors tilt u
vertical flight.

Bell XV-15 makes a transition to
...copter Textron)

With pods fully rotated, the XV-15 hovers in a slightly nose-down attitude.
(Bell Helicopter Textron)

The Grumman A2F-1, later to become the
A-6 Intruder, had tilting tailpipes to vector
engine thrust for reduced take-off distance
and better obstacle clearance.
(Grumman)

119

Plenum Chamber Burning was tried in a Pegasus and tested in a complete airframe suspended from a gantry. PCB was later incorporated in the BS100 engine which would have powered the Hawker P.1154. (British Aerospace)

In glorious technicolour, one of only six Bristol BS100 Plenum Chamber Burning supersonic thrust engines made. Each paint changes colour at a specific temperature to indicate component heating during test runs. The split front nozzle and moving ramp are visible.
(Rolls-Royce Bristol)

The McDonnell YC-15 blew its jets into the flaps rather than over them. The larger C-17, soon to enter production, will use the same technique. Here a Pratt & Whitney PW2037 engine is tested under a slice of C-17 wing.
(Pratt & Whitney)

VFW used this hover rig to test systems for the VAK191. It was powered by five Rolls-Royce RB108 lift engines.
(Rolls-Royce)

The Boeing YC-14 engines were mounted above and forward of the wings so that the jet exhausts blew over the upper wing and flap surfaces
(Boeing)

The NASA-funded QSRA used exhaust-blown upper wing surfaces and complex flaps to achieve STOL performance. (NASA)

Below insets: Based on the C-8A Buffalo the NASA Augmentor Wing Jet STOL Research Aircraft used two vectored nozzle Rolls-Royce Spey turbo-fans to generate lift force and thrust. (NASA)

The Hawker Harrier is sold to Spain as the AV-8S Matador. Seen before delivery are an AV-8S and a TAV-8S trainer.
(British Aerospace)

The Royal Air Force uses the Harrier II as the Harrier GR.5. The pilot has much better all-round vision. Visible here are zero-scarf engine nozzle, leading-edge wing root extension and longer wing.
(British Aerospace)

Sea Harriers are used predominantly by the Fleet Air Arm. Shown here is the version supplied to the Indian Navy. (British Aerospace)

Co-operation between Hawkers and McAir produced the Harrier II with lighter structure, new wing and lift improvement devices. It has twice the weapons load and range of the earlier variant. (British Aerospace)

The first prototype of the V-22
Osprey flew on 19 March 1989
powered by two Allison T406-AD-400
engines.
(Bell Helicopter Textron)

This artist's impression of the
Bell-Boeing V-22 Osprey shows a
simulated hostage rescue. The
wing trailing edges droop to
maximise effective disc area.
(Bell Helicopter Textron)

The Osprey as seen at first roll-out, temporarily painted
in US Marine camouflage colours.
(Bell Helicopter Textron)

The V-22 Osprey depicted in US Marines colours, and complete with a possible combination of
weaponry.
(Bell Helicopter Textron)

Bell and Boeing are also capitalising on their tilt-rotor work with the tiny Pointer remotely piloted vehicle.
Vertical take-off and landing allow it to operate from any site without launch ramps and catch nets, while
conversion to aerodynamic cruising flight gives it a longer endurance and greater radius of action.
(Bell Helicopter Textron)

7 PROPELLERS

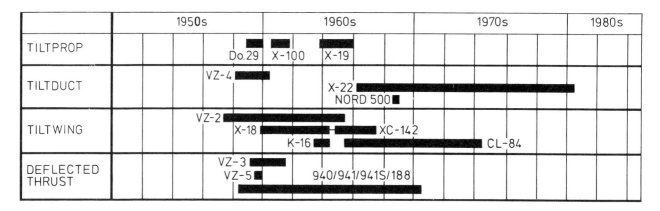

	1950s		1960s		1970s		1980s	
TILTPROP	Do.29	X-100	X-19					
TILTDUCT	VZ-4		X-22 NORD 500					
TILTWING	VZ-2 X-18	K-16	XC-142	CL-84				
DEFLECTED THRUST	VZ-3 VZ-5	940/941/941S/188						

Propeller driven Convertiplanes

The rotorcraft discussed in the previous chapter were all primarily helicopters or autogyros which used rotors for efficient vertical flight and converted wholly or partially to wingborne horizontal flight. This chapter discusses convertiplanes which are primarily designed for wingborne horizontal flight and which can convert in some way to hovering flight. The distinction between the two types lies in the difference between the rotor with its long articulated blades designed primarily for hovering, and the propeller with short rigid blades, coarse pitch and high rate of twist designed primarily for high-speed horizontal flight. Inevitably the rotors and propellers used in both types of convertiplane represent a compromise between their lifting and thrusting applications and the distinctions between rotors and propellers become blurred to the point where some are described by their manufacturers as 'prop-rotors'. It seems fairly clear, however, that the XV-3, XV-15, V-22 family are rotorcraft, whilst the aircraft included in this chapter are propeller-driven.

The propeller-driven convertiplanes may be subdivided into four categories: tiltprops, tiltducts, tiltwings, and thrust deflectors. The tiltprops are conventional aircraft in which the propellers may tilt so that their thrust supports aircraft weight. Tiltducts are very similar to tiltprops, but each propeller is surrounded by a duct which tilts with it. The duct can increase propeller thrust, especially when hovering. Vanes within the duct may be used for control of duct airflow, providing the tiltduct aircraft with an advantage in controllability over the tiltprop. Tiltwings are aircraft where the entire wing, engines, propellers and control surfaces tilt as a single unit. The tiltwing gains over tiltprop and tiltduct by having only a single pivot and tilting mechanism, but suffers from a number of complications and disadvantages. The thrust deflector has fixed props and employs over-large flaps to deflect the propeller slipstream downward to create vertical thrust.

Tiltprops

The earliest record of a serious proposal for a tilting propeller aircraft dates from the Second World War when Professor Focke designed the Focke-Achgelis FA269, an otherwise conventional aeroplane with two pusher propellers which tilted down beneath the wing to provide lifting thrust. A longer than usual tailwheel undercarriage provided clearance beneath the aircraft for the propellers to drop down. It is not clear from the available information how Professor Focke intended to power and control this early VTOL.

The FA269 concept was revived in the mid-fifties when the German Defence Ministry financed Dornier to build the Do 29 STOL research aircraft. The Do 29 was based on the existing Do 27 single-engined high-wing monoplane. The engine was removed from the nose and replaced by curved perspex panels affording helicopter-like forward and downward fields of view. Two Lycoming GO-480 six-cylinder horizontally opposed piston engines, each of 270bhp, were fitted beneath, and to the front of, each wing. Both engines fed into a power transmission system consisting of cross-shaft (for engine-out safety) and trailing shafts to pusher airscrews mounted behind the wings. The trailing shafts were driven by bevel gears at approximately 30 per cent chord so that the propellers could be hinged down behind the wing with their thrust acting through the centre of lift. Maximum tilt angle was 90 grad (81 degrees), but contemporary photos show 60 degrees in use.

The Do 29 first flew during December

Propeller-driven convertiplanes were flying from the mid-fifties through to 1980, with all groups most active during the sixties. All suffered from the high power requirement of small discs. Vibration, noise and mechanical failures were common problems. (Author)

The Dornier Do 29 could fly at very low forward speeds with the pusher propellers tilted downward. (Photo Deutsches Museum Munich)

1958. With propellers tilted and flaps down, stalling speed was only 15mph. The Do 29 could could take off in 80 feet and land in 50 feet. In this configuration, it had a high resistance to forward motion and a steep angle of approach.

In the USA, Curtiss-Wright had flown the VZ-7 flying platform and proved the lifting properties of suitably shaped propellers. They were also aware of a phenomenon known as 'radial force' which causes a propeller to produce a large force at right-angles to the airflow as its angle of attack is increased. They realised that the radial force could be used to add lift, and dubbed the effect 'radial lift-force'.

During the late fifties, Curtiss-Wright designed and built their X-100 to prove that radial lift-force could be used to advantage in a full-scale aircraft. The X-100 had a conventional 24 ft long aircraft fuselage of welded tube construction with fixed tailwheel undercarriage and T-tail. Short high-mounted wings of 16 ft span carried the two 10 ft diameter tilting propellers at their tips. The single Lycoming YT-53-L-1 engine was mounted in the centre fuselage and drove the propellers via a cross-shaft through the wings. Engine jet exhaust was piped to the tail where it was deflected by vanes for control in pitch and yaw during hovering. Hovering roll control was by different propeller pitch. Normal surfaces provided control in forward flight.

The X-100 was flown at a weight of

3,500 pounds by various pilots during 1960, completing 14 hours of flying time. In April 1960 it converted from a vertical take-off to horizontal flight, but hover was difficult to control because of the limited thrust in pitch and yaw provided by the deflector vanes. Testing ended in October 1961 and the X-100 was donated to the Smithsonian Institution.

Curtiss-Wright used the X-100 to provide data for the design of Model X-200, a fast four-passenger civil executive transport with VTOL capability. Two prototypes of the X-200 were already in build when Curtiss-Wright, aware of military interest in VTOL, offered the design to the USAF. The USAF bought the two prototype X-200s, and contracted Curtiss-Wright to convert them to military requirements under the designation X-19. Conversion involved the addition of ejector seats, rescue hoist and dummy refuelling probe and lengthening of the fuselage to permit better passenger access.

The X-19 had a monocoque fuselage of conventional aircraft appearance, 44ft long and of slender and streamlined shape. It had a long nose and a cockpit accommodating two pilots side by side. The addition of two ejector seats in a small cockpit cannot have improved working conditions. Behind the pilots there was a tiny cabin, only 4ft high by 4ft 6 inches wide and 8ft long, intended for four passengers or 1,000 pounds of cargo. The rear of the fuselage was occupied by the engines. The original intention was to use

133

The Curtiss-Wright X-100 conducted early tiltprop research, using 'radial lift-force' propellers. In this photo the props have been removed. The tail nozzles were used to deflect the turbine exhaust for pitch control
(NASM, Smithsonian Institution)

The Curtiss-Wright X-19A used four tilting propellers with broad paddle-like blades. Originally a private venture, it was purchased by the USAF and is seen here in Tri-Service trials colours.
(NASM, Smithsonian Institution)

license-built Wankel rotary engines, but these were abandoned in favour of two 2,650 shp Lycoming T55-L-7 turboshaft engines. The engines breathed air in through a duct above the rear fuselage and exhausted just below the tail. The X-19 had a tricycle undercarriage, the front wheel retracting into a well in the long nose and the main gear retracting into the sides of the fuselage behind the cargo space.

The flying surfaces consisted of two wings and a vertical stabiliser. Both wings were attached to the top of the fuselage. The front wing was of 20 ft span and very slender chord, while the rear wing was of 21ft span and of greater chord. Both wings had moving rear surfaces. The tall swept fin and rudder was above the rear of the fuselage.

At the tip of each wing there was a swivelling pod and propeller. The propellers were of 13 ft diameter and each had three broad paddle-shaped blades with generous twist. The blades were of advanced composite construction and each one consisted of a plastic skin over a foam filling on a central steel core. The starboard propellers were right-handed and the port propellers were left-handed, so as to cancel torque reactions and gyroscopic effects.

For transition from horizontal to vertical flight, the four wingtip pods were swivelled approximately 90 degrees by a switch on the control column and a hydraulic actuation system. In vertical flight and hover the trailing surfaces of each wing were drooped to minimise disc masking. Control in hover was by means of differential propeller pitch, port/starboard for roll, and front/rear for pitch. Yaw was controlled by making appropriate adjustments to pod tilt angles.

Control in aerodynamic flight was by means of the surfaces in the rear wing and rudder, control authority being phased from hover to normal as the pods tilted. Manual control was assisted by a mechanical stability augmentation system.

The X-19 was intended to weigh 8,000 pounds empty and to fly at weights up to 12,300 pounds. The empty weight grew to 10,000 pounds as modifications were incorporated, reducing range and payload by 50 per cent. Gross weight was limited by the design of the mechanical power transmission until such time as this could be uprated.

The first of the X-19s flew in hover on 20 November 1963, but this flight was prematurely terminated when the X-19 grounded itself. It remained grounded for repair of damage and improvements to the flight control system, and took to the air again for a conventional flight on 25 June 1964. The X-19 flew for a month and made its first controlled hover flight on 7 August. It then went back to the workshop for further work on the stability augmentation system.

Flying resumed in January 1965 with a partial conversion test, but the failure of a propeller caused further delays. The X-19 did not fly again until 31 July when it made an airworthiness test flight in hover before being moved to the FAA's Experimental Center at Atlantic City to proceed with transition testing. Less than a month into the test programme, on 25 August 1965, a transmission part failed during a hovering flight. This caused one rear propeller to become detached, putting the aircraft into an asymmetric lift condition which caused simultaneous pitch-up and roll. The crew wisely abandoned ship, owing their lives to the USAF's insistence on ejector seats. The aircraft was totally destroyed.

The first X-19 completed a total of 50

The X-19 made many flights, but most were of very short duration. It is seen here in low-level hovering flight. Propeller angles produce divergent downwash. Trailing edges are full down to minimise masking of propeller discs. (Department of Defense)

flights, a remarkable number considering that it had spent so much of its short life undergoing repair and modifications. In fact, most of those flights were of extremely short duration, averaging less than five minutes each. Total flying time was less than four hours.

The X-19 programme was abandoned on 12 December 1965. Only the first of the two prototypes had flown and that had not completed a full transition. Perhaps if the second aircraft had commenced testing it might have been allowed to continue flying, but a lot of work would have been required to overcome the limitations of the power transmission system and to upgrade the troublesome stabilisation system. The X-19 had been designed as a small civil aircraft and its small size had created problems. The pilots found the cockpit uncomfortable, especially during hover, and payload was so small that any additional weight due to modification or instrumentation put severe limitations on fuel load.

The first X-19 was completely destroyed when it crashed. The second was cannibalised and eventually scrapped.

Tiltducts

The tiltduct aircraft were similar to tiltprops, but used ducted propellers. The ducts were advantageous in augmenting propeller thrust and in providing additional lifting area in forward flight. There was a change in trim as the ducts were rotated but this could be offset by deflector vanes in the duct airstream. Control could be exercised both by moving the vanes and by changing the propeller pitches.

Doak, of Torrance, California, constructed their Model 16 Tiltduct under a contract from the US Army Transportation Research and Engineering Command with the military designation VZ-4DA. Completed in late 1957, it was one of the first 'flat-riser' VTOL aircraft. It had a slim 32ft fuselage fabricated from tubular steel, high-mounted short wings, tandem two-place cockpit with pilot in front and passenger behind and conventional aircraft tail. The ducts were of 4ft 8 inches outside diameter, 4 ft inside diameter and 2ft 9inches deep, with horizontal pitch trim flaps on their downstream airflow. Eight-blade fans in the ducts were driven from an 850 bhp Lycoming YT53 turboshaft mounted in mid-fuselage. Maximum weight was 3,200 pounds.

When hovering, roll was controlled by

differential propeller pitch. As in the Curtiss-Wright X-100, the turboshaft exhaust was piped to the tail and was deflected by stainless steel vanes to control pitch and yaw. Duct tilting during transition was controlled by a switch on the control column. Control in horizontal flight was by conventional control surfaces.

The first flight of the VZ-4 took place at Torrance Municipal Airport on 25 February 1958. On completion of initial trials, it was transferred to Edwards Air Force Base and completed 50 hours of flight testing there. In September 1959 it was transferred to the US Army for Army/NASA evaluation.

Flight test data showed that the VZ-4 required 800 shp in hover, dropping only a little to 700 shp at 30 knots, and then falling rapidly to a minimum of 200 shp at 80 knots. Stalling and buffeting tests showed a critical condition at 45 knots where the portion of the wing nearest to the ducts suffered upwash and came close to stalling.

The Doak 16 was among the most successful of the early VTOL research aircraft and provided NASA with much useful data on VTOL aircraft characteristics and power requirements.

Bell began work on ducted propellers for VTOL in 1953 and conducted a number of design studies for transport, observation, utility and rescue aircraft using ducted propeller technology. One of these studies, the D-190 rescue concept, started as a private venture and continued for four years, in close collaboration with the USAF Air Rescue Service and later with the encouragement of Air Research and Development Command. The D-190 was a 15,000 lb aircraft, looking very much like the subsequent XV-15 but with a tilting ducted propeller rather than a rotor on each wing. It was intended to be carried by a C-130 and to be used as a life-boat, descending to pick up survivors from the sea and returning to the C-130 to be carried home. A nine-seat passenger, liaison and light logistics support version of the D-190 was also proposed.

In 1957, the Navy awarded Bell a one-year contract to study the possibility of a VTOL ducted propeller assault transport. Continued research led to a design for a tandem ducted propeller VTOL transport of approximately 35,000 lb gross weight. This was submitted to the US Marines as the D-2005 in summer 1959 and as the similar D-2022 to the US Army in 1960. The D-2014 was a version with clamshell freight loading doors in the tail.

All of the US armed services were interested in procuring VTOL transport air-

The Doak 16 fully converted to horizontal wingborne flight. The duct behind the cockpit is the air intake for the mid-mounted Lycoming YT53 turboshaft. (Copyright reserved)

The Doak 16 is seen making a transition from vertical to horizontal flight. Power requirement dropped from 800 hp to 200 hp during transition. (Copyright reserved)

The Doak Model 16 or VZ-4DA tiltduct hovers in ground effect. The tail nozzle controlled both pitch and yaw. (Copyright reserved)

craft and they had a variety of technologies to choose from. In the autumn of 1959 the Ad Hoc Committee on VTOL Aircraft was formed by the US Department of Defence who invited industry representatives to a Princeton University Symposium. The Committee recommended the procurement of a number of V/STOL aircraft for research and trial operational use.

A competition was held in 1961 to select designs for 'tri-service' evaluation. A Bell/Lockheed technical proposal was not successful, tiltwings being preferred, but the US Navy, recognising that the tiltduct had more desirable hovering and transition characteristics, requested that a smaller version of a Bell/Douglas proposal be built and tested. On November 30 1962, Bell were awarded a 42 month contract to design, build and flight test two VTOL research aircraft for delivery April 1966. These would be known as X-22A.

The X-22A was 39ft long, had a 39ft wing-span, and its tall tail fin made it 20 ft high. It had a gross weight of 17,000 pounds. The cockpit seated two pilots and gave them an excellent helicopter-style field of view. Behind them the fuselage formed a large box capable of accommodating six passengers or a 1,200 lb payload, together with the large single fuel tank of 465 gallons capacity situated in mid-fuselage on the aircraft's centre of gravity.

In normal forward flight, the X-22A was of canard configuration, very unusual for the sixties, with a 23ft span front wing and a 39 ft span rear wing. The front wing and the outer portions of the rear wing were enveloped by the four ducted-propeller systems. For vertical and hovering flight, the four ducted-propellers were rotated about their horizontal axes, taking the front wing and outboard rear wings with them. The portions of wing within the ducts were used as fully-flying control surfaces to deflect the propeller slipstreams.

The X-22A was powered by four YT58-GE-8D turboshaft engines of 1,250 shp each, mounted two each side of the fuselage just ahead of the rear wing. Each was geared to a cross shaft within the rear wing to power the two rear propellers. A gearbox at the centre of the rear wing allowed power to be taken down a longitudinal shaft to a cross-shaft in the front wing which powered the two front propellers. The available thrust from the four ducted propellers exceeded aircraft laden weight by 35 per cent allowing a generous margin for control and allowing the aircraft to survive a failure in one of the four engines.

The four ducts were rotated for tran-

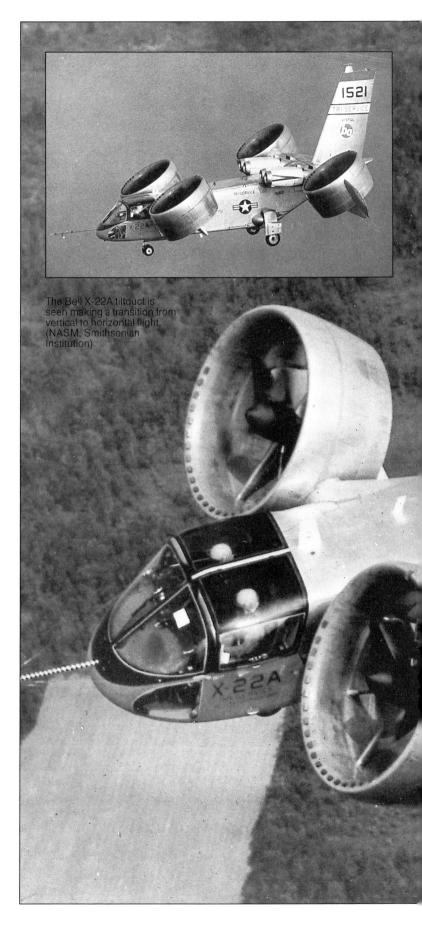

The Bell X-22A tiltduct is seen making a transition from vertical to horizontal flight. (NASM, Smithsonian Institution)

The X-22 flew with ducts only partially rotated when in low-speed flight. The small rotor atop the vertical stabiliser is a vertical speed sensor. (NASM, Smithsonian Institution)

139

sition by hydraulic activators under electrical control and could be locked in any position from 0 degrees to 95 degrees. Although separately activated, the four ducts moved together and no differential motion was possible. All four propellers rotated at the same speed.

Control was exercised by changing the pitch of each of the four propellers and by moving the four elevons. These eight variables were used to control the X-22 in normal flight, with ducts horizontal, and in hover, with ducts vertical.

In horizontal flight, pitch and roll were controlled by the elevons and yaw by differential variation of propeller pitch. For hovering flight, propeller pitch adjustments controlled pitch and roll while elevon movements controlled yaw. During transition, control functions were phased gradually as a function of duct tilt angle. The pilot was provided with artificial 'feel' in yaw during forward flight, but this was removed during transition to hover. Pitch and roll 'feel' were provided by a hydro-electric system which applied stick reactions proportional to g-forces. For hover, transition and low-speed flight, a stability augmentation system (SAS) was used to improve aircraft stability and handling characteristics.

The X-22A was equipped with a variable stability control system (VSCS) developed by the Calspan Corp. This allowed it to be programmed to behave like any other existing or projected VTOL aircraft for assessment of flight characteristics. The VSCS interacted with the Smiths Industries Head-Up Display and the Kaiser Electronics Head Down Display. Data inputs to the VSCS included those from a low-speed airspeed sensor (LORAS) invented by Calspan's Jack Bellman.

The first X-22A was completed on 25 May 1965. After static tests, it made a hovering flight in March 1966. It completed a series of STOL tests with ducts set at 30 degrees and with forward speeds up to 100 knots. On August 8 1966, a hydraulic failure caused it to land heavily. The crew were not seriously injured, but the X-22 was a write-off.

The second X-22A completed in January 1966, continued the flight tests from January 1967. At weights from 14,000 to 16,000 pounds, it logged 220 flights including 386 vertical take-offs and 185 complete transition cycles. It managed to hover at over 8,000 ft altitude, thus proving its claimed high sea-level thrust-to-weight ratio. It also achieved a forward speed of 315 mph, proving conclusively that the tiltduct could fly faster than a conventional helicopter.

In May 1969, it was turned over to the Navy who appointed the Calspan Corp to continue the flight test programme. They continued to fly it until 1980, logging some 200 flight hours and testing sensors and control systems.

The X-22A proved to be a very successful and versatile research tool, flying for at least fifteen years and providing much valuable information on VTOL systems. With only 1,200 lbs payload and 450 miles range, however, it was not developed as either a commercial or military transport.

The first X-22A was written off in the 1966 crash-landing. The second is scheduled to be donated to an aircraft museum.

The French company Nord also made a small research tiltduct machine, designated Nord 500. This was a truly minimal design, being only 22ft long and 20 ft wide and weighing only 2,760 pounds. The fuselage consisted of a cockpit, on a tricycle under-carriage and a high tail section enclosing the two 317 shp Allison T63-A-5A turboshafts, and carrying conventional vertical and horizontal surfaces. A radome on the nose probably housed a radio altimeter for measuring rate of descent.

Two large ducts took up most of the wingspan and each contained a five-blade propeller. On the downstream end of each duct, there was a diamond arrangement of four control vanes. These were intended to control the expansion of the airflow as it left the ducts in an attempt to enhance hovering thrust. Pitch was controlled by tilting the ducts collectively and yaw by tilting them differentially. Roll was controlled by the application of differential propeller pitch.

Two Nord 500 aircraft were made. The first performed static tests in April 1967 and the second made a tethered hovering flight on 23 July 1968. It went back to the wind tunnel for dynamic stability tests and development was suspended before it could fly again. The intended research program, into the benefits of expanding the airflow emerging from the ducts, was not carried out.

In Russia, a very small tiltduct aircraft was designed by the students of the Kazan Aviation Institute. A mock-up was built by S.P.Gorbonuv and was exhibited in Moscow during 1967. The aircraft had a short and slender fuselage which housed a sailplane-size cockpit in the nose and a 210 hp M-337 six-cylinder engine behind. Propulsion was by a 4ft diameter ducted propeller at the end of a tail-boom. There was no wing, 6 ft diameter propeller ducts being pivoted direct to the upper fuselage. Control was probably

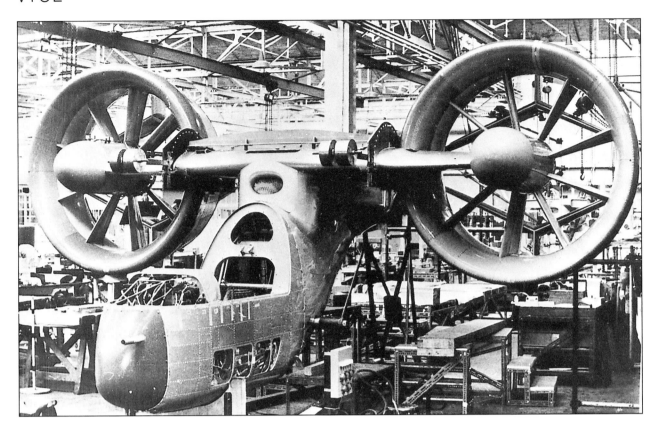

The Nord 500 on tethered trials. The surfaces beneath the ducts were intended to expand airflow in hover and compress it for forward flight. (Copyright reserved)

effected by combinations of propeller pitch and tilt, as in the Nord 500.

Tiltwings

The tiltwing type of aircraft appears very simple. The wing to fuselage attachment is replaced by pivot and jack, and the entire wing tilts, taking engines and propellers with it. In practice, this apparent simplicity carries complications with it. The propellers are mounted in line along the wing and cannot provide control in pitch, so an additional pitch control jet or rotor must be added. The ailerons are tilted with the wings and change their function from roll control in level flight to yaw control in hover, so aileron authority has to be transferred from lateral stick to rudder pedals. As the aircraft goes through a transition sequence or makes a short take-off with partial wing tilt, wing and rear stabiliser functions must balance. The rear stabiliser has to be inclined to match wing tilt. Cross-shafting between propellers must be added to assure engine out safety. The flight control system must select the appropriate controls for each mode of flight and must make the aircraft stable under all conditions. These complications make the tiltwing just as complex as other convertiplane VTOL aircraft.

The tiltwing has advantages during transition because the propellers force air at high speed over wings and flaps. This keeps the wing lifting at low aircraft speeds and reduces the apparent stall speed. The lift created by the wing under these conditions helps to support aircraft weight during transition. Wing lift is not significant during hover. The tilted wing is a disadvantage when hovering in gusty conditions, and tends to make control difficult when attempting a short landing.

The first of the tiltwing projects was the Convertawings Model B. Convertawings was a company founded by D.H. Kaplan who, like the founders of Transcendental, had worked for Piasecki. The Model B was designed to meet US Air Force and Navy specifications for a VTOL transport. It had a tilting wing with a rotor at each tip. The rotors were of small diameter, had four blades each and were to rotate at high speed, driven by two Boeing type 502 gas turbines. The Model B was partly built, and underwent static tests, but did not fly.

At the same time, Vertol were working on their Model 76. This too was built on a 1956 contract from the US office of Naval Research and the US Army, as the VZ-2A.

The VZ-2A fuselage was fabricated from metal tube. At the front it carried a cockpit resembling that of a Bell 47 helicopter,

complete with perspex bubble. The crew of two sat side by side and had dual controls. At the rear there was a tall T combination of stabilisers incorporating two ducted fans for pitch and yaw control. Overall length was 26 feet. The 26ft span wing was pivoted at one third chord to a mounting above the fuselage. An 860 hp Lycoming YT53-L-1 turboshaft mounted above the fuselage and just behind the wing drove a cross shaft which carried power to the two airscrews. The airscrews were just outboard of half-span. Each was 9ft 6 inches in diameter and had three broad paddle-like blades. The VZ-2 weighed 2,500 pounds empty and 3,200 pounds laden.

The VZ-2 was controlled in hover by the two ducted fans for pitch and yaw and differential propeller pitch for roll. As the wing tilted down to normal flight position, hover controls were phased out and the normal aerodynamic controls were phased in.

First vertical flight was made on 13 April 1957 and first horizontal flight on 7 January 1958. The first complete transition was on 15 July 1958. Testing at Vertol was completed on 23 September 1959 and the VZ-2 was shipped to Langley Research Centre for evaluation by NASA.

The Vertol Model 76 or VZ-2 tiltwing makes a transition at low altitude.
(Copyright reserved)

The VZ-2 shows its manoeuvrability in partly tilted configuration.
(Copyright reserved)

A wing stall problem during transition was cured by the addition of a drooping leading edge, trailing edge flaps were added to increase lift at partial tilt angles and the use of ailerons for yaw control in hovering flight was investigated.

The VZ-2 was still flying in 1961 and by then had made some 450 flights including 34 full conversions and 240 partial conversions. It continued to fly until it was retired in 1965 and transferred to the Smithsonian Institution in Washington DC.

The 1956 contract awarded by the US Army and Navy for Vertol to develop the VZ-2 was followed a year later by a US Air Force contract for Hiller to build a large tiltwing transport aircraft under the USAF experimental designation X-18. Hiller had already started work prior to funding and had opted to economise by using existing major assemblies. The fuselage and tail surfaces came from a Chase YC-122 transport aircraft, engines and propeller came from the XFY-1/XFV-1 tailsitter programme and various items from the Convair Tradewind were used. Hiller added their own 48ft span rectangular wing which had provision for extension to 60 ft for improved cruise efficiency. The wing had removable leading edge slats and dual ailerons, but no flaps. It was pivoted at one third chord and could be tilted hydraulically over the full 90 degrees in six seconds. Dual activating cylinders were controlled by a lever on the pilot's cockpit pedestal.

The X-18 had three engines. The two 5,850 shp Allison YT40-A-14 turboprops were mounted on the wings and drove 16 ft diameter contra-rotating three-bladed propellers. These engine assemblies, coming as they did from the single-engined tailsitter programmes, did not have provision for cross-shaft power transfer in the event of an engine failure. The third engine was a 3,400 pounds thrust Westinghouse J34 turbojet which was mounted in the rear fuselage and supplied gas to tail-mounted pitch control nozzles.

Control in hover was by means of tail nozzles in pitch, airscrew pitch in roll and ailerons in yaw. Control was transferred electronically to normal flying surfaces during transition.

The X-18 weighed 27,000 pounds empty and 33,000 pounds loaded, putting it in the heavyweight league of contemporary (and subsequent) VTOL aircraft. Each engine would have to carry up to 16,500 pounds as compared with the 12,000 to 14,000 pounds of the XFV-1 and XFY-1

The X-18 was completed and rolled out in December 1958. It was subjected to extensive ground tests to prove the operation of all systems and to determine vibration characteristics. These tests took place at Moffett, and on completion of the test programme, the X-18 was dismantled and moved to Edwards Air Force Base for its flight test programme.

First flight was on 24 November 1959 and during the following months the X-18 made some 20 horizontal flights, during which it proved to be a stable and controllable aircraft. In common with all VTOL aircraft, it had greater than unity thrust-to-weight ratio and it impressed test pilots George Bright and Bruce Jones with its dragster performance on the tarmac.

Partial transitions were attempted with wing tilt angles up to 33 degrees. The aircraft adopted a nose-up attitude with an additional 17 degrees of pitch, giving an effective 50 degrees of tilt. Going this far into transition, a substantial amount of control was transferred from the normal flight controls to the hovering controls. It was found that the hover controls were not adequate. In particular, the electric pitch change on the propellers was too slow and produced an unacceptable lag in roll control.

On its twentieth flight, the X-18 had a problem in one of the propeller pitch controls and entered a spin. Fortunately, this occurred at 10,000 feet and there was just sufficient height for the pilot to regain control. This incident caused the X-18 to be grounded. It continued to produce useful data in the VTOL Ground Effect Simulation Programme at Edwards from 1962 to 1964. These tests measured the effects of propeller downwash with wing vertical, and recirculation was found to produce an upward force of 10,000 pounds on the fuselage.

The X-18 was damaged by the failure of a test stand and was eventually dismantled and scrapped. It had flown only twenty times and never in vertical or hovering flight, but it did provide much useful information and test results for use in the LTV-Hiller-Ryan XC142A.

The US Navy contracted the Kaman Aircraft Corp to build a tiltwing, assigned the in-house number K-16B. This was to be another 'erector set' exercise and used the fuselage of a Grumman JRF Goose amphibious flying-boat. Kaman added to this a 34 ft span wing of their own design which tilted only to 50 degrees. Further downward deflection of thrust was by large full-span flaps. Two General Electric T58-GE-2A turboprops were to drive large 15 ft diameter propellers. The propellers were fitted

73078

with trailing edge surfaces which could be operated by a cyclic control so that the props could function as rotors, with longitudinal cyclic pitch used collectively to control aircraft pitch and differentially to control aircraft yaw. Roll would be controlled by differences in collective pitch. The K-16 was essentially a propeller driven tiltwing, but used thrust deflection and a tiltrotor type of control system.

The K-16 was completed and went to NASA Ames to be tested in the wind tunnel during 1962. It did not fly.

The XC-142A was the result of co-operation between LTV, Hiller, and Ryan. LTV or Ling-Temco-Vought has previous experience of slow wing-borne flight in the Vought XF5-U/V173 'flying pancake' and had used wing tilt to make small changes of incidence on the Vought Crusader carrier-borne jet fighter. Hiller had direct experience of tilt-wings in the X-18, and Ryan had been involved in many VTOL programmes including their own testrigs, the X-13 Vertijet and the Vertiplane.

The XC-142 was built to a specification issued by the US Department of Defense in 1961 for a VTOL transport aircraft to meet the needs of the Army, Navy and Air Force. The designation XC-142 demonstrates that this was not an X-series experimental aircraft, but the prototype of an intended production aircraft in the C or transport series.

The fuselage of XC-142 was box-shaped with a the large glazed area around the cockpit. It was 58ft long overall and fat enough to contain a cargo compartment of internal width 7ft 6 inches, height 7ft and length 30ft, with rear loading ramp. The proportions of the fuselage combined to give the impression of a small aircraft, yet the XC-142 had a gross weight of 41,000 pounds VTOL or 45,000 pounds STOL, quite a respectable size for a carrier resupply or battlefield aircraft. The landing gear was of tricycle type, the nosewheel retracting into a bay beneath the cockpit and the main gear into Hercules-type pods. At the tail, the fuselage maintained its width but tapered

This tail shot of the Hiller X-18 shows the jetpipe and nozzle used for pitch control. (Department of Defense)

The Hiller X-18 tiltwing used a Chase YC-122 fuselage and surplus tailsitter engines and props. Here it demonstrates a conversion sequence. (NASM, Smithsonian Institution)

VTOL

sharply in height, affording a wide ramp and good access. Above the rear fuselage, there was a tall fin and rudder with high-mounted all-flying horizontal stabiliser capable of large deflections. Behind the rudder was a horizontal 8 ft diameter rotor of symmetrical section to provide positive or negative vertical thrust for control in pitch when hovering.

The wing was of 67 ft span and slightly tapered. It tilted about a pivot at the top of the fuselage. Airflow was maintained by hinged fairings. The four 3,080 shp General Electric T64-GE-1 turboprop engines and their giant 15 ft diameter five-bladed airscrews were spaced so as to bathe the whole wing in their slipstream. Inside the wing, all four props were driven from a common cross-shaft for engine-out safety. Leading-edge slots and generous trailing-edge flaps permitted the wing geometry to be manipulated to prevent stall during transition.

The first of five XC-142s was rolled out on 17 June 1964. It flew conventionally on 29 September 1964, hovered on 29 December, and made a full transition on 11 January 1965. The five aircraft were delivered to the USAF in July and August 1965 and April, May and August 1966. Aircraft numbers 4 and 5 were each delivered within a month of their initial flights.

Aircraft performance included the carriage of 32 troops or 10,500 pounds of payload, speeds from 416 knots (478 mph) forward to 20 knots backward or 41 knots sideways, rate of climb 6,400 ft/min, altitude 25,000 ft, time to altitude 6 minutes to 25,000 ft, hover altitude 6,400 ft, radius of action 230 miles VTOL and 345 miles STOL, and ferry range 3,000 miles.

The USAF put the XC-142 through its paces during 1966 with cargo flights, cargo drops, live parachute drops, desert operations, mountain operations, live rescue and aircraft carrier landings. All of these operations were successful but continued operation of the five XC-142s showed that the design had the normal quota of minor problems. What may be a minor problem in aerodynamic flight, however, can become a major problem if it occurs while hovering, and four of the five aircraft made heavy landings sufficient to cause damage, one of these involving three fatalities. Two accidents were attributed to mechanical failure and two to pilot error.

Mechanical problems centred on the power transmission cross-shaft and gearboxes, which would not tolerate wing flexing, and on the shaft taking power back to the tail rotor. It was this which failed and caused the fatal crash.

The LTV-Hiller-Ryan XC-142A made a most impressive spectacle when hovering. It was much larger then it appears. Not recorded by the camera is the associated crescendo of engine and propeller noise. (USAF Museum)

The XC-142 had to be well clear of the ground before attempting a transition, because at low level and low speed it could fly into its own recirculation. In low-speed flight the horizontal stabiliser was tilted to match wing tilt. (USAF Museum)

25921

TRI-SERVICE

Five XC-142s were made. Here three of them fly in formation during trials. Although they appear very compact, they were large aircraft with 67 ft span. (USAF Museum)

149

Aerodynamic problems were encountered when flying at low altitude with wing tilt set between 35 and 80 degrees, because aircraft speed was slow compared with the rate at which downwash spread out over the ground and the aircraft could fly into the resultant updraught. Any asymmetry caused one wing to hit the updraught before the other and this happened at the Vought plant early in the test programme, causing the aircraft to hit the ground with one wing.

Hovering over desert was a good way to create a sandstorm, but not a good way to retain visibility and distinctly unkind to the engines as they breathed abrasive dust. Slow forward flight obeying the downwash constraints was no problem as the dust was left behind. Propellers were slightly eroded by sand and dust, but were easy to repair.

The generous glazing of the cockpit gave an excellent all-round view, but pilots felt insecure in such a gold-fish bowl. In sunny conditions greenhouse heating of the cockpit was extreme and crews would leave the rear ramp down for ventilation. Later, several glass panels were painted over to reduce solar heating.

Vibration and noise were problems.

Low level flight over desert terrain kicked up a lot of dust. The XC-142 here is flying fast enough to leave the dust (and recirculation) behind. (Vought)

The uppermost windows of the XC-142 were painted over to reduce heating. Hinged fairings smoothed out airflow between fuselage and tilted wing. The wings had complex leading and trailing edge flaps. (USAF Museum)

Hovering, even with four large propellers of combined area 700 square feet, still represented a high disc loading of 57 pounds per square foot and required tremendous power. The resultant vibration caused premature component failures and the noise from the propellers and tail rotor would be a great operational handicap in any military action requiring stealth. Internal noise was so bad that it reduced crew efficiency. Pilot workload was high, mainly due to a complex throttle system, but pilots still found the XC-142 easier to fly than a helicopter.

During trials, XC-142s were flown by 21 civil and 18 military pilots. There were 296 contractor flights totalling 186 hours and 219 military flights totalling 233 hours. Total flying time was 420 hours.

One XC-142 was shipped across the Atlantic and flew to the Paris Air Show during May and June of 1967. Great interest was shown in it, but no orders resulted. Nor were there any orders received from any of the three US armed services. Many of the minor problems could be easily solved and reliability could have been improved, but this particular type of aircraft with its high disc loading would always be prone to vibration

and noise. The technology was expensive when compared with the very reasonably priced Hercules, which could carry three times the payload over twice the distance, and did have STOL performance.

It seems clear that the XC-142 was everything that a tiltwing could be, but that it suffered, as all propeller driven VTOL aircraft must, by being inefficient and noisy in hover.

The surviving XC-142A is on display at the USAF Museum at Wright-Patterson Air Force Base, Dayton, Ohio.

The Canadian firm Canadair had pursued a programme of VTOL R&D over the seven years 1956 to 1963 and had proposed the CL-62 tiltwing in answer to the NATO NBMR4 specification of 1961. In 1963, the Canadian Department of Defense joined with Canadair to finance the construction of the CL-84.

The CL-84 Dynavert was a tiltwing with only a quarter the weight of the XC-142 at 8,100 pounds empty, 12,200 pounds VTOL and 14,700 pounds STOL. It had two propellers of 14 ft diameter, giving a disc area of 300 square feet and a VTOL disc loading of 40 pounds per square foot. With only 70 per cent of the disc loading of the XC-142, the

The XC-142 carried out deck
landing trials with success.
(USAF Museum)

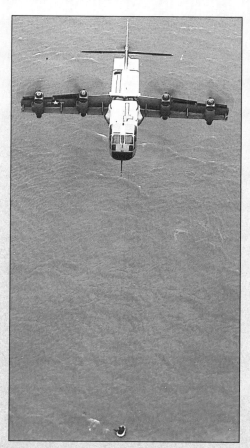

Despite its large size, the XC-142 was able to manoeuvre with sufficient precision for air-sea rescue missions. (USAF Museum)

CL-84 had a chance of reducing noise and vibration to manageable proportions.

The fuselage of the CL-84 was 47 feet long, incorporating a conventional aircraft cockpit, a box-shaped forward fuselage with rear loading ramp and a tail boom. The boom carried a wide horizontal stabiliser with end-plate vertical surfaces and a central vertical fin. Behind the fin two contra-rotating rotors provided vertical thrust for pitch control in hover. The undercarriage was unusually long with the ability to arrest fairly high sink rates without airframe damage. The nose-wheel retracted beneath the cockpit and the main gear into wide sponsons.

The wing was rectangular and of 33ft span. It was hinged at two thirds chord to the top of the fuselage and carried the two 1,450 shp Lycoming T53-LTC1K-4A turboprops and 14 ft diameter four-blade airscrews. Wing geometry could be modified by Kruger flaps which drooped the leading edge and by generous full-span flaps.

Control was conventional in horizontal flight. In hover, lateral stick controlled roll via differential propeller pitch, longitudinal stick controlled pitch via the tail rotor, and the rudder pedals controlled yaw via flaperons. Height was changed by a combination of throttle and collective propeller pitch.

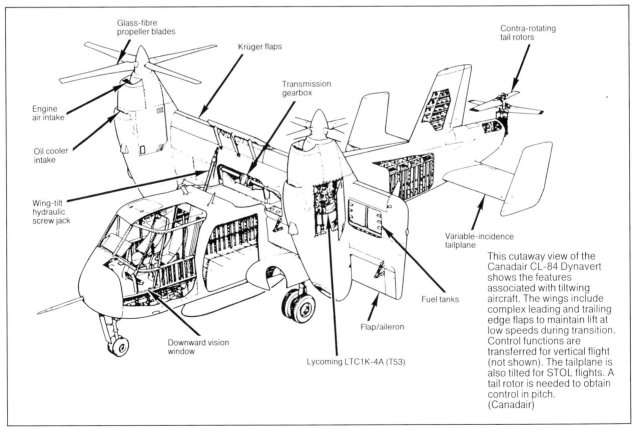

Glass-fibre
propeller blades

Krüger flaps

Contra-rotating
tail rotors

Engine
air intake

Transmission
gearbox

Oil cooler
intake

Wing-tilt
hydraulic
screw jack

Variable-incidence
tailplane

Fuel tanks

Downward vision
window

Flap/aileron

Lycoming LTC1K-4A (T53)

This cutaway view of the Canadair CL-84 Dynavert shows the features associated with tiltwing aircraft. The wings include complex leading and trailing edge flaps to maintain lift at low speeds during transition. Control functions are transferred for vertical flight (not shown). The tailplane is also tilted for STOL flights. A tail rotor is needed to obtain control in pitch. (Canadair)

Left: The first CL-84, CX8401, is seen in hovering flight. The stray surface is the wing-to-fuselage fairing which lifted with the wing at highter tilt angles. (Canadair)

The CL-84 makes a transition to forward flight. At slow forward speeds during transitions and STOL operation, Kruger flaps enhanced wing performance and the horizontal stabiliser tilted to match wing tilt. (Canadair)

The propellers of 8401 look somewhat oversize in level flight. Landing gear is only partially faired. (Canadair)

VTOL

The CL-84 prototype was built in only two years and made its first flight in May 1965. It continued flying until September 1967, being flown by 16 pilots for a total of 145 flying hours. It was evaluated by the US Triservice team along with the X-19, X-22 and XC-142.

A further three CL-84 aircraft were ordered by the Canadian Government in February 1968 under the designation CL-84-1. These were very similar to the prototype CL-84, but had dual controls, additional avionics, external hard points and a modified fuel system for long-range operation.

The CL-84-1 could carry pilot plus 1,600 pounds of fuel and 2,500 pounds of payload VTOL, or 3,230 pounds of fuel and 3,200 pounds of payload STOL. A 35 knot wind increased the VTOL payload from 2,500 to 5,000 pounds, with wing tilt reduced from 86 degrees to 45 degrees. Given a 250 ft take-off run, it could ferry itself 2,100 nautical miles at 235 knots using additional internal and external fuel tanks. This is just sufficient for a Gander/Shannon Atlantic crossing with nominal reserves.

Successful demonstrations were given to the US Navy in February 1972, including flying displays given at the Pentagon from a 100 foot square helicopter pad, and a series of VTOL and STOL operations on the USS *Guam*.

The CL-84 in hover was a stable gun platform; it is seen here scoring a hit during gunnery trials. In a real battlefield situation, one might not wish to hover within range of the enemy. (Canadair)

Left: The CL-84 in civil guise as CF-VTO-X demonstrates its air-sea rescue capability. (Canadair)

The CL-84 carries out deck landing trials. VTOL was much vaunted for shipboard use, especially on smaller carriers and assault craft. (Canadair)

In level flight, the tail rotors of the CL-84 were feathered and stopped, their blades aligned fore-and-aft for minimum drag. (Canadair)

A further version, the CL-84-1C, had an uprated version of the Lycoming T-53 known as the LTC1S-2 and rated at 1,800 shp. The additional power permitted VTO at 15,000 pounds gross weight, of which 4,200 pounds could be payload.

CL-84 flying operation continued through to blind flying trials using Smiths Head-Up and Head-Down Displays in June 1974.

CL-84-1, registration CX8402, can be seen at the National Aviation Museum in Ottowa.

Deflected Thrust

Flaps may be used to produce lift in either of two different ways. The conventional operation of flaps is to enhance the lift of the wings in normal but slow aerodynamic flight. The propeller pulls the aircraft through the air, and the wings and flaps deflect air downward, creating lift.

A different and less common use of flaps is to deflect the propeller slipstream downward, producing lift from thrust without forward motion. To make best use of this effect, the propellers should be large so as to blow the maximum mass of air at low velocity, and the flaps should trap all of the airflow and deflect it downward. The large propellers and generous flaps make deflected thrust VTOL and STOL aircraft easy to recognise. They tend to look either like flying buckets or like tiltwings without tilt. There were three propeller-driven aircraft which supported an appreciable fraction of their weight on deflected thrust. The Ryan Vertiplane and Fairchild Fledgling were flying buckets, and the Breguet 940, 941 and 941S series were tiltwings without tilt.

In 1956, the US Army, via the Office of Naval research, awarded Ryan a contract to build their Model 92 Vertiplane under the military designation VZ-3RY. The contract called for a reconnaissance and liaison aircraft which could operate from unprepared terrain.

The VZ-3 had a slender 28ft fuselage of metal construction with an enclosed cockpit,

Ryan staff put finishing touches to the VZ-3 Vertiplane. The broad blades of the Harzell wooden propellers are apparent. (Ryan)

The VZ-3 Vertiplane was tested by NASA in their large low-speed wind tunnel at Ames. This photo shows the flaps fully extended to form deflector buckets.
(Ryan)

the roof and screen of which were attached with the aid of an external frame. The engine, a 1,000 shp Lycoming T53-L-1 turboshaft, was situated in mid-fuselage. The tail was similar to contemporary light VTOL aircraft in having vertical and horizontal stabilisers arranged in a T. A tail wheel undercarriage was fitted.

The wing, of 23 ft span, had endplates and was equipped with double flaps which could be extended and drooped to such an extent that the combined surface resembled the bucket of a Pelton wheel. Two Harzell metal three-bladed propellers were mounted ahead of and below the wing, so that their slipstreams blew into the buckets and were deflected vertically downward.

As in the Doak 16 and Curtiss-Wright X-100, the engine exhaust was piped to the tail where a nozzle deflected it to control pitch and yaw at low speeds. Roll was controlled by differential propeller pitch.

After three months of testing in the wind tunnel at Ames, the undercarriage was changed to a tricycle type and a small ventral fin was added to improve directional stability.

The VZ-3 first flew on 21 January 1959 at Moffett Field with Pete Girard at the controls. Flying continued until a mishap on 13 February necessitated grounding for repairs. Testing was resumed later in the year and speeds from 26 knots to 110 knots were recorded. It would not hover in still air because of insufficient engine power, but it could put on a convincing simulation if headed into a light breeze.

It was handed over to NASA in February 1960. On its first flight with NASA, an unplanned manoeuvre prompted the pilot to eject. The VZ-3 crashed and was very badly damaged. It was rebuilt, with a stringer and fabric nose section and an open cockpit. It resumed flying in 1961 and carried out a programme of tests to investigate the low-speed handling characteristics of VTOL aircraft.

Fairchild were also contracted by the US Army to build a bucket-plane. Their M-224-1 Fledgling, designated VZ-5FA, was 34 ft long and had a wing of span 33 ft. It used four Harzell three-blade metal propellers driven by a 1,024 shp General Electric YT58-GE-2 turboshaft engine. The pilot sat in a small open cockpit in the nose and there was room for an observer or monitoring equipment in a jump-seat behind. The fuselage swept sharply upward to the rear and the Fledgling could either sit on its tricycle undercarriage in a

The VZ-3 was reconstructed with tricycle landing gear, open cockpit and additional ventral stabiliser. It is seen in level flight with flaps up. (Ryan)

The VZ-3 flies at very slow forward speed with flaps full down. Here the nose transparency is covered and the insturumentation boom is unbraced. The Vertiplane was rebuilt several times and photos usually differ. (Ryan)

The Fairchild VZ-5 Fledgling was designed to the same requirement as the Ryan Vertiplane, but did not get further than tethered trials. (NASM, Smithsonian Institution)

conventional if high-tailed attitude, or it could sit on its two main wheels and tailskid with its nose in the air, giving the wing a 30 degree angle of attack to enhance the bucket effect for vertical take-off. Pitch was controlled by small rotors at the top of the T-tail.

Tethered trials of the Fledgling were conducted late in 1959. It is thought not to have flown in free flight.

The French Breguet 940, 941 and 941S also used deflected thrust to produce lift directly but were very different aircraft. They

were designed as military STOL tactical transports and were very similar to the XC-142 in size, weight and configuration. Wings were high-mounted and the four engines and large propellers were spaced out so as to blow slipstream over the whole wing. Propellers were linked by a cross-shaft as in VTOL types for safety. The wings did not tilt; the wing, engines and propellers remained fixed and the propeller slipstreams were deflected downwards by a cascade of flaps and slots which were lowered from the

trailing edge across the whole wing. The 940, 941 and 941S were not powerful enough to achieve VTOL and they lacked any system for controlling hovering flight, but they did support a large fraction of their weight on slipstream alone and were able to demonstrate impressive STOL performance.

The Breguet 940 Integral was an experimental aircraft built to test the thrust deflection system. It was a transport aircraft in its own right and had a 50 ft long box-like fuselage with upswept tail and loading ramp.

It had a straight wing of 59 ft span carrying four engines and large propellers, spaced out so that the entire wing was bathed in propeller slipstream. Multiple full-span flaps could be lowered to deflect the slipstream vertically downward. The Integral weighed 17,000 pounds loaded, and was powered by four 400 shp Turbomeca Turmo II turboshaft engines. It first flew on 21 May 1958.

The Breguet 941 was larger, with 75 ft fuselage and 76 ft span wing. Its maximum

Left: The Breguet 940 Intergral used compound full-span flaps to deflect the propeller slipstream downwards and directly convert thrust to lift. This view shows the 940 with flaps fully lowered on both wings and tail. A modification to the fuselage dorsal area seems to be in progress.
(Copyright reserved)

Breguet used their experience with the 940 to build two prototypes of the larger Model 941. A 941 prototype is seen here in civil paint, taking off with full-span slipstream-deflecting flaps down.
(Copyright reserved)

Left: The Breguet 940 Integral is seen here in level flight with compound flaps in the 'up' position.
(Copyright reserved)

A Breguet 941S in military paint is seen landing. The thrust deflection gives it a nose-down attitude, and the descent path being much shallower than it would appear.
(Copyright reserved)

loaded weight was 44,000 pounds and it was powered by four 1,250 shp Turmo IIID engines. The same principle of thrust deflection was used and multiple section flaps could be lowered across the whole trailing edge. Two prototypes of the 941 were built. These did not have a working rear loading ramps. The first flew on 2 June 1961. When flying with flaps fully down, it had a distinctive nose-down attitude which made it appear to be flying into the ground.

The American McDonnell company obtained a licence for the manufacture of the 941 and, during the summer of 1964, demonstrated the 941 in the USA as the McDonnell Model 188 Prototype. They emphasised military applications and advertised that the Model 188 would be built to American military standards.

A developed version, the 941S, had 1,500 shp engines and a maximum take-off weight of 58,000 pounds. The 941S was intended for military use and had a nose radome and rear loading ramp. Four were made and flew during 1967. McDonnell demonstrated the 941S in the USA as the Model 188E, this time emphasising civil short-haul STOL applications.

Conventional aircraft

In discussing VTOL aircraft, it is important not to lose sight of the competing conventional aircraft. Many of the propeller-driven types discussed in this chapter were assessed during the mid-sixties for use by the US armed forces, and one of the prime applications for VTOL transports was fleet resupply.

The aircraft chosen by the US Navy for resupply was the Grumman C-2A. This was a conventional twin-engined transport aircraft with deck-landing capability. The C-2A Greyhound cost very little to develop. It used the wings, tail surfaces, engines, landing gear

McDonnell took out a licence to build the 941S as the McDonnell Model 188. Here a 941S is disguised as the Model 188 Technology Demonstrator. Once again, the aircraft is flying nose-down and is not descending at a steep angle. Good judgement of flare was essential.

and cockpit of the existing Grumman E-2A Hawkeye, with an enlarged pressurised fuselage. It was 57 ft long and had wings of 81 ft span, folding to 29 ft for deck storage. Its maximum loaded weight was 55,000 pounds and it could take off with a payload of 15,000 pounds from land or 10,000 pounds from a carrier.

The C-2A first flew on 18 November 1964 and the Navy took delivery of nineteen aircraft during the sixties.

In June 1983, the Navy awarded Grumman a $678 million contract for a further 39 aircraft. These were identical to the original C-2A with detail improvements to avionics, corrosion protection and passenger comfort.

The first was delivered on schedule in January 1985 and deliveries should be complete in 1989.

The success of the Greyhound is a salutory lesson to proponents of VTOL. The Greyhound cost very little to develop, was a straightforward and quite ordinary design, it won the original contract, and it was so successful that it won the second contract twenty years later. It is difficult to justify the vast sums spent on VTOL research against economic designs like the Greyhound. It is also difficult to see how the original requirement for only twenty aircraft could justify major expenditure.

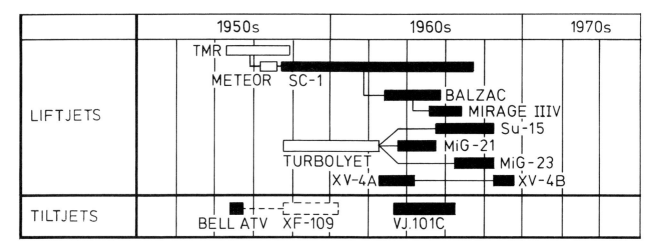

	1950s	1960s	1970s
LIFTJETS	TMR — METEOR — SC-1 — TURBOLYET — XV-4A	BALZAC — MIRAGE IIIV — Su-15 — MiG-21 — MiG-23 — XV-4B	
TILTJETS	BELL ATV — XF-109	VJ.101C	

The first jet VTOL aircraft had been the tailsitter Ryan X-13 Vertijet and the SNECMA Coleoptere. These used the same jet engine to provide both lifting thrust and propulsion by the very simple expedient of tilting the whole aircraft. Tailsitters were not practical because the pilot was tilted to an uncomfortable position and had a restricted field of view during hovering flight, just when he needed the maximum of vision and control. Subsequent generations of VTOL jet aircraft remained horizontal both in normal flight and in vertical or hovering flight and were termed 'flat-risers'.

The first generation of flat-risers used liftjets. These were highly specialised jet engines of very light weight and capable of producing high thrust for the short time required for take-off and transition to horizontal flight. In normal flight the liftjets were shut down and the aircraft was driven by a separate propulsion engine and for a vertical landing the liftjets were started again. Variations on the liftjet theme included thrust augmentation and use of the same engines for lift or propulsion by switching their exhausts from one outlet to another.

Refinements of the liftjet led to a further generation of aircraft, the tiltjet. This used liftjets to get off the ground, but could then tilt the liftjets through 90 degrees to use them for propulsion, saving the weight of an additional propulsion engine, but adding the tilt mechanism and invoking a more complex control system.

Liftjets

The liftjet principle was very simple. Nothing had to move or tilt. All that was needed was a conventional aircraft with a few lift engines added somewhere near to the centre of gravity. For short take-off applications, the lift jets would not have to support the total weight, since a thrust equal to only half the weight would still take 25 per cent of the take-off run. For vertical take-off, the jets should be able to support aircraft weight plus 20 per cent so as to have a margin for control. In vertical and hovering flight, a control system, for instance puffer pipes and valves, would be required. A VTOL liftjet aircraft would be able to lift a greater payload by making an appropriate take-off run, giving it VTOL, STOL or CTOL capability.

The liftjets had the advantages of being simple and versatile, and were expected to have the performance of a conventional aircraft in horizontal flight. Lift-jet research aircraft appeared in Britain, France, the USSR and the USA.

The British liftjet story began at Rolls-Royce with a test rig known as the TMR, or Thrust Measuring Rig. Bland names such as this are often used by engineers as a subterfuge to confuse the accountants who approve (or veto) their funding allocations. In reality the TMR was designed as a flying machine capable of controlled free hovering flight; it even received the military serial number XJ314.

Like the early Ryan and SNECMA rigs, the TMR was designed only for hovering flight and its structure consisted of a four-legged metal framework which bore a great resemblance to an old-fashioned bed, giving rise to the popular nickname, 'Flying Bedstead'. The frame supported two Rolls-Royce Nene Jet engines mounted tail-to-tail. The exhaust of one Nene was angled through 90 degrees to pass vertically down through the Bedstead's centre of gravity. The exhaust of the other Nene was split in two and each pipe was angled vertically down, one each side of the centre of gravity. This arrangement ensured that both engines produced thrust

Lift and tilt jets were flying from the mid-fifties until 1970.
Most of the activity centred on liftjet types, which were easier to make and control. (Author)

The Rolls-Royce Thrust Measuring Rig or 'Flying Bedstead' was the earliest free-flying test rig. Plumbing from engine compressors to reaction control jets is clearly visible. (Rolls-Royce)

through the centre of gravity, and while failure of either would cause loss of lift, at least the TMR should remain upright during its forced descent. The pilot sat on top of the engines. Four outrigger pipes carried the 'puffer' jets which used air bled from the engine compressors to control vehicle attitude. A tubular frame above the pilot's head was for attachment of restraint cables during initial tethered tests. It was too flimsy to give any protection to the pilot if this tall and top heavy vehicle should fall over.

The Bedstead weighed 6,000 pounds empty and 7,500 pounds with pilot and 10 minutes fuel. The engines produced 3,720 pounds of thrust each, pitch nozzles 290 pounds each and roll nozzles 40 pounds each. This gave a total lift of 8,100 pounds, an excess of only 8 per cent over gross weight. This, combined with the extreme throttle lag of these early centrifugal engines, made control of height extremely difficult, though life became easier as fuel was burned and the machine became lighter. With tanks almost empty, there was 30 per cent excess of

thrust over weight, permitting vertical manoeuvres up to 0.3g.

The pilot had full authority over the two throttles which, of course, controlled the rate of rise or sink. He was also in direct control of rate of yaw, via rudder pedals which inclined the pitch nozzles sideways. The two-channel electrical autostabiliser had full authority in roll and pitch. The pilot could use his control column to introduce electrical roll and pitch demands into the stabilisation system, but he did not have any manual override.

The Bedstead made tethered flights during 1953 and 1954 and made its first free flight on 3 August 1954 with Rolls-Royce chief test pilot R. T. Shepherd in the hot seat. Further flights were made by RAE pilot, Squadron Leader R. A. Harvey, again at the Rolls-Royce test facility at Hucknall near Derby. The Bedstead was rock steady in pitch and roll, pitch control was good, but roll control was weak. It was easy to move forwards or sideways by applying a little pitch or roll, but the thrust requirement increased rapidly in both cases, and good throttle co-ordination was essential.

In five months of flying the Bedstead flew 23 times, logging some three hours in the air. It was withdrawn for modifications and then moved to RAE Farnborough for further flying. There were no tether facilities at RAE, so the modified XJ314 could not be properly tested before being tested in free flight. It was found to be unstable in pitch and the cause could not be found. It later crashed, killing the pilot.

A second Bedstead, XK426, was used for turbulence tests at Hucknall from 22 November 1957, but crashed only a week later. Parts from it were used to repair XJ314,which had been moved to RAE Bedford.

The surviving Bedstead, XJ314, is on temporary loan from the London Science Museum to the Royal Museum of Scotland who have it on display at East Fortune near Edinburgh.

Whilst the Bedstead programme was under way, a Rolls-Royce team led by Dr A. A. Griffith were working on the RB108 lift engine. This produced 2,130 pounds of thrust yet weighed only 270 pounds, a thrust to weight ratio of almost 8:1, and was first run in July 1955. A single RB108 was mounted vertically in a special bay in the centre fuselage of Meteor PR9 VZ608 for air-testing. A door above the engine bay admitted ram air to prove that the engine could be restarted in mid-air. VZ608 may be seen at Newark Air Museum, near Nottingham, England.

The British Ministry of Supply held a design competition for a VTOL research aircraft to be lifted by the new engine. Various companies responded, including Fairey, with a version of the FD1, and Percival, with a version of the Provost. The contract was won by Shorts of Belfast who were funded to build two VTOL research aircraft powered by the new engine. Work started in August 1957 on project PD11, which resulted in a tiny delta-winged aircraft, the Short SC1.

The fuselage of the SC1 was only 25 ft long, but was of relatively large cross-section for most of its length, being 5 ft in height and 4 ft 6 in wide. The nose was fully glazed, offering the pilot excellent all round vision. There was a small equipment bay to the rear of the cockpit and behind this the centre fuselage accommodated four lift engines mounted vertically on gimbals which permitted them to swivel fore and aft. The rear fuselage housed a fifth engine for horizontal propulsion, with dorsal air intake.

The engine air intakes for the four lift engines consisted of a set of louvres in the upper fuselage above the engines and a set of gills further forward. The louvres were normally sprung shut, but would suck open when the lift engines were running. The gills could be opened by the pilot in forward flight so that ram air would spin the lift engines up to speed.

Like Ryan, Shorts chose to use a delta wing for strength and lightness. In the SC1 the wing was mounted fairly low on the fuselage. No horizontal stabiliser was fitted and the SC1 had only a small, almost vestigial fin, a large part of which was rudder. Additional fin area was added early in the test programme.

A long fixed tricycle undercarriage was fitted. The SC1 was to study hovering, transition and low-speed flight, so there was no need to carry the weight of retractable

The four lift engines of the SC-1 supplied compressor air to a ring main, the large bore pipe encircling them. Air from the ring main was ducted to reaction control jets in wings, nose and tail. The fifth engine, used for propulsion in horizontal flight, is in the tail.
(Shorts)

Early hovering trials were performed over a grid which diverted hot exhaust gases to prevent recirculation and re-ingestion. Main landing gear is angled aft for VTOL flight.
(Shorts)

The Short SC-1 meets its ancestor, the Flying Bedstead. Progress in engine technology is underlined by the tiny size of the SC-1 with its four lift engines against the much larger Bedstead with its two Nenes. The two machines were approximately equal in weight and total thrust.
(Shorts)

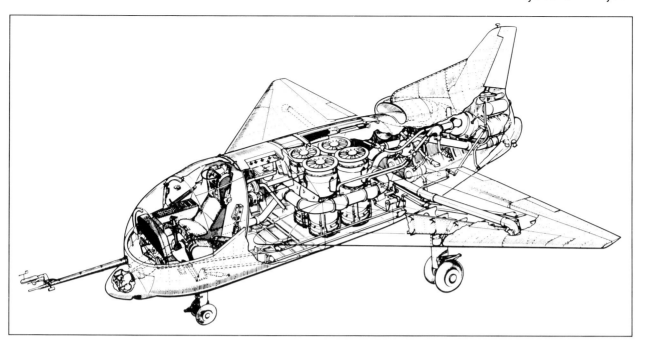

gear. The main wheels could be set by the pilot in a forward position for conventional take off or rearward for vertical take off. In the forward position they were locked but when in the rearward VTOL position they were free to castor.

Air-bleeds from all four lift engines were fed to a ring main and via four pipes to nose, tail and wing tip puffer valves, which were used to control attitude in hovering flight. The air system could also be used to start the engines, the normal procedure being to use air from a ground trolley to start the propulsion engine and then to use air bleed from that to start the four lift engines.

The SC1 was fitted with a comprehensive autostabiliser system permitting various levels of manual, semi-automatic and automatic control. For safety, the automatic system was triplicated and in theory would tolerate component failure without malfunction. There was also a system whereby the pilot could mechanically uncouple the autopilot and assume fully manual control.

The SC1 weighed 6,260 pounds unladen, could take off vertically with a 10 per cent thrust margin at a gross weight of 7,700 pounds and could take off conventionally with a wing loading of 38 pounds per square foot at 8,050 pounds gross weight. Total thrust available for vertical lift, including the four lift engines and the four control nozzles was 8,600 pounds.

Two SC1 aircraft were made, the first having serial XG900 and the second serial XG905. XG900 was fitted with propulsion engine only, and after taxi trials at Short's Belfast facility was shipped to Boscombe Down. Here it made its first flight horizontally on 2 April 1957 with Tom Brooke-Smith at the controls. XG905 remained in Belfast and was fitted with the first set of lift engines for tethered trials in a test gantry. It made its first tethered vertical take-off on 26 May 1958 and its first free flight vertical take-off and landing on 25 October 1958. For early VTOL flights a special steel platform was used to accept the engine exhaust gases and direct them away so as to avoid re-ingestion and loss of engine efficiency.

During 1959, XG900 was tested in conventional flight at lower and lower speeds, and XG905 was tested in VTOL flight at higher and higher speeds. When XG900 had got down to 75 knots and XG905 had got up to 80 knots, it was clearly time to try a transition. On 6 April 1960 Tom Brooke-Smith took off from RAE Bedford in XG905 conventionally, converted to hover and converted back for a conventional landing. XG900 made its first vertical flight on 20

July 1960 and vertical-horizontal-vertical flights followed.

The SC1 appeared at the SBAC air display at Farnborough in 1960 and flew the English Channel both ways to appear at the French display in 1961. The Farnborough show provided the VTOL fraternity with a new learning experience. The SC1 was now able to take-off vertically from an unprepared site without the aid of the platform, and this was demonstrated with a take-off from the grass by the runway. The grass had been mown for the display and the hovering SC1 picked up the mown grass and recirculated it into the lift-jet intakes. These were protected against foreign object ingestion by wire mesh, which caught the grass. The SC1 grew a small haystack on its back, blocking the intakes and causing it to lose thrust and sink to the ground. The lesson was learned that it is better to eat debris and put up with engine erosion, rather than try to stop it.

Both aircraft were used in long and successful research programmes. XG900 spent the years 1961 to 1964 in a programme designed to test handling qualities in hover and transition. It was tested both with direct mechanical control of aerodynamic and reaction controls, and in 'Nozzles Electrical' mode with mechanical control of aerodynamic surfaces and electrical autostabiliser control of reaction nozzle valves. The 'Fully Elecctrical' mode was not used because the high control sensitivity needed for nozzle control in hover could have caused instability in conventional flight. Control power, sensitivity and damping were evaluated for rate damping and quasi-attitude modes of autostabiliser characteristic and were compared with AGARD recommendations. It was found that the ability to tilt the lift engines fore and aft, intended primarily as a means of accelerating and decelerating horizontally through transition, were also a great advantage in pitch axis control. Because only the engines, rather than the whole aircraft, had to be tilted the stick sensitivity could be reduced, thereby permitting greater damping and higher stability in pitch.

Concern was expressed at the high pilot workload during transition from horizontal to vertical flight. Because the engines were thirsty even when idling, lighting the lift engines had to be left as late as possible. The lighting procedure took much of the pilot's attention, as did the related changes of trim and the deterioration of handling at low speed. These distractions occurred just when the accurate flying necessary for a good landing was needed.

XG905, meanwhile, was fitted with

The SC-1 hovers at low altitude over the runway. Some scorching is apparent, but surprisingly little debris is thrown up.
(Shorts)

VTOL

equipment capable of controlling it in fully automatic landing and was used by the BLEU (Blind Landing Experimental Unit) for work on poor and zero visibility landing. This was at the time when the Trident (Smiths Industries) and the VC10 (Elliotts) were competing to be the first aircraft certificated for completely blind civil landings. VTOL blind landing was a high priority, since it might be expected that a VTOL aircraft, at zero speed, might be safer to land blind than a conventional aircraft at 100 knots. A VTOL blind landing aircraft could land almost anywhere in an emergency.

weight ratio of 16:1. There was no demand in Britain for this engine, but Rolls-Royce found a partner in the French Dassault company. NATO wanted a supersonic VTOL fighter aircraft and had issued Nato Basic Military Requirement NBMR3. Various individual companies and consortia proposed configurations for NBMR3 aircraft. Few actually completed designs and only Dassault got as far as building an aircraft.

Dassault were already very successful builders of supersonic aircraft. They had opted for a slender delta wing and had flown the tiny Mirage I in June 1955. This had

On 2 October 1963, XG905 proved one fallacy in the triple channel autostabiliser design philosophy: if all three channels use the same technology and design, then simultaneous failure is possible. In the event all three gyros malfunctioned, and XG905 crashed killing the pilot. It was rebuilt and joined XG900 at Bedford in 1967 for further research work.

XG900 is at the Science Museum, Wroughton, near Swindon, England and XG905 is on display at Ulster Folk and Transport Museum, Cultra, Holywood, County Down, Northern Ireland.

The Rolls-Royce VTOL programme proceeded smoothly enough with the TMR and its Nene engines and the SC1 with its RB108 liftjet engines. The RB108 had a thrust to weight ratio of 8:1 and Rolls were already planning a developed version with a thrust to

grown into the Mirage III, a 15,000 pound Mach 2 single-seat fighter, by late 1956. They proposed to use the new Rolls lift engine in an even larger version which, at 30,000 pounds, would be one of the heavier jet fighters of its era.

To gain VTOL experience, Dassault started with an existing airframe and available engines. The airframe was that of the Mirage III prototype, III-001, and the engines were the Rolls-Royce RB108s already used in the SC1. The outcome was a scale model, weighing some 15,000 pounds, of the proposed 30,000 pound final design. This was designated V 001, the V standing for Vertical and 001 being the airframe number. The airframe 001 was already known by the nickname 'Balzac', derived from a well-publicised telephone number, Balzac 0001.

The Balzac retained the general features

The Dassault Balzac V-001 was a rebuild of Mirage III-001 with eight lift engines in mid-fuselage. Balzac was a liftjet technology demonstrator for Dassault's NATO NBMR3 submission, the larger and heavier Mirage IIIV. (Copyright reserved)

174

Balzac lifts clear of the ground in early tethered hovering trials. Two of the four raised intake ducts can be seen. Each feeds air to two liftjets.
(Copyright reserved)

'Allo'? Ici Balzac zero-zero-zero-un.' The name Balzac came from the similarity between the airframe serial and a well-known telephone number.
(Copyright reserved)

of the Mirage and had a 24 foot span slender delta wing with 60 degrees of sweep, large sharply swept tail fin, and a slim pointed nose with single-seat cockpit set well forward and semicircular air intakes on each side. The fuselage was lengthened a little to 43 ft and the centre section was made taller and much wider. Eight 2,160 pound RB108 lift engines were fitted in two parallel rows of four. The rows were separated to allow the intake ducting for the propulsion engine to pass between them, and in each row the front two engines were separated from the rear two by the main gear retraction bay. With the lift engines taking up most of the centre fuselage, there was no room for the original

10,000 pound thrust Atar propulsion engine, so a much smaller, 5,000 pound thrust, Bristol Orpheus engine was fitted in the remaining space in the rear fuselage.

With test pilot Réné Bigand at the controls, the Balzac made its first tethered hover on 12 October 1962, followed by a free flight hover on 18 October. After completing hovering trials, it made a conventional all-horizontal flight on 1 March 1963. It then progressed rapidly to a transition on 18 March and a full transition cycle vertical-horizontal-vertical on 29 March. The Balzac continued flying until a fatal crash on 27 January 1964. After a rebuild, it went on flying until written-off in another fatal crash on 8 September 1965. It had flown for almost three years and during this time provided much useful data to be used in finalising the design of the larger Mirage IIIV.

The Mirage IIIV (III for three and V for Vertical) was twice the weight of the Balzac. It had the same general layout and overall shape, was 59 feet long and had a wingspan of 29 feet. The wings were slightly cranked to reduce the sweep by a few degrees at mid-span. Engine installation was very similar, this time using eight of the new 5,400 pound thrust Rolls-Royce RB162-31 lift engines and a SNECMA TF-104 turbofan propulsion engine capable of 12,000 pounds thrust, or 20,000 pounds thrust with afterburning.

Two Mirage IIIVs were built. IIIV-01 **175**

Balzac is seen in free hover.
Special long-stroke landing
gear was fitted for hovering
trials.
(Copyright reserved)

The boxes seen under
Balzac's fuselage are
deflectors which were fitted
to the liftjet exhausts for short
take-off trials.
(Copyright reserved)

The Dassault Mirage IIIV was larger and heavier than Balzac, but very similar in appearance. Mirage IIIV 01 is seen here hovering at low level. The four intake doors each feed air to two liftjet engines.
(Copyright reserved)

flew in hover on 12 February 1965. The TF-104 engine was replaced by a TF-106 and IIIV-01 was flown horizontally to Mach 1.35. First transition was not until March 1966. The second aircraft, IIIV-02, had a Pratt and Whitney TF30 turbofan engine and flew on 22 June 1966. Dassault's aim of building a Mach 2 VTOL fighter was achieved on 12 September 1966 when IIIV-02 flew at Mach 2.04. Aircraft 02 was lost in a crash on 28 November 1966.

The Balzac and both Mirage IIIVs used much of the technology developed in the Short SC1. Like the SC1, they used lift engines grouped close to the centre of gravity for lift, a separate propulsion engine in the tail and control jets at nose, tail and wingtips for attitude control. The lift engine

air intake covers were rear-hinged to admit ram air for engine starting. Since all designs were of similar configuration, the comprehensive control parameter measurements made during the SC1 programme were broadly applicable to V-001 and IIIV control system design. The Dassault aircraft had one significant advantage over the SC1. They had eight lift engines, where the SC1 only had four. In the event of a lift jet failure, the engine diagonally opposite must also be cut so that the aircraft stays upright. In the SC1 losing one engine and cutting another would halve the lift and cause a heavy landing. The Dassault aircraft would suffer only 25 per cent loss of lift, with much less serious consequences.

The Mirage IIIV was the only NBMR3

Mirage IIIV 02 is anchored by a chain so that the lift engines can be ground tested. The exhausts pass though the grid into a pit and are conducted away though a tunnel.
(Copyright reserved)

aircraft to fly, it achieved its design objectives and it was declared the winner jointly with the Hawker P.1154, which was only a design study. In theory, the NATO countries should then have placed orders but in fact they did not. The IIIV had VTOL capability and it had Mach 2 performance, but had to carry eight lift engines, associated structure and additional fuel. The total weight penalty was some 3,000 pounds, equivalent to almost a 50 per cent reduction in payload and range.

Both Balzac V-001 and Mirage IIIV-02 were destroyed in crashes. Mirage IIIV-01 may be seen at the Musée de L'Air at le Bourget in Paris, France.

The Soviets had a VTOL test rig, known as the Turbolyet. This was designed by A. N. Rafaelyants and is thought to have been used for a test programme during the late fifties. It used a single turbojet with its axis vertical, from which a tubular framework extended fore and aft and to each side. The four arms of the framework each carried a sturdy long-travel landing leg with castor and, further outboard, a reaction jet. An enclosed box-shaped cockpit sat on the forward arm. The exact test dates are not available, and it is not known if the programme resulted in VTOL research aircraft.

Soviet work on liftjet engines continued, and lift engines were installed in several experimental fighter aircraft during the mid-sixties. These did not have true VTOL capability and used the lift engines to support only part of their weight, so as to obtain STOL performance. Three such aircraft were seen at the Domodyedovo Air Day in 1967, and these were liftjet versions of the MiG-21, Mig-23 and Su-15 designs.

The MiG-21 was a medium-size short-range interceptor fighter with a sharply swept delta wing and conventional tail surfaces. It weighed 17,000 pounds loaded, was 47 ft long and had a wingspan of 25 feet. The liftjet test vehicle was made from a MiG-21 by adding two vertically mounted lift engines in a bay in mid-fuselage. The engines were similar to the Rolls-Royce RB108 but were rather larger with approximately 8,000 pounds thrust each. The liftjet air intakes were covered by a rear-hinged door similar to that on the Dassault aircraft, and jet exhaust below the fuselage was deflected by louvres. The standard MiG-21 suffered from lack of control at low speed and the liftjet version must have had some form of control enhancement. External fuselage pipes were visible and may have fed compressor air to

Mirage IIIV 02 is seen in hovering flight. 02 differed from 01 in having longitudinally hinged intake doors for the liftjets.

nose and tail reaction nozzles. Blown wing surfaces may have been used for roll control. The landing gear was fixed and of wider track than usual. The aircraft was seen to fly slowly, approximately 50 knots, at Domodyedovo in July 1967.

The MiG-23 was a much larger aircraft and had its air intakes each side of the fuselage to permit a large radome to be fitted in the nose. The early prototypes included a swing-wing version and a liftjet version, these being two possible ways of combining high performance and STOL. The liftjet version had mid-mounted delta wings and a mid-fuselage lift engine bay similar to that used on the MiG-21, again using rear-hinged upper door and controllable exhaust louvres.

Sukhoi applied liftjets in the Su-15, and showed a version with three lift engines mounted in-line in mid fuselage. There were two rear-hinged intake doors on the upper fuselage, one for the front engine and one for the other two. The engine exhausts were covered by longitudinal doors in normal flight. Like Mikoyan, Sukhoi abandoned liftjets and used swing-wings instead.

The Italian company Fiat and the Japanese company NAL both made liftjet test rigs, but neither went on to build aircraft. North American flew the Hoverbuggy, a hover rig powered by two J85 engines mounted together with reaction jets on four outriggers. It weighed 3,800 pounds. Test pilot Van Shephard made a captive flight on 1

This is the Sukhoi Su-15DPD, a liftjet version of the Sukhoi Su-15. MiG also used liftjets in versions of the MiG-21 and MiG-23. All of these types were thought to be STOL rather than VTOL. (Novosti)

In retrospect it is hardly surprising that the swing-wing version was chosen for production. The lift engines would have supported only half the aircraft weight, reducing the take off run by only 30 per cent and were dead weight once airborne. As in the Mirage, payload and range would have suffered badly. The swing-wing gave STOL performance and when airborne would pay for itself by providing economical long-range cruise.

November 1965 and free flights soon after. The Hoverbuggy was used for general VTOL research work.

Bell Aerospace made a combined liftjet and rocket platform known as the Lunar Landing Training Vehicle (LLTV). This enabled NASA astronauts to practice lunar landing techniques. The liftjet, a CF 700-2V of 4,200 pounds thrust, supported five sixths of the weight of the platform. This left one-sixth to be supported by the rockets, so as to simulate lunar gravity. Two early versions known as LLRV were flown in 1962-4, and three LLTV were used by the Apollo programme from 1967 on.

The Lunar Excursion Module (LEM) used to land on the moon in 1969 was a rocket-powered platform which was capable of hovering for a few seconds while the crew selected a landing site. It was non-aerodynamic.

Augmented Jets

In the USA, work on liftjets was approached in a rather different way. Where Rolls-Royce had concentrated on making very light special-purpose lift engines the American approach was to divert the thrust of the propulsion engines, and to use that thrust in the most effective possible way. It was known that mixing hot jet engine exhaust gas with cold air increased engine thrust, this effect being known as jet augmentation. Von Karman's analysis, made in 1949, predicted the amount of thrust augmentation to be expected from any given mixing ratio and the additional augmentation which could result from subsequent controlled expansion.

Von Karman's method is an approximation which simplifies the augmentation process so that it can be analysed using reasonably straightforward application of momentum theory and Benoulli's theorum. The following verbal explanation is based on von Karman's algebra.

The exhaust of the jet engine is directed into a large tube. As it flows down the tube it mixes with the air in the tube and carries it along. The total momentum of the exhaust gas is shared between the gas and the air, and the efflux that emerges from the tube is a mixture of gas and air with exactly the same momentum as the original jet. This process adds no thrust and loses no thrust. At the mouth of the tube, air is sucked in to replace that which has been swept away down the tube. It is the momentum added to this air as it is sucked in which creates additional thrust.

The area of the tube has to be at least twice the area of the jet in order to obtain an increase in thrust. If the tube is five times the jet area, thrust should increase by 20 per cent, and at ten times, thrust should be up by 36 per cent.

If the mixture of gas and air is allowed to expand after mixing, pressure energy will be converted to additional momentum lift. In theory, an area ratio of five to one with subsequent expansion gives 32 per cent augmentation and an area ratio of ten should give 75 per cent augmentation.

The simplified theory takes no account of the high temperature of jet exhaust gases and it might be expected that further expansion would create further lift by converting thermal energy to momentum.

There is no flaw in the von Karman theory, but it does assume that exhaust gas and air mix fully and continue down the tube. Incomplete mixing will reduce airflow and degrade augmentation and this sets a limit on the practical advantage to be gained.

Laboratory tests of various designs of augmenter jet and tube geometry gave very promising results. Single-stage devices gave up to 50 per cent augmentation, multiple injectors approached 100 per cent, and a three-stage device multiplied thrust by 2.3. These were very useful gains; worth trying on a full-size aircraft.

Lockheed's Georgia Division set up a privately financed programme and tested a wind-tunnel model in 1959. They then built a flying test rig powered by two Fairchild J44 turbojets rated at 1,000 pounds static thrust each. The rig lifted a total weight of 2,600 pounds off the ground. On the face of it, this looks like 30 per cent augmentation, but of course the engines could have produced more (or less) than rated thrust for the duration of the test. The rig was later uprated by the substitution of Continental J69 engines and was used for two years to provide data for use in control system design.

Lockheed put a proposal to the US Army in August 1959 for a battlefield surveillance and target acquisition system based on their Model 330 Hummingbird augmented thrust VTOL design study. US Army awarded them a contract for two aircraft in July 1961 and gave the Hummingbird the designation VZ-10. When military designations were revised in July 1962 this was replaced by the designation XV-4A.

The XV-4A Hummingbird was 32 feet long and had a fat fuselage 4 ft wide and 5 ft high and of rounded square cross-section. A conventional two-place cockpit occupied the nose. The bulk of the fuselage was occupied by the mixing chamber for the jet augmenter system, and hatches along upper and lower fuselage opened when the system was in use. The two 3,300 pound thrust Pratt and Whitney JT12A-PW-3 turbojet engines were mounted on the sides of the centre fuselage at shoulder height. The tricycle undercarriage main gear retracted into the engine nacelles. Flying surfaces consisted of slim 26ft span mid-mounted wings and a T tail.

The engines exhausted rearward for propulsion but could be diverted by a valve in each jet-pipe to feed the ejector system. This was a system of pipes and downward-pointing nozzles distributed along the top of the mixing chamber. The two engine exhausts fed separate nozzle systems, these being interleaved so that failure of one engine would not affect the distribution of lift. The ejector system had to withstand engine exhaust temperatures and was fabricated from stainless steel and titanium. Engine compressor air was used to control the boundary layer around the mixing chamber inlet.

The control system was conventional and used compressor bleed to supply air to nozzles at nose and tail and at both wingtips. No change of control function was needed at transition, apart from turning off the air bleeds in normal flight.

The Hummingbird weighed 5,000 pounds empty and 7,200 pounds for vertical take-off. The engine thrust at 6,600 pounds fell to 6,000 pounds at the nozzles due to duct losses and was increased by the augmentation system to more than 7,500 pounds to provide a 5 per cent excess of lift over weight. Augmentation was thus 25 per cent gross but only 14 per cent nett. Figures

as high as 45 per cent had been measured in test rigs, but only in configurations which were too heavy to fly.

The XV-4A hovered in a nose-high attitude because of the 12 degree rearward inclination of the ejectors. For transition to horizontal flight, the nose was dropped through the horizontal to 10 degrees down, so that ejector thrust angled 22 degrees backward, providing a useful forward component. As the aircraft attained forward speed, one engine was diverted from lift to thrust. The remaining engine continued to generate lift, evenly distributed by the interleaved nozzles. The asymmetry of single-engine thrust was minimised by outward-angled jet-pipes. When flying speed was reached, the second engine was diverted from lift to thrust and the mixing chamber doors were closed.

The XV-4A first flew in a conventional flight on 7 July 1962. First tethered hover was on 30 November 1962, free hover on 24 May 1963 and first transition on 8 November 1963. On a conventional flight, early in 1963, the Hummingbird reached 12,000 feet altitude in only 50 seconds. It was destroyed in a fatal crash on 10 June 1964.

The funded programme of work had been completed, the XV-4A had demon-

The Lockheed XV-4A Hummingbird used the jet augmentation principle to increase the static thrust of its jet engines. When hovering, both engine exhausts were diverted to suck air in through the doors along the top of the fuselage and blow it out through the doors beneath the fuselage. (Lockheed)

strated thrust augmentation and had achieved hover, transition and horizontal flight. The actual thrust augmentation achieved was only 14 per cent nett, very much less than the expected 40 per cent. Better nozzle systems were available, but would require further work to reduce them to flyable weight.

At the time the Hummingbird programme started, engines had been heavy and any way of increasing thrust was highly desirable. The augmentation system turned out to be very bulky, the mixing chamber occupying most of the fuselage, and quite heavy. By 1964, engine technology had advanced and adding lift engines yielded more lift per pound weight than augmentation. The one advantage of augmentation, that the extra

thrust came from nothing more than stationary sheet metal, was negated by the fact that this sheet metal was stainless steel and titanium welded into expensive complex shapes.

The surviving XV-4A was grounded for conversion to liftjets. After weighing the merits of various numbers and combinations of engines, Lockheed went for a six-engined modification where four engines were added and used for lift only, while the existing two engines and deflector valves could be used for either propulsion or lift. Considerable work and experimentation was done to find the best engine angles for entrapment of a lift cushion beneath the fuselage.

The modified aircraft was designated XV-4B Hummingbird II, and was powered by

The XV-4A Hummingbird is seen here in conventional flight with air intake doors closed and both engines producing forward thrust. During transition one engine produced thrust and the other was diverted to generate lift. (Lockheed)

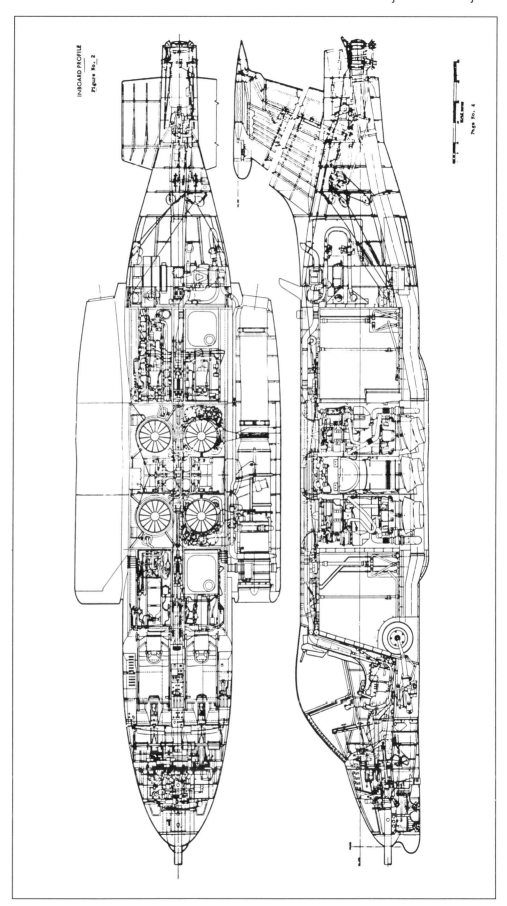

INBOARD PROFILE
Figure No. 2

Page No. 4

This sectioned view of the Lockheed Hummingbird shows it in its later form as the XV-4B with four J85 engines for lift only and two for lift or propulsion. The reaction jets for pitch and yaw control can be seen at nose and tail. (Lockheed)

183

Left: One XV-4A was rebuilt to become the XV-4B Hummingbird II, with four liftjet engines and two engines used either for lift or propulsion. It is suspended on an elaborate safety rig. The Lockheed test pilot is B.J.Dvorscak. (Lockheed)

The XV-4B Hummingbird II incorporated many modifications. Along with the liftjet conversion, fuel tankage was increased the reaction control system was improved and horizontal surfaces were added at rear fuselage and on the vertical stabiliser. (Lockheed)

six General Electric J85-GE-19 engines with a total thrust of 18,000 pounds. These occupied only the middle of the previous mixing chamber, leaving plenty of space for additional fuel tanks. With more engine thrust available and more fuel to lift, VTO weight was increased to 12,600 pounds.

The control system was updated with a fly-by-wire dual redundant autostabilisation system and a variable stability control system with manual override.

The XV-4B was rolled out on 4 June 1968. It was scheduled for five months of flight tests at Lockheed before being delivered to the USAF. From January 1969 it would be used by North American Rockwell for instrumentation and flight research at Edwards Air Force Base. It was lost in a crash on 14 March 1969. A second, new XV-4B was ordered, but appears not to have been built.

A decade later, Rockwell International designed and built their XFV-12A augmented-thrust VTOL research aircraft for the US Navy. The XFV-12A was a canard with symmetrical tapered foreplane and swept wings. It used the thrust augmentation principle, but instead of having a mixing chamber, flaps were lowered to form boxed slots in the foreplanes and wings. Engine air and exhaust was blown from nozzles into the slots, and 50 per cent augmentation was expected. The XFV-12 was rolled out on 26 August 1977, but is not thought to have flown.

Tiltjets

In 1954, while Convair, Lockheed, and Ryan were pioneering tailsitters, Bell Aircraft

Corporation's Niagara Frontier Division of Buffalo, NY, were assembling their private venture Model 65 ATV (Air Test Vehicle) from a variety of parts. The fuselage came from a Schweitzer sailplane, and the 36ft span wing was from a Cessna 170 high-wing cabin monoplane. To these was added a lightweight twin-ski landing gear. The engines, a pair of Fairchild J-44 turbojets of 1,000 pounds thrust each, on loan from the USAF, were mounted one each side of the fuselage and were pivoted at the aircraft centre of gravity. A separate Turbomeca Palouste turbocompressor supplied compressed air to control jets at the wingtips and tail. The valves for the control jets were linked directly to the conventional control surfaces and operated with them, giving a smooth transition from aerodynamic-plus-puffer control in normal flight to puffer only control when hovering.

The ATV made its first free flight on 16 November 1954, soon after the XFY-1 Pogo, and completed over twenty flights during which it proved to have ample control in pitch, yaw and roll, for take-off, hover, low-speed flight and landing. Especially impressive was its ability to hover at low level and turn within its own wingspan. It was fitted with wheeled landing gear and made conventional flights during 1955. In horizontal flight, the ATV could reach a safe altitude at which to attempt partial conversions toward hovering flight. Full conversions were not possible because of inadequate engine thrust at altitude. The ATV programme ended during 1955 and the Model 65 was donated to the Smithsonian Institution.

The ATV gave Bell valuable practical experience of VTOL flight and led to Air Force sponsorship of the project D-188 tiltjet

The Bell Model 65 VTOL Air Test Vehicle was a private-venture tiltjet. It flew horizontally and vertically but did not complete a transition. Bell pioneered the reaction control system, using gas from a separate Palouste turbine. (NASM, Smithsonian Institution)

This montage shows how the Bell VTOL ATV would have made a transition. The reaction jets can be seen at wingtip and tail. (NASM, Smithsonian Institution)

supersonic fighter, designated XF-109. This was of approximately Starfighter size and shape. It had short high-mounted tapered wings each carrying two engines in a tilting pod at its tip. Two lift engines were mounted vertically just behind the cockpit and two more engines were mounted horizontally in the rear fuselage to provide thrust in forward flight, and had their thrust deflected downward during hover. The XF-109 had reached only the mockup stage when funding was halted in 1959.

It was left to the German company EWR (Entwicklungsring Sud GmbH), based in Munich, to produce the first tiltjet fighter design. EWR, a combination of Bolkow (helicopters), Heinkel and Messerschmitt (both of whom had built jet fighter aircraft), were awarded a contract on 29 September 1959 by the Federal Ministry of Defence, following a design competition for an interceptor held in 1956.

After studying the various possible methods of thrust vectoring, engine swivelling and combinations of lift and thrust engines, they chose to use six engines in pairs, one pair in the forward fuselage to produce lift only, and one pair at each wingtip swivelling to provide either lift or thrust. The pairs of engines would be arranged at the apexes of an equilateral triangle, so that during hover, aircraft attitude in pitch and

roll could be controlled by relative adjustment of engine throttles. Control in yaw would be by differential tilting of the engine pods, one forward and one back. In theory, this would produce a very simple system, with no need for the puffer ducting, nozzles and valves of other designs. Against this, the control systems would be more complex and would have high authority with little or no possibility of reversion to manual control.

In practice, the precise control of jet engine throttles required for fine adjustment of aircraft attitude had yet to be demonstrated. Gas turbine engines, especially the early ones, were notoriously slow to respond to the throttle, especially if sudden changes in thrust were demanded. It was known that altitude could be controlled by slow and very fine adjustments of the throttle, but EWR were also very aware that attitude control needed relatively large and instantaneous changes in thrust. The whole project would hinge on the ability to control attitude with thrust, and the feasibility of the control concept could be proved only by practical demonstration.

In the Spring of 1960, EWR constructed the *Wippe* or 'See-saw', which was a test rig with a single degree of freedom, in pitch only. It consisted of a horizontal beam with a transverse horizontal pivot at one end. An engine was mounted vertically at the centre

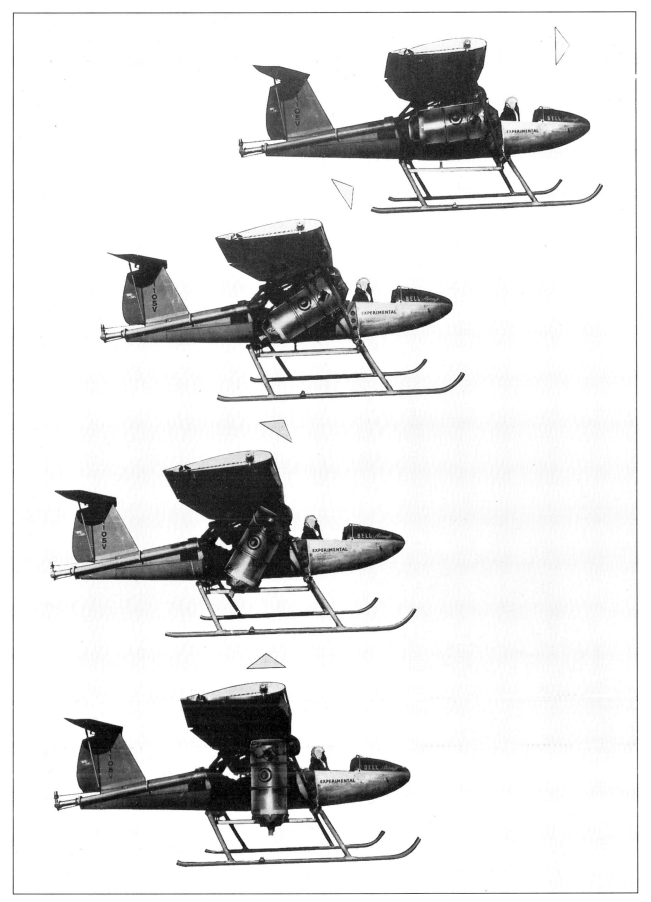

The VJ101C relied heavily on the ability to control attitude by the use of very fine engine throttle movements. This test rig, the *Wippe*, or see-saw, was used for preliminary single-axis tests of the control system.
(Photo Deutsches Museum Munich)

The VJ101C hover rig was used to test control systems and to evaluate ground effects. The RB108 engines look tiny in the 35 ft long rig.
(Photo Deutsches Museum Munich)

of the beam, and a simple cockpit at the free end of the beam. The 'pilot' was able to practise controlling hover in pitch and, with a later modification, in both pitch and roll. Several engine control systems from various companies were tested for their ability to hold the beam in a stable 'hover' against various deliberate disturbances including step inputs via the pilot's controls and the dropping of weights from the beam. The 'See-saw' rig was also used to evaluate ground effects such as recirculation.

The 'See-saw' rig was followed by the hover rig, which consisted of a steel tubular

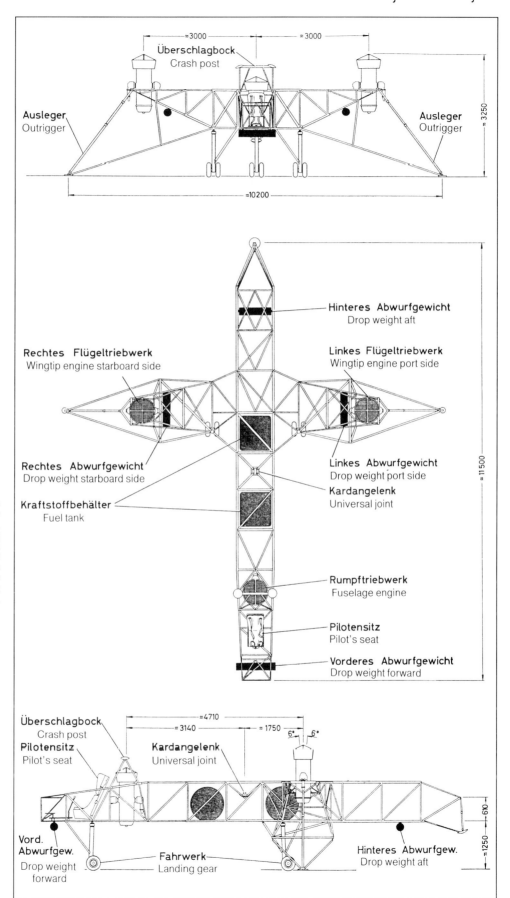

This three-view of the VJ101C hover rig shows how the layout of pilot's seat, landing gear and engines simulated that of the actual aircraft. The drop weights were released individually to test the reaction of the control system to sudden disturbances.

Überschlagbock
Crash post

Ausleger
Outrigger

Ausleger
Outrigger

≈3000

≈3000

≈3250

≈10200

Hinteres Abwurfgewicht
Drop weight aft

Rechtes Flügeltriebwerk
Wingtip engine starboard side

Linkes Flügeltriebwerk
Wingtip engine port side

Rechtes Abwurfgewicht
Drop weight starboard side

Linkes Abwurfgewicht
Drop weight port side

Kardangelenk
Universal joint

Kraftstoffbehälter
Fuel tank

Rumpftriebwerk
Fuselage engine

Pilotensitz
Pilot's seat

Vorderes Abwurfgewicht
Drop weight forward

≈11500

Überschlagbock
Crash post

Pilotensitz
Pilot's seat

Kardangelenk
Universal joint

≈4710

≈3140

≈1750

6° 6°

Vord.
Abwurfgew.
Drop weight
forward

Fahrwerk
Landing gear

Hinteres Abwurfgew.
Drop weight aft

610

1250

framework 35 ft long and 33ft wide, supporting pilot's cockpit and three engines in the relative positions they would assume in the actual aircraft, one just behind the pilot and one at each wingtip. The engines used in the hover rig were the small lightweight Rolls-Royce RB108 each of 2,100 pounds thrust, optimised purely as lift engines. The layout of landing gear also represented that intended for the VJ101C.

For the initial series of trials starting in May 1961, the hover rig was supported by a universal joint at its centre of gravity on a telescopic column. This gave it four degrees of freedom – pitch, roll, yaw and altitude – sufficient for further pilot training both with direct manual control and through the auto-stabiliser system. Altitude was controlled by collective throttle movements, roll by differential port/starboard throttle movements and pitch by differential front/rear throttling. The wingtip engines were pivoted about a horizontal transverse axis and could be tilted differentially, one forward and one back, up to 6 degrees from the vertical, to control yaw. Three drop weights were mounted on the structure, one on each wing and one in the tail. Dropping one of these weights produced an instantaneous change in centre of gravity and tested the ability of the control system to respond to sudden disturbances.

After completing trials on the telescopic column, the hover rig was flown free for the first time in March 1962. For free hover tests, a canvas 'underbody' was added to simulate the presence of wings and fuselage in ground effect. As the jet effluxes of a hovering aircraft strike the ground, the hot gases spread out in sheets across the surface until they collide and form upward fountains, which then impinge on wings and underbody to generate additional lift. Simulation of this extra lift and its effect on stability was one of the objects of the hover rig. The hover rig made successful flight tests in all seasons and weather, encountering heat, wind, rain and snow. The results were excellent and proved the controllability of the rig both in manual mode and with automatic flight system engaged. Two flight systems were tried, one from Minneapolis Honeywell and one from Perkins-Elmer Bodensee works. Both gave excellent results.

The first experimental aircraft, the VJ101C-X1, was already in final assembly. It was a single-seat fighter aircraft, very similar in size to the F-104 Starfighter at 22 ft span, 54ft length and 13 ft height, but rather lighter at 14,000 pounds loaded. The wings were set high halfway along the fuselage, and were swept back 39 degrees. Each wingtip

carried a pod with two engines mounted one above the other and capable of swivelling between horizontal and vertical to provide either forward or upward thrust. Two further engines were buried in the fuselage immediately behind the cockpit to provide lift only. They were shut down in forward flight, and restarted by opening their forward-facing cover door which rammed in sufficient air to spin them up for ignition. All six engines in the VJ101C-X1 were Rolls-Royce RB145s without reheat, X1 being intended for hover and low to medium speed tests. Control was as in the hover rig, by a combination of thrust modulation and differential pod tilt.

The RB145 engine was developed by Rolls-Royce in collaboration with MAN Turbomotors from the RB108 liftjet. It had a static thrust at sea-level of 2,750 pounds, later increased by use of reheat to 3,560 pounds. Rolls were also responsible for the development and testing of the swivelling pod assemblies. The pod swivels had to carry heavy loads and allow the passage of fuel and controls. Each pod had to be very compact for minimum drag and had to breathe effectively from zero speed to high supersonic speeds. Rolls' solution to the breathing problem was to optimise the intake fairings for high speed flight, and to move each fairing forward exposing slots through which the necessary additional mass of air could flow at low speed and hover.

X1 started its trials mounted on an improved telescopic rig which permitted limited motion in all three linear axes as well as in pitch, roll and yaw. This facilitated dynamic test and the development of control systems and allowed many improvements to be incorporated. Flight both in and out of ground effect could be simulated by adjustment of three jet efflux deflectors. After rig trials, X1 conducted rolling tests during March 1963. Unlike most other VTOL types, X1 first flew in hover, on 10 April 1963, long before its first aerodynamic flight which took place in August 1963. After making a number of partial transitions, the first full 'verticircuit' consisting of vertical take-off, transition to aerodynamic flight, transition back to hover and vertical landing was made on schedule on 8 October 1963.

Evaluation of X1 continued through 1964 with 40 aerodynamic flights, 24 hovering flights, 14 full transitions and demonstration flying at the Hannover Air Show on 3 May. VJ101C-X1 exceeded Mach 1 in level flight, being the first VTOL aircraft to do so. It was lost on 14 September 1964 during a conventional take-off, the crash being caused

Tethered trials of the VJ101C and its systems were conducted on this safety rig. The column is telescopic and gives freedom of vertical motion. The linkages give freedom in pitch, roll and yaw. Pit covers may be left in place to simulate ground effects or removed to simulate flight at altitude. (Photo Deutsches Museum Munich)

The VJ101C makes a hovering flight. The very level attitude is maintained by the high authority autostabiliser. (Photo Deutsches Museum Munich)

191

The VJ101C hovers over the airfield prior to making a transition to horizontal flight. (Photo Deutsches Museum Munich)

The VJ101C in conventional aerodynamic flight. Although two of its engines were used only for lift, the VJ101C still had two-thirds of its power available for manoeuvring and high-speed flight. (Photo Deutsches Museum Munich)

by a fault in an electronic unit. Test pilot George Bright ejected safely.

Meanwhile, VJ101C-X2 was nearing completion and started rig tests late in 1964. X2 had four Rolls-Royce RB145-R afterburning (reheat) engines in the wing tip pods and two RB145 without reheat in the fuselage. Use of reheat in conventional flight would permit fully supersonic performance, while use of reheat during take off would increase the maximum VTOL weight to some 18,000 pounds. X2 flew in hover on 12 June 1965 and aerodynamically on 12 July. It met its design objectives in October 1965 when it successfully completed a transition from hover to horizontal flight with afterburners operating.

EWR-Sud's American Chief Test Pilot, George Bright, did most of the test and development flying on the hover rig and the VJ101C. He reported some initial problems in controlling the hover rig. Because he had helicopter experience, he was applying all the corrections needed to fly a helicopter. In fact, the hover rig did not need continuous over-correction and after ten minutes flight experience with reduced control sensitivity, he found it was a very easy craft to fly, both manually and through the autostabiliser systems. Various modes of automatic control could be selected. The 'pure rate' system responded to a constant control deflection with a constant rate of attitude change, and the 'attitude' system converted a constant control deflection to a constant attitude. For instance, holding the control column over to the right would create a constant rate of roll in the 'pure rate' mode, while in the 'attitude' mode it would cause a constant bank angle. A third mode called 'integrated rate with attitude hold' provided a more subtle combination of characteristics. The pure rate system was similar to, but superior to, the control response of a helicopter. The integrated rate with attitude hold was even better, and both rate modes were excellent for use at air displays where the object is to impress the crowd with dramatic manouevres. In real flying, George Bright found the attitude mode to be much more useful.

Take-off was a hands-off manouevre, and constant deflection of the stick would cause a constant pitch or bank angle, resulting in forward or lateral movement. The attitude mode was more fuel-efficient, since the control system could make a smoother changes of attitude than the pilot and would hold a given attitude without continual corrections. It was also safer, because it kept the attitude within predetermined safe limits.

The VJ101C test programme was very successful, attained all its objectives and produced an aircraft capable of vertical take-off and landing in combination with high supersonic performance. It remains one of the fastest VTOL aircraft to date, and its vertical take off weight of 18,000 pounds against an unladen weight of 13,000 pounds allowed for 5,000 pounds of fuel and payload, a respectable load for VTOL fighters of the early sixties. The VJ101C did not lead to serious production aircraft and it is hard to find a reason why such technical success should lack military application. Perhaps some of the answer lies in the complex project structure of EWR, who were also involved in many other projects including German F-104 starfighters, the VFW VAK191 and the VJ101D. The VTOL VAK191 was to fly at a later date, in the early seventies, with a combination of vectored thrust and lift engines. The VJ101D prototypes, also VTOL, were only partly built and used one propulsion plus five lift engines. This lack of commitment to a single design must have confused potential customers. In addition, it is not clear what sort of customer would want to buy supersonic VTOL fighters. Several specifications and operational requirements documents existed, but an Air Force would want to buy supersonic conventional fighters, while the Army and Marines would want small light VTOL strike aircraft.

VJ101C-X1 was extensively damaged in the September 1964 take-off accident and was not rebuilt. VJ101C-X2 is at the Deutsches Museum in Munich, Germany, where it is suspended in mid-air near to an F-104 Starfighter permitting easy visual comparison of features and size.

9 VECTORED & DEFLECTED JETS

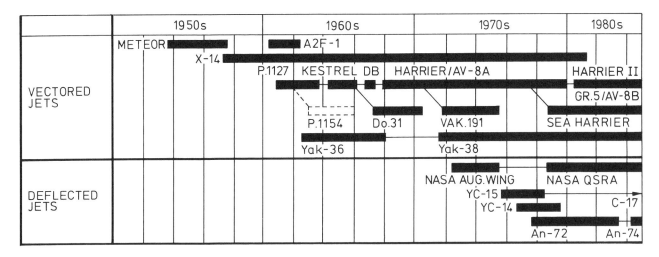

	1950s		1960s		1970s		1980s	
VECTORED JETS	METEOR ▅▅▅	X-14 ▅▅▅▅▅	▅▅ A2F-1 P.1127 ▅▅ KESTREL DB ▅▅	HARRIER/AV-8A ▅▅▅▅		HARRIER II ▅▅▅ GR.5/AV-8B	
			P.1154 ┄┄┄ ▅▅▅ Do.31	VAK.191 ▅▅▅	SEA HARRIER ▅▅▅▅	
			Yak-36	Yak-38 ▅▅▅▅		
DEFLECTED JETS				NASA AUG.WING ▅▅ YC-15 ▅▅▅	NASA QSRA ▅▅▅	
				YC-14 ▅▅▅	C-17 ▅▅	
				An-72 ▅▅▅	An-74 ▅▅	

The general principle of vectored jet thrust was well known and was tried as a means of reducing take-off run in several aircraft during the fifties. The tail-sitting Ryan X-13 Vertijet used thrust vectoring to control its attitude, and various aircraft used jet thrust in conjunction with diverter vanes for pitch and yaw control.

There were obvious advantages in using the same engine both to propel an aircraft and to lift it by thrust vectoring. The problem lay in the difficulty of designing a thrust vectoring system which was practical. An obvious way of deflecting thrust used a jet engine with a hinged tailpipe. For normal flight the tailpipe would be horizontal and in hover it would be vertical. For the aircraft to balance in hover, the centre of gravity had to be over the hinge, putting the weight of the engines ahead of the centre of gravity. This forced the rest of the aircraft weight to move rearward, no great problem in a research aircraft, but unacceptable in a combat machine which requires pilot, radar and other electronic items to be well forward.

Two VTOL vectored thrust research aircraft, the Bell X-14 and the Yak-36, had engines ahead of the centre of gravity. The Yak-38 used lift engines at the front with deflected thrust at the rear. It was the Bristol aero-engine company who combined a number of interesting ideas to produce a jet engine with a vertical thrust line through its own centre of gravity, at the same time accidentally advancing conventional engine technology by a couple of decades. The Bristol Pegasus engine powers the famous Harrier, and has also been used in combination with lift engines in both fighter and transport aircraft.

True vectoring of jet exhausts has been around since before 1960 and is still in use. Vectored jets use nozzles which are part of the engine to turn the jet exhaust gas downward, while deflected jets use external flaps or similar devices.
(Author)

Gloster Meteor IV serial RA490 was fitted with a vectored thrust system. The special Nene engines were mounted well forward so that the exhausts could be diverted to nozzles beneath the engine nacelles and in line with the aircraft centre of gravity.
(Westland)

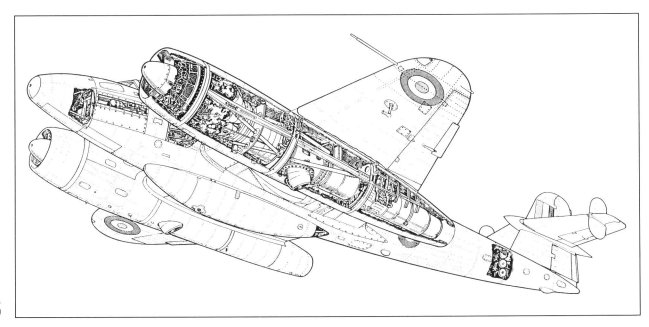

Gloster Meteor IV RA 490 was fitted with a jet deflection system to reduce landing speed. In this photo the additional jetpipes can be seen emerging beneath the nacelles. (Westland)

Tilting Pipes

During the years 1948 to 1952 the British Gloster Meteor IV twin-jet fighter flew with Metropolitan Vickers F2/4 Beryl Engines, and this aircraft, serial RA490, became known as the Beryl Meteor. In July 1952 it was transferred to the Westland Aeroplane Company at Yeovil for a jet deflection system to be installed.

The engine nacelles were extended forward to accommodate special Nene 101 engines well forward of the centre of gravity. The jetpipes extended back through the nacelles and valves permitted the exhausts to be directed either rearward or down through pipes which emerged through the bottom of each nacelle.

The installation was completed in July 1953. After tests at Yeovil, RA490 was transferred to RAE in August 1954 for the jet deflection research programme, at Farnborough 1954-56 and at Bedford 1956-57. Jet deflection reduced the stalling speed of the Meteor and it was possible to fly it at 70 knots. Without deflection, airspeed had to be kept above 100 knots.

RA490 suffered the ignominious fate of being used for firefighting practice from April 1957, a sad end for a distinguished research machine.

In 1957 Grumman had a team working under Lawrence M. Mead on a proposal for a Naval STOL all-weather attack airplane. This grew into a tadpole shape with nose radar, side-by-side cockpit, forward mounted J52 engines and long slender tail. Having the engines forward had two advantages. The engine exhausts could be angled out and down to put their thrust vectors through the centre of gravity, negating any tendency to pitch or yaw when flying with one engine out. It also permitted the use of hinged jetpipes, since with pipes angled the thrust vector could still be kept lined up with the centre of gravity. The pipes were arranged to droop by 23 degrees for take-off and reduced lift-off speed from 86 to 75 knots. The distance to clear a 50ft high obstacle was reduced by several hundred feet. This satisfied US Marines requirements and added very little weight, thus not prejudicing Navy missions.

The aircraft was built as the A2F-1 and one of the first items to be evaluated was the tiltpipe system. In fact, with available engine thrust of only 17,000 pounds the vertical component of about 8,000 pounds was useful only at low aircraft weights, in the region of 25,000 pounds, and negligible at the fully laden weight of 54,000 pounds. This meant that the only real benefit of tiltpipes came during landing, and since landing performance was satisfactory without tilt, the feature was discontinued. With more powerful engines the story might have been different.

The A2F-1 became the A-6 Intruder, one of the most successful attack aircraft of all time, providing rare proof that forward

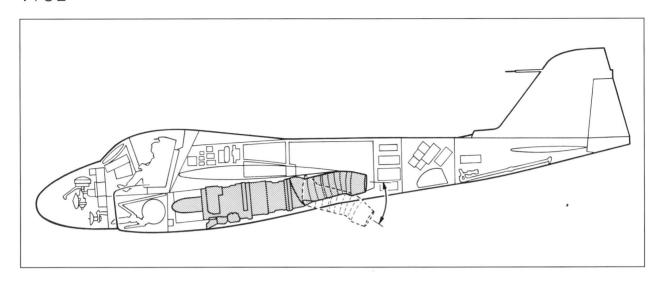

The A2F-1, which became the A-6, had vectoring tailpipes. Lowering them 23 degrees from the normal cut lift-off speed by 8 knots and shortened obstacle clearance by several hundred feet. The tailpipes were only a short distance aft of the centre of gravity position. The change in trim due to thrust vectoring was taken up by geared elevators which acted only with flaps down.
(Author)

Below left: The X-14 in low-level hover. Because it had no ejector seat, hover was restricted to very low levels or to altitudes high enough for recovery to aerodynamic flight. These restrictions helped the X-14 to survive from 1957 to 1981.
(NASM, Smithsonian Institution)

The Bell X-14 was the first aircraft to use jet exhaust vectoring to achieve VTOL flight. It is seen here in an early form, but after the longer landing gear was fitted.
(NASM, Smithsonian Institution)

engines are practical for some types of mission. It is more usual to have the engines further aft, where deflection would cause severe pitch problems.

Jet Vectoring with Conventional Engines

In July 1955 Bell Aerospace won a US Air Force contract to build their X-14. This would test Bell's method of thrust vectoring, which used a planar array of vanes which could be rotated in-plane to deflect the thrust. The significance of in-plane rotation was that no net work was done on the vanes during rotation, and therefore very little control power was required.

The X-14 fuselage was 25ft long. Two 1,750 pound static thrust Armstrong Siddeley ASV8 Viper turbojet engines were slung under the nose, exhausting through the vane cascades beneath mid-fuselage. The pilot sat high over the centre of gravity in an open two-place cockpit. From cockpit back the rear fuselage and tail surfaces were from a Beech T-34 Mentor, and the 34 ft span

mid-mounted wing came from a Beech Bonanza. A short tricycle undercarriage was fitted, this soon being replaced by much longer legs. The original gross weight was 3,100 pounds, which grew to 4,300 pounds as more powerful engines became available. Control was by means of engine air bleed to reaction jets at wingtips and tail.

During the second half of 1956 the X-14 engines and control system were ground tested and the phenomenon of 'suck down' was discovered. The X-14's landing gear was very short and the exhaust gases flowed at high velocity out between wings and ground, causing a large area of low pressure which pulled the aircraft down, negating the lift obtained from engine thrust. The effect may be simulated by blowing up through a cotton-reel at a large coin resting on top of it. Suck-down was only significant when the wings were close to the ground and was cured by lengthening the X-14's landing gear.

The first flight of the X-14, in hover, took place on 17 February 1957, with Bell test pilot David Howe at the controls. Hovering trials were followed by tests of conventional aerodynamic flight perform-

The X-14 hovers close to the ground. Although it had a two-place cockpit, only one seat was fitted. Early on it lacked the thrust to lift two crew and later the space was taken up by autostabiliser and instrumentation. (NASM, Smithsonian Institution)

ance. Partial transitions were first attempted from conventional horizontal flight at a safe altitude of 5,000 feet. The first full transition sequence took place at low level on 24 May 1958.

On completion of testing by Bell, the USAF took delivery of the X-14 and shipped it to NASA's Ames Research Laboratory at Moffett Field. NASA's plans to install additional equipment for control and instrumentation required greater lifting ability than the two Vipers could provide and plans were made to change them for J85s.

Meantime two British test pilots, Bill Bedford and Hugh Merewether, arrived at Ames. They would soon be flying a small British experimental aircraft known as the P.1127 and were to fly the X-14 to gain experience in handling jet VTOL flat-risers. Both spent some time learning on the NASA simulator, and Merewether was first to qualify for a solo X-14 flight. During his flight he experienced a gyroscopic coupling effect, and got so deep into it that the control system lacked the ability to recover. He bent the X-14 quite comprehensively, but his hosts were very polite about it and explained that the X-14 would have been grounded in any case for the change to J85s.

Merewether's accident taught the British more about VTOL than a thousand hours of successful flying would have done. It was the lessons learned from this one event that caused major changes to the P.1127's engine and control system, contributing greatly to the success of its descendent, the Harrier.

After repair and installation of two 2,680 pound thrust General Electric J85-GE-5 turbojets, the X-14 became the X-14A. This continued with test and pilot training for a decade. In 1971 the J85-GE-19 engines of the XV-4 became available, permitting a further upgrade. The test and training programme continued at Ames through to 29 May 1981 when the X-14 suffered a hard landing and minor fire.

During its twenty-year flying lifetime, the X-14 thrust had grown from 3,500 pounds to 6,000 pounds and its weight from 3,200 pounds to 4,300 pounds. The excess of thrust over weight was 10 per cent for the X-14, 30 per cent for X-14A and 40 per cent for X-14B.

During its two decades of test flying the X-14 was used for the development of a Variable Stability Control Augmentation System (VSCAS). This used an analogue computer to control a second reaction jet system which operated alongside the manually-operated control jets. This system allowed the X-14 to be programmed to behave as though it were any particular VTOL aircraft, permitting pilots to train for other types on the small and inexpensive X-14. As the X-14 did not have an ejection seat, all hovering was performed either at ground level or at over 2,500 ft. The X-14 survived many mishaps without major damage. No pilots were injured in X-14 flying.

The X-14 has to be one of the most successful research aircraft of all time, flying for more than twenty years and contributing greatly to a variety of other VTOL programmes both in providing technical input and in pilot training.

The X-14 is still at Ames, though in

The Yakolev Yak-36 'Freehand' had two engines mounted well forward with their exhausts vectored by vane cascades below the centre of gravity. The surfaces lowered from the fuselage reduce reingestion and shield the tyres from hot exhaust gases. (Novosti)

damaged condition. It is scheduled to be moved to the Army Aviation Museum, Fort Rucker, Alabama.

Similar to the X-14 though rather larger, was the Russian Yakolev Yak-36. This had a similar configuration with two engines under the front fuselage, and rotatable cascade thrust directors directly beneath the centre of gravity. It was seen in 1967 at the Domedyedovo Air Show, and was a mature design. It was presumably preceeded by simpler research vehicles similar to the X-14.

by reaction jets, but was equally likely to have been achieved by blowing of the ailerons. There were lift-enhancing strakes beneath the front and centre fuselage, and two further strakes beneath the tail, possibly to improve longitudinal stability.

Two Yak-36 have been seen and as many as twelve may have been built. The Yak-36 programme started in 1962 and probably continued until 1971. The Yak-36 was developed into the Yak-38 shipboard fighter.

The Yak-36 begins to lift off, creating a substantial heat haze. The reaction jets at nose and tail would control pitch and yaw. Roll may have been controlled by blown ailerons. (Novosti)

The Yak-36 had a fat oval cross-section front fuselage, presumably housing two R-11 or R-13 engines of 8,000 to 10,000 pounds thrust each. The cockpit had a conventional fighter-type canopy, forward of the centre of gravity. The rotatable cascades were below centre of gravity and at the fuselage sides with some 4 ft of separation between their centres. The rear fuselage was more slender and had a swept fin with high-mounted horizontal tail surfaces. The fuselage was only 34 ft long, but overall length including swept fin and 8ft nose boom was 53ft. The wing was mid-mounted and of cropped delta form with a span of 27 feet. In vertical flight, the Yak-36 was controlled in pitch and yaw by air bleed and reaction jets at the tail and at the tip of nose boom. Control in roll could be

Vectored jets

In 1957, Hawker Aircraft were looking at ways of becoming involved in VTOL. At that time the official British approach was to use separate lift engines together with complex autostabilisers. Hawker's Chief Engineer, Sir Sydney Camm, was not happy with the dead weight of lift engines and he preferred simple controls which would be easier to keep working under battlefield conditions.

Sir Sydney heard of the Bristol work and obtained a brochure on the BE53, which then consisted of an Orpheus driving a fan, with only the fan air applied through vectoring nozzles. He passed this to Ralph Hooper, who developed some airframe ideas around it. After toying with STOL applications,

Hooper thought of adding a bifurcated jetpipe and vectored rear nozzles. This doubled the available lift force and made VTOL designs feasible. Neither idea was new. Bifurcation appeared in a Hawker patent and vectored rear nozzles in a Bristol patent. Both had been made and flown, bifurcation in the Sea Hawk and vectored hot nozzles in the Bell X-14. What Hooper did was to apply these ideas to the BE53, doubling the available lift and making it a practical proposition for VTOL.

The project was designated P.1127 and was developed by Hawkers in very close co-operation with Bristols.

The P.1127 almost designed itself. The engine had to be at the centre of gravity with nozzles each side of the fuselage. The wing had to be high, so that the nozzles could work. The cockpit had to be ahead of the engine and had to be narrow, flanked by large intakes, so that the engine could breathe. With a high wing, the main landing gear retracted into the fuselage. It had to be behind the engine, which took up all room midships, and it had to have a narrow track to avoid incineration. Wing-mounted stabilisers were required to stop the aircraft falling over, and stabiliser length and weight could be reduced by using anhedral. To save weight, the wing was of small area, and to give it good strength for light weight, a cropped delta shape was used. The tail surfaces were conventional.

Previous VTOL jet aircraft had been very difficult to design and had included difficult design decisions and compromises. The P.1127 went together so well that it just had to be right.

In 1959 Hawkers decided to go ahead

with two P.1127 prototypes as a private venture. Later in the year, the British government started to help a little with funding and by provided facilities at the Royal Aircraft Establishment (RAE), Farnborough, for the wind-tunnel testing of scale models. The results of the tests indicated that transition from hover to forward flight would be unsafe because of a pitch-up effect.

In the USA, NASA were funded for VTOL work and the X-14 programme was under way. NASA took an interest in the Hawker project and offered to build a model and test it in their large slow-speed wind tunnel at Langley, Virginia. The model was electrically powered and was flown in tethered flight by four pilots, one each for pitch, roll, yaw and power. The model was flown through accelerating and decelerating transitions and test reports were favourable, apart from a problem with directional stability at high angles of attack.

NASA also provided training facilities for Hawker test pilots Bill Bedford and Hugh Merewether on the VTOL simulator at Ames, and on a variable stability helicopter which could be programmed to simulate VTOL flight. They were also invited to try the X-14, and it was the experience gained in flying (and bending) this aircraft that convinced them of the need for powerful controls and elimination of gyroscopic effects.

The visit by Hawker's test pilots to NASA Ames to fly the X-14 caused Hawkers to put pressure on Bristols to use contra-rotating shafts so as to eliminate gyroscopic effects. This, and Sydney Camm's insistence on simplicity, made the P.1127 controllable without autostabilisation. Experience with the X-14 also drove the pilots to demand the

The first prototype Hawker P.1127 was completed in July 1960. The 'pen-nib' fairing behind the rear nozzle can be seen. This feature was soon abandoned. (British Aerospace)

203

VTOL

availability of large control forces, again a significant factor in making the P.1127 controllable, since it could be made to recover faster from any unplanned rate of rotation.

The first P.1127, serial XP831, was completed in July 1960, but had to wait until September for its engine to be delivered. The Pegasus engine was at an eary stage in its development, with only 11,000 pounds of thrust. XP831 was lightened by stripping it of non-essential equipment, and weighed 10,000 pounds including pilot and a few minutes fuel. With a ten per cent excess of thrust over weight, controlled hover was be feasible.

The P.1127 hovers over the grid. Radios were removed to save weight and replaced by the cable link seen attatched to the starboard outrigger.
(British Aerospace)

The P.1127 makes a tethered flight. The temporary extensions to the outrigger wheels gave a more predictable unstick sequence.
(British Aerospace)

Vectored & Deflected Jets

Bedford flew XP831 in tethered hovering flight on 21 October 1960. The tethers were a nuisance, and were soon removed. First free hover was on 19 November 1960. The second P1127, XP836, was used for conventional flight trials and made its first flight on 7 July 1961. The two aircraft explored their respective flight regimes until their speed ranges overlapped. Bedford made the first full transition from vertical to horizontal flight and back to vertical on 12 September 1961. Tests were also made with a short take-off run, to demonstrate that greater take-off weights were possible.

XP836 lost a fibreglass front nozzle during a flight on 14 December and Bedford had to eject. The aircraft was destroyed when it crashed. XP831 is on display at the RAF Museum, Hendon, England.

The P.1127 cockpit was conventional with the addition of the nozzle control lever next to the throttle. (British Aerospace)

XS688 is portrayed here both
as a P.1127 and as the first
Kestrel FGA Mk1 in Tripartite
Nine colours.
(British Aerospace)

Three P.1127's fly in
formation. The first prototype
is in the foreground, the
other two belonging to the
Development Batch.
(British Aerospace)

Four Tripartite Kestrels fly in
formation.
(British Aerospace)

The British government purchased the two P1127 prototypes and funded a development batch of four more. These were fitted with the 13,500 pound thrust Pegasus 3s and were used for further development work. XP984 may be seen at RNEC Manadon.

A further nine aircraft were funded equally by Britain, Germany and the USA for operational evaluation. These were known as the Kestrel FGA (Fighter, Ground Attack) Mk1, and had the Pegasus 5 with 15,500 pounds of thrust. Trials took place during 1964 and 1965. One aircraft crashed early on, the British retained two for further work. XS695 may be seen at RNAS Culdrose in Cornwall, England.

The remaining six went to the USA where they were designated XV-6A for evaluation in competition with the Lockheed XV-4 Hummingbird and the Ryan XV-6 Vertifan. An XV-6A is on permanent display at the Smithsonian Institution.

The Kestrel was developed into the Harrier, which remains the only VTOL fighter to enter service in the West.

207

Seven of the nine Tripartite
Kestrels can be seen in this
line-up.
(British Aerospace)

Two Tripartite Kestrels are
seen here on field trials.
(British Aerospace)

Vectored Jets with Lift Engines

The vectored jet, when used on its own, has to provide enough thrust to lift the total aircraft weight, but in forward flight is throttled back to only a small fraction of maximum thrust. This is acceptable in a single-engined aircraft such as the Harrier, but for multi-engined aircraft there is no point in vectoring the thrust of all engines. Liftjets weigh less than vectored jets per pound of thrust, and weight can be saved by using a vectoring engine for propulsion and vectoring engine plus liftjets for lift.

Two aircraft were built using a combination of vectored thrust and lift jets. Both German, these were the Dornier Do 31 transport and the VFW VAK 191 fighter.

The Dornier Do 31 programme was funded by the German government, with the object of producing a light military transport with VTOL capability. The word 'light' in this context is by comparison with conventional transports. The Do 31 would be required to carry a payload of three to four tons, and gross VTO weight would be in the region of 50,000 pounds, making it the heaviest of Western VTOL aircraft.

Studies made by Dornier during the early sixties eliminated the helicopter because it lacked speed and the tiltwing because of its mechanical complexity. Combined propeller drive and jet lift provided efficient cruise at low altitude but not at high altitude. This left the combination of jet propulsion with jet lift, which would meet all requirements, provided that an absolute minimum of time was spent in inefficient jet-borne hovering flight.

Dornier were very aware that a transport aircraft required the best possible mix between propulsive and lifting thrust. They decided to go for a mix of two vectored-thrust engines for propulsion and lift, and lift-jets to make up the remaining lift. Ideally, they would have liked fairly small vectored-thrust engines which provided just enough propulsion, so minimising weight. At that time there was no choice and they had to use the heavier BS53 Pegasus. The remaining lift jet requirement was made up with eight Rolls-Royce RB162s, which boasted a 16:1 thrust to weight ratio.

The Pegasus, as usual, made its own decisions. The engines could not be fuselage mounted, so had to be fitted to the wing. This forced the use of a high wing to allow the nozzles to vector. The two engines had to be spaced from the fuselage, again to allow room for the nozzles, but not so far as to create impossible yaw when flying on one engine.

The RB162's were not so choosey. They could be mounted anywhere so long as their net thrust acted through the centre of gravity. The actual location had no significance in free flight, since, in the event of an engine failure, the one diagonally opposite would also be shut down, thus retaining symmetry. When in ground effect, it would be useful if the liftjet exhausts combined in some way which created additional under-fuselage lift.

Dornier chose to fit the RB162s in wing-tip pods, four in each pod. This gave them the option of making the aircraft with or without liftjets, and even of making the lift-pods removable. It gave some promise of lift enhancement, since the jet exhausts should spread out across the ground and collide under the fuselage, creating a higher pressure and contributing a useful additional amount of lift. It also permitted a new control concept to be used. The lift engines in each pod were fitted with nozzles which could be deflected 15 degrees forward or backward. Since the pods were at the wingtips, differential nozzle tilt between the pods would control yaw, and differential throttle would control roll. Pitch would still have to be controlled using air bleed and nozzles, and Dorner chose to use a single up and down nozzle extending from the tail.

These decisions determined the overall configuration of the aircraft, and the required payload and cruising speed would decide most aspects of the design. The airframe designers could now go ahead and design the aircraft structure. The control system designers were not yet ready to go ahead. They needed more information on the control arrangements and they needed, in particular, to know how the liftjet deflection and throttling would affect the control requirements. Their questions were answered in three stages. First, they worked with 'see-saw' type thrust balance rigs, similar to the VJ101 *Wippe*, to optimise single-axis control. Then they went on to a 'systems test rig', which was a small free-flight hover test rig, and finally to a 'large hover rig', which was representative of the full-size aircraft in hover and ground effects.

The 'systems test rig' was a large skeletal structure with one square space-frame girder forming a fuselage and a second girder representing the wings. Although known as the *Kleines Schwebegestill* or small hover rig, it was actually close in size to the final aircraft. It was supported on a long-legged tricycle wheelgear, with a fourth leg

Dornier's small hover rig was powered by four RB108 lift engines. It is seen here on the telescopic test stand. (Photo Deutsches Museum Munich)

The small hover rig is seen in flight. The nose-down attitude produces a rearward component of thrust for forward motion. (Photo Deutsches Museum Munich)

at the tail as a safety bump. The pilot sat among the tubework in the 'nose', with a panel of instruments suspended in front of him. The 'wings' carried four Rolls-Royce RB108 liftjets, two fixed vertically inboard to represent the Pegasus, and two outboard to represent the lift pods. Compressor air was fed to a pair of nozzles, one up, one down, in the 'tail'.

The systems test rig or small hover rig was checked out on a telescopic stand which permitted roll, pitch, yaw and vertical motion for initial tests of the control system. It flew in free hover from June 1963 and made 247 free flights in the course of developing the Do 31 attitude stabilizer. Work included the examination of the effects of real aerodynamic disturbances and the effects of simulated component failures.

In parallel with small hover rig tests, the complete hydraulic and electrical system was built full-size on a three-axis table which simulated on the ground all expected in-flight motions.

The large hover rig was much closer to the actual aircraft. It had a tubular steel framework for a fuselage, with cockpit and forward fuselage covered-in to resemble the actual aircraft, but with open girderwork tail section. The wings and engines were 'real'.

Two Pegasus 5-2 vectored thrust engines were fitted at the inboard stations, and three RB162 liftjets were fitted in each wingtip pod. The full complement of eight liftjets was not needed because the large rig weighed some six tons less than would the actual aircraft.

The large hover rig was fitted with the same control systems that would be used on the aircraft and it had representative size, mass and inertias. It also had a similar external surface shape in order that it should behave in a representative manner when in ground effects. A removable hatch in the underbelly allowed it to be mounted on the telescopic pedestal for systems checkout and ground-run tests.

The big rig was put through some 200 ground tests. The first series of ground tests took place with the rig mounted on the telescopic stand with freedom in pitch, roll, yaw and vertical motion. During these tests, the autostabiliser parameters were adjusted to optimise control performance and to eliminate some dangerous oscillations. It is always easier to diagnose such problems on the ground, where suitable test and monitoring equipment can be used, than in the air. It is also much safer.

The tests on the telescope stand had taken place over a pit which allowed the engine exhaust gases to escape, and therefore simulated flight out of ground effect. Ground tests continued with engine runs to assess recirculation and re-ingestion. These

tests were conducted with the big rig weighted down to the runway, so as to simulate engine run-up prior to vertical take-off, with the Pegasus nozzles at various angles. The nozzles had 110 degrees movement and were fitted so that the level flight position was 10 degrees down from horizontal, permitting selection of any angle from 10 degrees to 120 degrees (i.e., 30 degrees forward of vertical) in 5 degree increments.

With the lift engines at take-off thrust and the main engines at high thrust, the nozzles were rotated in 5 degree increments from the 10 degree position. Up to 85 degrees all was well, but at 90 degrees, the lift engine intake temperatures rose by 20 to 30°C. Past 90 degrees, the main engine inlet temperatures also increased, as exhaust gases were re-ingested. The main engines found and swallowed all available loose pieces of concrete, only to centrifuge them out of the cold forward nozzles. Very little material reached the core of the engine.

Because of the adverse effects of re-ingestion on engine temperatures, nozzle angle was limited to 90 degrees for take-off. Test pilot Drury Wood's first attempt at free flight produced a spectacular display of fire-breathing from both main engines, and the rig settled back to the ground amid clouds of gas and smoke. Subsequent investigation showed that the nozzles had overshot the 90 degree mark, causing re-ingestion.

A second attempt on 8 February 1967,

The large hover rig used the wings and engines of the Do 31 with a temporary fuselage structure. (Photo Deutsches Museum Munich)

with nozzles limited to 85 degrees was more successful. It was a STOL flight with a 50 metre take-off run, a 100 metre 'hop' at 8 metres altitude and a rather hairy landing caused by nose-wheel flutter.

The third flight attempt was aimed at getting the rig up out of its own gas cloud. On full throttle it jumped into the air whilst accelerating forward, and was held in an autostabilized hover at 15 metres height for 2 minutes. At this stage, hover involved a 5 degree nose up attitude since the lift engines were inclined 5 degrees aft and the main engines were at the 85 degree setting, 5 degrees aft.

The next flights were used to fine-tune the autostabiliser and to convert to full manual control, all with the 85 degree nozzle limit. During further flights, nozzle angles beyond 85 degrees were tried. This improved the aircraft attitude in hover, bringing the nose down and improving pilot vision. With nozzles at 115 degrees, the aircraft was level and could make a three-point landing. Greater angles were undesirable for landing since the nosewheel would touch first.

The large hover rig helped greatly in developing the autostabilisation system, first on the ground and then in the air, and permitted gradual acclimatisation to manual control. It also tested performance in the event of multiple autostabilisation failures. The rig was returned to the telescopic pedestal to check out the actual control system to be used on aircraft E3.

The Do 31 aircraft had a tubular fuselage, 68 ft long, with rounded glazed nose and upswept tail. The two man crew sat side by side in the nose and had dual controls. Joystick controls were used, rather than the column and wheel more common in transport aircraft. The joystick permitted easier control when hovering and was compatible with the use of ejector seats. Behind them the freight compartment was 30 ft long by 7ft wide by 7ft high and could be loaded via a ramp which lowered out of the rear fuselage. A large fin carried high horizontal surfaces. The high-mounted wing was of 59ft span and carried the two Pegasus engines at inboard stations and a pod of four lift engines at each tip. Tricycle landing gear was used, with the main gear retracting into the rear of the Pegasus nacelles.

The main engines were Bristol Siddeley BS53 Pegasus B.Pg. 5-2 vectored thrust turbofans, each rated at 15,500 pounds static thrust. The lift engines were 4,400 pound Rolls-Royce RB162-4D liftjets. Total rated thrust was therefore 66,200 pounds. The actual amount of thrust available would of course vary with temperature and altitude, and a certain amount of thrust was reserved to make the aircraft controllable. Safe vertical take-off weights ranged from 43,000 pounds at 86°F and 5,000 ft to 60,000 pounds at freezing and zero feet. Under common European conditions, the Do 31 could take off safely at 50,000 pounds or more.

The large hover rig is seen in flight. The rig provided useful information on permissible engine exhaust angle settings.
(Photo Deutsches Museum Munich)

Above right: Do 31 E1 was used for horizontal flight trials. The horizontal stabiliser was high-mounted to keep it clear of the Pegasus exhausts.
(Photo Deutsches Museum Munich)

This underside view of the Do 31 E1 in flight shows the Pegasus nozzles turned down to enhance lift at low speed. When lightly laden, the two Pegasus engines could support most of the weight.
(Photo Deutsches Museum Munich)

The failure of a lift engine did not require any special action, since the control system would automatically adjust port and starboard pod differential throttles to control roll, and collective throttles to control height. The loss of 4,400 pounds out of 66,000 pounds was not serious, an advantage of having many small lift engines. The failure of the Pegasus when hovering would be more of a problem, since 15,500 pounds represented almost 25 per cent of the available lift, and its loss would cause asymmetric lift leading to a rapid rate of roll. In the event of a Pegasus failing, the system was programmed to run the lift engines that side flat out at an emergency thrust in excess of their normal rating and the surviving propulsion engine at maximum thrust, with the remaining lift engines run at less than maximum thrust and providing roll control.

Three aircraft were built. Do 31E1

to climb away from some fighter and trainer aircraft, and it had the ability with nozzles at 120 degrees to sink at 125 knots forward and 8000 feet per minute downward, useful if under attack.

Do 31E3 made its first conventional flight on 14 July 1967 and made four conventional flights to check out systems. After some necessary modifications, E3 resumed testing. It made its first hover on 22 November 1967, a transition from vertical take off to horizontal flight on 16 December and a transition from horizontal flight to vertical landing on 21 December 1967. It continued test and demonstration flights for several years and during 1969-70 was evaluated by scientists and engineers from NASA. The programme was terminated in April 1970.

The Do 31E3 which made the vertical flight tests and conversions may be seen at

was to be used for horizontal flight trials, Do 31E2 was a ground test airframe and Do 31E3 would conduct the hovering and transition trials.

Do 31E1 was rolled out on 10 February 1967. It was fitted with Pegasus main engines but had no lift engines. The horizontal flight trials turned out to be a routine shake down without incidents. Although it could not hover, the vectored thrust capability of the Pegasus proved useful for control of taxi speed and for braking. In the air, the high 0.6 thrust to weight ratio permitted E1

the Deutsches Museum in Munich, Germany.

The VFW VAK 191 was originally designed as the Focke-Wulf Fw 1262 in response to German government requirement VAK 191B, which specified a subsonic VTOL tactical reconnaissance fighter. This was developed further by VFW in collaboration with Fiat, whose G-91 it would replace, under an agreement between the German and Italian governments in 1964. Italy withdrew in 1968, and VFW-Fokker continued the programme with subcontract assistance from Aeritalia.

Do 31E3 hovers with Pegasus nozzles pointing down and liftjets operating. (Photo Deutsches Museum Munich)

The third VAK191 was
delivered in an appropriate
manner.
(VFW Fokker)

VTOL

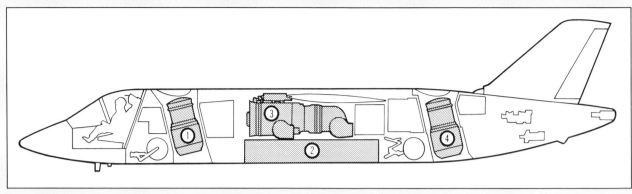

This sectioned view of the VAK191 shows how the compact installation of the three engines leaves a convenient internal weapons bay beneath the centre of gravity
(Author)

1 Rolls-Royce RB162 liftjet engine
2 Cargo bay
3 Rolls-Royce RB193 vectored lift/thrust engine
4 Rolls-Royce RB162 liftjet engine

The cutaway view shows the finer details of the VAK191. An important feature is the sliding intake which is optimised for high-speed flight and slides forward to admit more air for vertical flight. Slides are visible at 35, 163, and 164. The reaction control jets can be seen at nose, tail and inboard of wingtips.
(VFW Fokker)

1 Aerial matching unit
2 Amplifier
3 TACAN navigation unit
4 Flight data recorder
5 Radiotelephoine
6 Flight control unit
7 Horizontal reference unit
8 Heading control equipment
9 Yaw vane
10 Pressure bulkhead
11 Cabin overpressure valve

12 Rudder bar
13 Control column
14 Nozzle angle preset stop
15 Nozzle angle selector
16 Main engine throttle
17 Lift engine throttle
18 Aileron-flap link control lever
19 Cabin air-conditioning equipment
20 Heat exchanger
21 Turbo-refrigerator
22 Water separator

23 Air conditioning distribution duct
24 Martin-Baker Mk 9 ejector seat
25 Cockpit canopy jack
26 Air distributor
27 Electric cables
28 Reservoir evacuation circuit
29 Fuel filler
30 Forward liftjet
31 Operating jack for upper air intake doors
32 Polyester upper intake doors
33 Door operating mechanism

34 Polyester air intake duct
35 Upper slide for translating air intake cowl
36 Main engine compartment ventilator
37 Main engine accessories
38 Control cables
39 Main vectored thrust engine
40 Control cable pullies
41 Air bleed from main engine to reaction jets
42 Fuselage centre section
43 Wing mounting points
44 Duct for reaction jet air (main engine circuit)
45 Linkage from air motor to rotating nozzles
46 Duct for reaction jet air (lift engine circuit)
47 Fuel filters
48 Air bleed to nozzle motor
49 Air motor
50 Air motor control jack
51 Rotating nozzle drive shaft

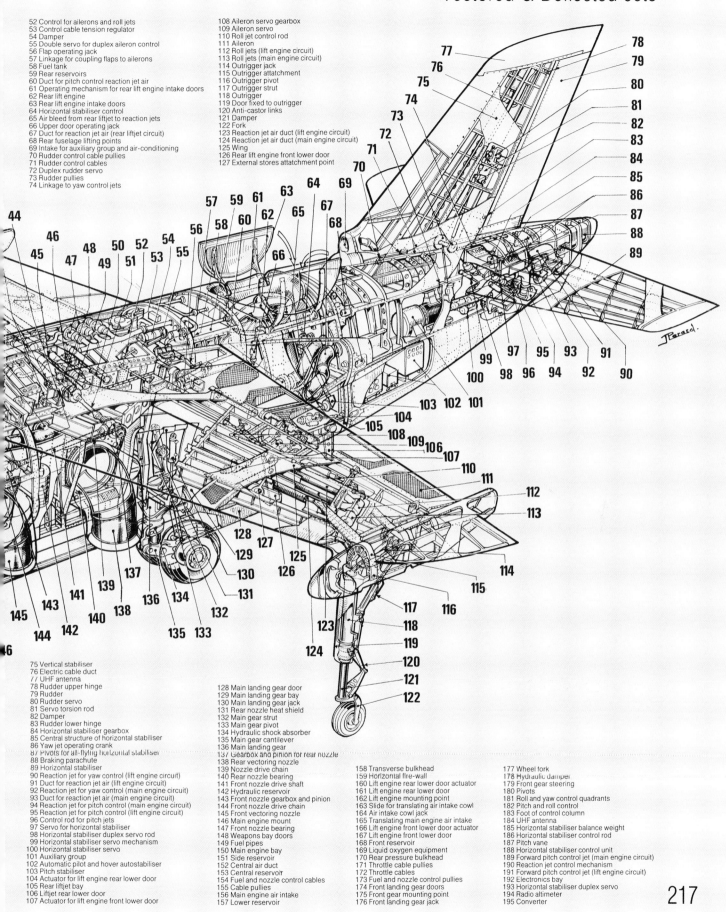

52 Control for ailerons and roll jets
53 Control cable tension regulator
54 Damper
55 Double servo for duplex aileron control
56 Flap operating jack
57 Linkage for coupling flaps to ailerons
58 Fuel tank
59 Rear reservoirs
60 Duct for pitch control reaction jet air
61 Operating mechanism for rear lift engine intake doors
62 Rear lift engine
63 Rear lift engine intake doors
64 Horizontal stabiliser control
65 Air bleed from rear liftjet to reaction jets
66 Upper door operating jack
67 Duct for reaction jet air (rear liftjet circuit)
68 Rear fuselage lifting points
69 Intake for auxiliary group and air-conditioning
70 Rudder control cable pullies
71 Rudder control cables
72 Duplex rudder servo
73 Rudder pullies
74 Linkage to yaw control jets

108 Aileron servo gearbox
109 Aileron servo
110 Roll jet control rod
111 Aileron
112 Roll jets (lift engine circuit)
113 Roll jets (main engine circuit)
114 Outrigger jack
115 Outrigger attachment
116 Outrigger pivot
117 Outrigger strut
118 Outrigger
119 Door fixed to outrigger
120 Anti-castor links
121 Damper
122 Fork
123 Reaction jet air duct (lift engine circuit)
124 Reaction jet air duct (main engine circuit)
125 Wing
126 Rear lift engine front lower door
127 External stores attachment point

75 Vertical stabiliser
76 Electric cable duct
77 UHF antenna
78 Rudder upper hinge
79 Rudder
80 Rudder servo
81 Servo torsion rod
82 Damper
83 Rudder lower hinge
84 Horizontal stabiliser gearbox
85 Central structure of horizontal stabiliser
86 Yaw jet operating crank
87 Pivots for all-flying horizontal stabiliser
88 Braking parachute
89 Horizontal stabiliser
90 Reaction jet for yaw control (lift engine circuit)
91 Duct for reaction jet air (lift engine circuit)
92 Reaction jet for yaw control (main engine circuit)
93 Duct for reaction jet air (main engine circuit)
94 Reaction jet for pitch control (main engine circuit)
95 Reaction jet for pitch control (lift engine circuit)
96 Control rod for pitch jets
97 Servo for horizontal stabiliser
98 Horizontal stabiliser duplex servo rod
99 Horizontal stabiliser servo mechanism
100 Horizontal stabiliser servo
101 Auxiliary group
102 Automatic pilot and hover autostabiliser
103 Pitch stabiliser
104 Rear liftjet bay
105 Rear liftjet bay
106 Liftjet rear lower door
107 Actuator for lift engine front lower door

128 Main landing gear door
129 Main landing gear bay
130 Main landing gear jack
131 Rear nozzle heat shield
132 Main gear strut
133 Main gear pivot
134 Hydraulic shock absorber
135 Main gear cantilever
136 Main landing gear
137 Gearbox and pinion for rear nozzle
138 Rear vectoring nozzle
139 Nozzle drive chain
140 Rear nozzle bearing
141 Front nozzle drive shaft
142 Hydraulic reservoir
143 Front nozzle gearbox and pinion
144 Front nozzle drive chain
145 Front vectoring nozzle
146 Main engine mount
147 Front nozzle bearing
148 Weapons bay doors
149 Fuel pipes
150 Main engine bay
151 Side reservoir
152 Central air duct
153 Central reservoir
154 Fuel and nozzle control cables
155 Cable pullies
156 Main engine air intake
157 Lower reservoir

158 Transverse bulkhead
159 Horizontal fire-wall
160 Lift engine rear lower door actuator
161 Lift engine rear lower door
162 Lift engine mounting point
163 Slide for translating air intake cowl
164 Air intake cowl jack
165 Translating main engine air intake
166 Lift engine front lower door actuator
167 Lift engine front lower door
168 Front reservoir
169 Liquid oxygen equipment
170 Rear pressure bulkhead
171 Throttle cable pullies
172 Throttle cables
173 Fuel and nozzle control pullies
174 Front landing gear doors
175 Front gear mounting point
176 Front landing gear jack

177 Wheel fork
178 Hydraulic damper
179 Front gear steering
180 Pivots
181 Roll and yaw control quadrants
182 Pitch and roll control
183 Foot of control column
184 UHF antenna
185 Horizontal stabiliser balance weight
186 Horizontal stabiliser control rod
187 Pitch vane
188 Horizontal stabiliser control unit
189 Forward pitch control jet (main engine circuit)
190 Reaction jet control mechanism
191 Forward pitch control jet (lift engine circuit)
192 Electronics bay
193 Horizontal stabiliser duplex servo
194 Radio altimeter
195 Converter

217

VTOL

The VAK 191 could at first sight be mistaken for a P.1127 variant, since it was very similar in shape and layout. It was 48 ft long compared with the P.1127's 42 ft, but had slightly smaller wings at 20 ft against 22 ft span.

The pilot's cockpit, as in the P.1127, occupied the front of the fuselage, the top of the canopy blending with the upper surface of the fuselage. This gave a poor rearward field of view and left only a very small cross-section forward of the cockpit, severely restricting any future radar installation.

The vectored thrust propulsion engine was adapted by Rolls-Royce and MBU from the RB193. It developed 10,000 pounds of thrust (contemporary Pegasus 15,000 pounds), and was much smaller than the Pegasus, permitting a cargo bay to be installed beneath it and more fuel to be carried in the fuselage both forward and aft of it.

To make up the lifting capability there were two 5,600 pound thrust RB162-81 lift engines, again developed in co-operation between Rolls-Royce and MBU. These were fitted in two bays, one in the forward fuselage and one towards the rear. Each was inclined to exhaust 14 degrees aft of vertical.

Total lift thrust was 21,000 pounds, giving a 20 per cent thrust margin at the VAK 191's maximum vertical take-off weight of 17,600 pounds.

An auxiliary engine, a Klockner-Humbold-Dentz T112 mounted in the tail, provided 300 horsepower to start the main engines and to provide electrical power when the main engines were not running. This made the VAK 191 less dependent on ground support equipment and gave it greater dispersal capability.

The air intakes for the liftengines were covered by semicircular doors hinged at the sides. There was no need to use ram air to spin the lift engines up to speed, since on-board starting was provided. Lift engine exhausts were covered by pairs of transverse-hinged rectangular doors.

The air intakes for the vectored thrust engine were at the sides of the fuselage just behind the cockpit. Whereas the Harrier had great 'elephant ear' intakes designed to gulp the maximum amount of air in hover, the VAK 191 had small semicircular intakes optimised for fast forward flight. The front 3 ft section of each intake was separate from the fuselage, and could slide forward about 10 inches, creating an additional slot through

The three VAK191B's are seen together during trials. The general layout was very similar to the P.1127, but the intake doors for the additional lift engines are a significant difference. (VFW Fokker)

which the engine could breathe during transition and hover. This was similar in principle to the translating intake used on the VJ101C.

Control was by means of reaction nozzles at nose, tail and wingtips using air bled from the compressors of all three main engines. The control system included a duplex electro-mechanical autostabiliser with automatic reversion to direct mechanical control in the event of a failure in either channel.

The VAK 191 was more complicated than the P.1127/Kestrel/Harrier family, but had several advantages. It could survive engine failure during vertical flight, making a heavier than normal landing. If either lift engine failed the other would be shut down and 10,000 pounds of lift would be available from the RB192, while if the RB192 failed the lift engines could support 11,000 pounds. The centre of gravity did not have to be so finely balanced, since any offset could be compensated by differential adjustment of lift engine throttles. The auxiliary power unit allowed greater field dispersal. These were real advantages, but of secondary significance when applied to a fighter aircraft since they affected only the way in which it was operated but did not provide additional combat performance.

It had been planned that six prototypes of the VAK 191 should be built, but only three were actually completed. The first of these was rolled out in April 1970, and flight trials progressed from tethered hover to free hover, with a transition from hover to normal flight on 26 October 1972. The lift engines were shut down in flight, the aircraft reached 300 knots in level flight and the lift engines were successfully restarted. All three prototypes flew.

When it was designed, the VAK 191 had potentially greater payload and range than the P.1127/Kestrel, but by 1972 the Pegasus was producing 21,500 pounds of thrust, and the Harrier GR3 could equal the VAK 191 take-off weight and payload. Further development promised to improve Harrier performance even further.

The German government changed its priorities and abandoned its VTOL fighter requirements. The three VAK 191 aircraft were assigned to the Panavia MRCA programme as testbeds for avionics and control systems. As in the Soviet Union, liftjets gave way to swing wings, which paid their way through the whole flight envelope instead of just at take-off.

The Do 31 transport and the VAK 191

The second VAK191B hovers over the runway. Debris guards may be seen over both lift engines, the main engine normal intake and main engine auxiliary intake. The auxiliary intake was formed by sliding the intake ducts forward. (VFW Fokker)

The VAK191 is seen in conventional flight. The three aircraft were later used in the development of the MRCA Tornado.
(VFW Fokker)

fighter each combined vectored thrust and liftjets.

In the case of the VAK 191 this was not a good choice. Later development of fighter aircraft showed that dogfight manoeuvrability is primarily a function of thrust to weight ratio. Any aircraft carrying the weight of the engines needed for vertical take-off should be able to take advantage of the extra installed thrust in combat. The VAK 191 lift engines were not available in normal flight and were just so much dead weight.

The choice of vectored thrust and liftjets for the Do 31 was much more appropriate. In forward flight a transport aircraft needs only sufficient thrust for economic cruise. All other VTOL thrust should be obtained for as little weight as possible and specialised lift engines are the right answer. The Do 31 suffered from having too much vectored thrust. Had the lighter RB193 been available, a better compromise could have been made between vectored and lift thrust and the reduced engine weight would have increased payload and range.

Deflected jets

In aircraft designed for STOL, it is not necessary for thrust to exceed weight, so long as the combination of direct engine lift and wing lift can support aircraft weight at low forward speeds. There were a number of attempts to combine the powered lift of the vectored or deflected jet with the aerodynamic lift of the aircraft wings.

Engine exhaust was used to produce direct lift force in three ways. It was turned down by vectored nozzles, or deflected downward by the flaps, or blown over flaps and pulled down by Coanda effect. Combinations of exhaust and flaps were capable of generating lift considerably in excess of engine thrust at low forward speeds, giving flap deflection methods an advantage over simple vectored jets.

Engines were also used to enhance lift by blowing fan air (or even exhaust gas) over the wings and flaps. It is difficult to separate the effect of direct momentum lift, due to air blown downward, from that of lift enhancement by boundary layer control. Figures for lift contributions are usually estimates.

Air was also blown over control surfaces, to enhance control at low speed. Additional direct lift force was gained by drooping the surfaces.

The various methods all had their costs, in complexity, in the space taken up by any ducting and in thermal problems. The 'cold' fan air bled from the front of an engine was hot enough to affect structural strength. The jet exhausts were at very high temperatures and surfaces in contact with them had to be made from expensive high-temperature materials, such as titanium, stainless steel and nimonic alloys.

Deflected jet research began in Britain, in 1963, with the Hunting H126. Later research was conducted in North America, by NASA and the Canadian Department of Industry Trade and Commerce (DITC), with two de Havilland Canada DHC C-8A Buffalo conversions. The USAF held a design competition during the late seventies for their Advanced Medium STOL Transport (AMST) requirement and this led to the American Boeing YC-14 and the McDonnell YC-15 prototypes. The Antonov An-72 met a similar requirement in Russia.

The Hunting H126 was an early blown-surface research aircraft. It was designed to test the results of work on jet flaps done by the National Gas Turbine Establishment and the Royal Aircraft Establishment.

The H126 had a 50 ft long fuselage of deep draught. A single-seat cockpit was placed well forward. with the Bristol Orpheus jet engine beneath it. The wing was high mounted, 44 ft in span and of slender chord. Its trailing edge consisted entirely of flaps and ailerons. There was a single fin of large area and a high-mounted tailplane.

The hot gases from the Orpheus entered a plenum chamber in the lower fuselage and were ducted up into the wing where they exhausted through a series of fish-tail nozzles in the flaps and ailerons. The jet flap system was designed to be used full-time, providing thrust in normal flight with flaps up, and lift at low speeds with flaps lowered and ailerons drooped.

The hot gases were also exhausted through nozzles on the sides of the fuselage to generate additional thrust, and through attitude control nozzles at wingtips and tail. In low-speed flight, roll was controlled by the wingtip nozzles and pitch and yaw were controlled by vertical and horizontal nozzles in the tail.

The H126 was completed in August 1962 and first flew in March 1963. When the flaps were lowered, the lift of the jetflaps at the trailing edges of the wings caused the aircraft to assume a nose-down attitude, so that in level flight it appeared to be diving at a steep angle. After a six-month period of shake-down trials at Huntings, the H126 was handed over to RAE for their jetflap research programme.

The H126 may be seen at the Aerospace Museum, RAF Cosford, West Midlands, England.

The NASA Augmentor Wing Jet STOL Research Aircraft was a joint venture between NASA and DITC, the Canadian Department of Trade Industry and Commerce, to research civil STOL aircraft techniques. It was based on a de Havilland Canada DHC-5 Buffalo. The Buffalo was a high-winged STOL transport with upswept rear fuselage and high T-tail, and was a turboprop development of the radial-engined DHC-4 Caribou. The Buffalo had been made to a US Army requirement as the C-8A and four were delivered for evaluation. When the USAF took over responsibility for intra-theatre transport, the requirement was cancelled and the three surviving C-8A's were handed over to NASA. NASA and DITC funded Boeing Commercial Airplane Company to make the conversion, which included rebuilding the wings and fitting new engines.

The turboprop engines of the Buffalo were replaced with two 9,000 pound thrust Rolls-Royce Spey 801SF turbofans. Both the fan and the core of each engine were used to generate lift force. The exhaust from each engine core was bifurcated and directed through two Pegasus-type vectoring rear nozzles, which could be rotated to generate lift force or thrust. The air from the fan of each engine was bled through two bypass air offtake ducts and used to feed air to the blown surfaces of the wings.

The wings were reduced in span to 79 ft and were rebuilt to incorporate a variety of lift-enhancing devices. The leading edge had full-span slats. The trailing portion had an air distribution system feeding augmentor flaps and blown ailerons. The augmentor flaps ejected air which mixed with the airflow over the wings to enhance lift. The blown ailerons allowed effective roll control at low speeds and were drooped with the flaps to enhance lift.

The Augmentor Wing first flew on 1 May 1972. It completed proof-of-concept trials during 1974 and was used to develop the STOLAND terminal guidance system in 1974 and 1975. It was still in use at NASA Ames in 1986.

NASA later funded the QSRA, or Quiet Short-haul Research Aircraft, which again was based on a C-8A Buffalo and was converted by Boeing Commercial Airplane Company. The QSRA used a system where the jet exhausts were blown over the upper wing surfaces and pulled downward by Coanda effect when the flaps were lowered.

The QSRA had a new wing which made extensive use of boundary layer control both at the wing leading edge and to increase aileron power at low speeds. The engines were four 7,860 pound thrust Avco Lycoming F102 turbofans, and their exhausts were blown over the upper surfaces of the wings. Lowering the flaps drew the exhausts downward by Coanda effect to create additional lift. Lift force was generated partly by deflected jet thrust, as in true VTOL types, and partly by additional induced circulation of air about the moving wing.

The QSRA first flew on 6 July 1978, and joined the Augmentor Wing Jet Research Aircraft at Ames. It was claimed to be quieter than conventional aircraft on landing and take-off, mainly because the wing shielded engine exhaust noise from the ground. The QSRA was still at Ames in 1986.

This close-up view of the NASA Augmentor Wing Buffalo shows the vectored jet exhaust, the blown flaps and the drooped ailerons. (NASA)

BOEING / DE HAVILLAND

The NASA QSRA upper-surface-blowing Quiet Short-Haul Research Aircraft at roll-out. (NASA)

In 1971, the USAF Tactical Air Command drew up a specification for an Advanced Medium STOL Transport (AMST). This was intended as a replacement for the C-130 Hercules, with improved STOL capability, payload, speed, flotation, cargo compartment size and costs. Against competition from Bell, Fairchild, and Lockheed, designs from McDonnell Douglas and Boeing were chosen to be built for evaluation.

McDonnell's entry for the AMST competition was the YC-15. McDonnell already had a licence for the Breguet 941 propeller-driven deflected thrust STOL transport, and had gained considerable experience of this configuration. The YC-15 was a logical extension of the 941 concept, with fanjet engines replacing the propellers of the 941. The fuselage internal dimensions were determined by the AMST specification and resulted in a fat fuselage 120 ft long with DC-10 nose and with upswept tail and loading ramp at the rear. The tail surfaces comprised a tall fin carrying the horizontal stabiliser high up and away from the jet exhausts. Tail surfaces were of large area to enhance control at low

speed. Tricycle landing gear consisted of dual nosewheel and tandem dual main wheels retracting into wide external pods.

The wing was high mounted and of 110 ft span. Cost was kept to a minimum, with a straight, tapered design. Super-critical section was chosen to permit high speeds and greater internal fuel storage. The leading edge of the wing had full-span hydraulically operated slats. At the trailing edge, the jet deflection flaps were double-slotted and extended over the inner 75 per cent of the span. The remainder of the span was occupied by large ailerons. A lift spoiler was fitted in front of each aileron.

The engines were four 16,000 pound thrust Pratt & Whitney JT8D-17 turbofans slung beneath the wings at quarter and half span, and mounted well forward so that their exhausts could fan out before hitting the flaps. The jet exhausts were fitted with mixer nozzles which diluted the high temperature exhaust with cool ambient air to reduce flap heating. The flap temperatures were still high enough to demand fabrication from titanium.

For low speed flight during take-off and

The two Boeing Advanced Medium-range STOL Transports make an impressive sight. The AMST winner was to have replaced the Hercules, but the 'Herc' was more cost-effective and is still in service. (Boeing)

landing, the leading edge slats were extended and the flaps were lowered into the jet exhausts to obtain maximum lift, which came half from conventional wing lift and half from deflected jet thrust, both directly and due to its effect on the flaps. The lift spoilers were used to obtain a steep angle of descent for a short landing. They were also used to control the aircraft during descent. Roll was controlled by differential spoiler action and rate of descent by collective spoiler action.

Two prototype YC-15s were made and the first flight took place on 28 August 1975. Performance included speeds up to 518 mph and payload to 78,000 pounds. The YC-15 competed with the Boeing YC-14 in fly-offs during 1976 and 1977 and was declared the winner, but funding cuts caused the AMST programme to be cancelled in favour of repurchase of the more economic Lockheed C-130 Hercules. The YC-15 visited Europe to appear at the Farnborough Air Show during the 1977 bicentennial celebrations.

The Boeing YC-14 was designed to meet the same AMST requirement. Boeing chose to go with a two-engine upper-surface-blowing (USB) approach. Again, fuselage size was dictated by the requirement, and the YC-14

had a fat fuselage about 130 ft long. General configuration was similar, with tricycle landing gear consisting of dual nosewheel and four-wheel main gear units retracting into large sponsons. The high T-tail had a double-hinged elevator to give smoother airflow at extreme deflections. The YC-14 wing was high-mounted and had greater span at 130 ft, but was more slender and had the same area as that of the YC-15.

Engines were two 51,000 pound thrust General Electric CF6-50D turbofans. They were mounted ahead of the wings and above them, so that the jet exhausts blew over the upper wing surfaces. The flaps, when lowered, formed a smooth curve which drew the exhaust gases downward by Coanda effect so that they were deflected downward to produce direct lift force. Wing lift was enhanced by full-span Kruger leading edge flaps and by blowing engine compressor air from holes in the leading edge to obtain boundary layer control. Spoilers were used to supplement the ailerons in low speed roll control and to control the sink rate on landing approach. Thrust reversal was upward. This reduced the tendency to raise a dust storm on unprepared strips and enhanced mechanical braking by pressing the aircraft down onto the ground.

Two YC-14s were built and the first flew on 9 August 1976. During 1977 the YC-14 demonstrated its ability to take off in 600 feet and land in 400 feet. It took off in 1,000 ft with 27,000 pounds of payload. Operation from soft dirt fields was possible and the thrust reverser position eliminated debris problems. The high bypass ratio turbofans and their overwing placement made the aircraft quite quiet. In 1977 the YC-14 made a bicentennial tour of Europe, showing off its STOL performance and load lifting ability in England, Germany and France.

One YC-14 is in storage at Davis-Monthan Air Force Base in Arizona, the other is in an aircraft museum nearby.

The Soviet counterpart of the YC-14 was the Antonov An-72. The An-72 was very similar in configuration, but was much smaller, with a length of 87 ft, wingspan of 85 ft and maximum take-off weight of 73,000 pounds. The Japanese also flew a USB aircraft based on a Kawasaki C-1.

The deflected-thrust STOL types of aircraft were more subtle in their approach. The brute force methods of VTOL were modified to co-operate with aerodynamic effects and generate greater lift, with modest forward speeds and good STOL performance. Aircraft weights were much greater, and the AMST contenders were able to take off at a STOL gross weight of 170,000 pounds and payload typically 27,000 pounds.

Although the AMST winner, the YC-15 was not purchased, it is currently being developed as the C-17. The An-72 has been stretched to produce the An-74, which is in use for arctic survey.

10 SURVIVORS

VTOL

Of all the test rigs, experimental aircraft and prototypes, very few have made it into production. Many came near. The XC-142 and CL-84 tiltwings were very close to being workable production designs, and the Dornier Do 31 would have been an ideal choice for anyone shopping for a VTOL jet transport. The Mirage IIIV won the NATO competition but was not bought. The VJ101C was an excellent supersonic VTOL design, but again did not sell.

It is not enough to design and develop an aircraft. It has to sell, and for it to sell there has to be a customer with a requirement which was met and money to spend.

The customers for fighter aircraft were the air forces, who, if faced with a choice, preferred large, fast, conventional aircraft fully equipped with all the latest in avionics and all-weather capability. Lightweight VTOL fighters did not interest them, and the larger ones such as the Mirage IIIV could not carry enough weapons far enough.

Potential buyers of transports included the armies, for battlefield use, the navies, for fleet resupply, and the air forces to service dispersed VTOL fighters. Army users were usually constrained to purchasing only lightweight aircraft, and the air forces held the purse-strings for larger ones. The air forces preferred to spend the money on strategic transports, leaving the armies without light battlefield transports. The Naval application for fleet resupply could equally well be met by much cheaper conventional types. Resupply of dispersed VTOL fighters needed several tons of fuel and weapons to be moved for each mission, and it was generally easier to do this with less vulnerable surface transport.

VTOL aircraft were not easy or cheap to make. Along with all the compromises of conventional aircraft design, they needed further compromises so that they could work in vertical flight and in transition. Engine power or thrust had to be capable of lifting aircraft weight. This demanded greater engine power, with more weight and cost. Control systems had to work in all three flight regimes, with smooth transfer during transition. Highly reliable autostabilisation was usually needed. With the engines running at hovering power, vibration and noise were problems. Vibration could cause fatigue and reduce airframe life. Noise was one feature of VTOL flight which took customers by surprise. Specifications, brochures and photos gave the impression of ideal battlefield aircraft hovering gently in mid-air. In reality the power required to hover was so great that all VTOL aircraft made a tremendous

For the *Daily Mail* Air Race, a
Harrier took off from St
Pancras Railway Station,
near the Post Office Tower,
London and flew the
Atlantic . . .
(British Aerospace)

. . . to land at a car-park near
the Empire States Building
and win the outward leg of
the race. The aircraft was
refuelled in flight.
(Rolls-Royce, Bristol)

A Harrier hovers over a field during trials. The suck-in doors around the inlets help the engine to breathe at low forward speeds.
(Rolls-Royce, Bristol)

amount of noise, much more than that of a conventional aircraft running up its engines prior to take-off.

Against this background it is hardly surprising that very few designs made it to the market place. In fact only three of the aircraft types described in previous chapters have so far led to quantity production. The P.1127 Kestrel became the Harrier, the Yak-36 contributed to the design of the Yak-38 Forger, the An-72 STOL transport was refined to become the An-74. Two more types are scheduled to enter volume production shortly. The XV-15 has been developed into the V-22 Osprey and the YC-15 has grown into the C-17.

231

Harriers working from a
dispersed site. The under-
fuselage stores also act as
lift-enhancement devices.
(Rolls-Royce, Bristol)

Harrier

The P.1127/Kestrel/Harrier programme had a chequered career. Early on it did not get much official backing and it was only the perseverance of individuals that kept the programme going. It took only ten years to get the Harrier from the drawing board into service with the armed forces, but it required another twenty years of development jointly by McDonnell Douglas and British Aerospace to produce the more acceptable Harrier II. During the three decades of development, the programme has suffered from the stops and gos of political funding. A lot of effort was diverted into the P.1154 supersonic version, only to be cancelled. On the American side a lot of work has been done on advanced derivatives, again cancelled. Perhaps it is true to say that the Western world can only afford one VTOL fighter.

Or, perhaps nearer to the truth, it can afford only one VTOL engine. The Pegasus engine was the key to the Harrier. It was the engine that came first and the airframe just grew around it. The weight of the aircraft was always limited (for VTOL) by engine thrust, and every extra pound of thrust gained by engine development was eaten by increases in airframe weight, fuel weight and weapons load. The pressure to develop the engine was enormous, but there were no other customers and the entire cost of engine development had to be borne by the one programme. It is always expensive to develop advanced technology for low-volume markets.

During the development of the Harrier, the thrust of the Pegasus increased progressively from 8,000 pounds to 21,500 pounds, but all the time users wanted more range and more payload and there was

A Harrier makes an approach during British Navy deck-landing trials. (British Aerospace)

The US Marines trials were held aboard assault ship USS Guam. (Rolls-Royce, Bristol)

VTOL

continual pressure to increase take-off weight. One way of increasing take-off weight was to use STOL. The Harrier had been designed specifically to take off vertically, however, and to convert to horizontal flight in mid-air. When used in the STOL mode, it had difficulty at take-off because of the small wing area and because the centre-wheel undercart design prevented its nose from being rotated upward during take-off. Braking was not designed for the high deceleration demanded in a short landing.

Fortunately, the short take-off problem was solved by using an up-turned runway known as the ski-jump, which provided rotation and a ballistic trajectory. Landing was no problem, because the weight after a mission was only the empty weight plus fuel reserve, about 13,000 pounds, and it would be possible to land vertically. The Harrier became STOVL, Short Take-Off Vertical Landing.

The Harrier is now famous as the only VTOL jet aircraft to enter service in the Western world, proof that it is the best of all the many attempts at jet VTOL. It is flexible in deployment and has a superb record in simulated and real battle situations.

The two-place Harrier trainer
for the US Marines was the
same as that for the RAF.
(British Aerospace)

It is in service with the British Royal Air Force as the Harrier GR Mk1 and GR Mk3, with the Royal Navy as the Sea Harrier FRS Mk1, with the US Marines as the AV-8A (Harrier Mk50), with the Spanish Navy as the AV8-A Matador (Harrier Mk50) and AV8-8S Matador (Harrier Mk55) and with the Indian Navy as the Indian Sea Harrier FRS Mk51. Tandem two-seat trainer versions are known as the T Mk2, 2A and 3 (RAF and RN), TAV-8A or Mk54 (US Marines and Spanish Navy), TAV-8S or Mk55 (Spanish Navy), and Indian Harrier T Mk60.

The Harrier has been developed jointly by British Aerospace and McDonnell Douglas to become the Harrier II. There was little freedom within the VTOL concept to make

The very first AV-8B is assembled.
(Rolls-Royce, Bristol)

fundamental changes, but the design modifications, notably weight reduction, increase in wing area and the development of lift improvement devices (LIDs) have led to a doubling of payload and range. The Harrier II is entering service with the RAF as the Harrier GR Mk5 and with the US Marines as the AV-8B and TAV-8B.

Forger

The Yak-38 Forger, originally designated Yak-36MP is the only Russian operational VTOL fighter. It was developed from the Yak-36, but there is no physical resemblance.

The fuselage of the Yak-38 is quite long at 52 ft, and is of fat, uniform cross-section for much of this length. This would imply a large internal volume, but much of this is absorbed by full-length ducting for intakes, propulsion engine and exhaust arrangements.

The propulsion engine is in mid fuselage with vectoring nozzles towards the rear of the fuselage. Two lift engines in the front fuselage provide additional lift and allow the total thrust vector to pass thorugh the centre of gravity. This is an exceptionally neat way of addressing the problems of jet VTOL and results in a compact and convenient fuselage layout. It is especially suitable for subsonic aircraft where the thrust required for VTOL greatly exceeds cruising thrust, since the lift engines provide the VTOL additional thrust with only a small weight penalty. It has the disadvantage that the extra VTOL engine power is not available to assist in manoeuvring in conventional flight.

The lift engine bay, main landing gear and heavy fuel load take up much of the fuselage space. The wing is mid-mounted and at 25ft span is smaller than that of the Yak 36. There are strakes along the underside of the fuselage, probably for lift enhancement. Further strakes along the top of the fuselage may help to prevent the lift engines from re-ingesting their own exhausts.

The method of control is unclear. There are no reaction nozzles visible at wingtips, nose or tail. Pitch may be controlled by differential engine throttling. Roll and yaw might be imparted by suitable movements of blown surfaces.

As a hybrid lift-jet/vectored thrust design, the Yak-38 requires full-time autostabilisation. It is thought to be limited to VTOL and unable to take advantage of STOL techniqes to increase its weapons load or range. It has been seen to make rolling take-offs at about 35 mph, not fast enough to generate any useful lift, but sufficient to

Several Yak-38 Forger VTOL fighter aircraft and a Ka-27 Helix helicopter are seen on the deck of the Soviet assault ship *Novorossiysk*. (via UK MoD)

prevent reingestion of the liftjet exhausts by the main and liftjet air intakes.

The Yak-38 is of comparable weight to the Harrier, but is thought to have smaller weapons load and range. Mission tasks include maritime air superiority and reconnaissance. An attack role is possible, though strikes against shipping or land-based targets would be limited by weapon load and range. It appears to carry only limited avionics and is unlikely to be able to penetrate land defences.

The Yak-38 first flew in the early seventies, and has been deployed for naval use since 1976, with about twelve examples now in service on each of the four aircraft carriers, *Kiev*, *Minsk*, *Baku* and *Novorossiysk*.

Coaler

The Boeing YC-14 STOL transport was too

expensive to replace the economical Lockheed Hercules, but its Russian counterpart, the Antonov An-72 had more success. This was developed into the An-74, which is replacing the aged Il-14 in arctic survey operations.

The An-74 is a little longer and heavier than the An-72 prototypes, and has added outboard wing sections which extend the span from 85 to 105 ft. With the longer wing, fuel consumption is reduced and the operational range is greatly extended. The flight deck crew comprises two pilots, engineer and navigator. The An-74 carries additional communication and navigation equipment and a large plotting table which permits the recording of ice-floe positions. The cabin is usually equipped for general arctic duties, with the rear available for cargo and the front divided between seating and sleeping accommodation.

Although the An-72/74 are not VTOL

The cameras of Royal Navy Frigate *Torquay* capture this photo of a Yak-38 hovering over Soviet warship *Kiev*. The doors above and below the lift engines are open, and the port propulsion engine nozzle is vectored downward. Roll control is probably by nozzles. (Royal Navy).

types, they can support about half their weight on engine thrust. They do not have VTOL control systems and flight at low speed is controlled by the normal aerodynamic flying surfaces. At low speed, the controls have less effect and aircraft attitude is more critical. The An-74 is fitted with special instruments which display angle of attack, yaw and vertical speed to assist the pilots to maintain the correct attitude during slow flight.

early Transcendental Model 1 G which flew in 1954-5, moving to the Bell XV-3 programme which got airborne in 1955 and continued through to 1965, and the XV-15, started in 1973 and still flying.

During the XV-15 programme, Bell joined forces with Boeing Vertol to submit a tiltrotor design in the Joint Services Advanced Vertical Lift Aircraft (JVX) programme. Bell's continuous involvement in tiltrotors from 1951 and Boeing's experience

Most of the aircraft seen here on *Kiev* are the single-seat Forger-A. The exception is aircraft 04, which is a two-seat Forger-B. (Royal Air Force)

C-17

The McDonnell Douglas C-17 will be a large transport based on the YC-15 and of general appearance similar to that of a C-141 with vertical winglets at the wingtips. As in the YC-15, lift will be enhanced more by the aerodynamic interaction of engine exhausts and flaps than by actual deflection of engine thrust.

Osprey

The Osprey is the result of four decades of design and development, starting with the

with the Vertol 76 tiltwing and many heavy helicopters won them a contract from the Naval Air Systems Command in April 1983. Their tiltrotor design became known as the V-22 Osprey during 1986 with an incentive award from the Navy in May and Department of Defense approval of a full-scale development programme in December.

The V-22 Osprey, flew first on 19 March 1989 and is due to enter service in 1991; it is the first practical application of Bell's forty years of continuous tiltrotor research and development. It is designed to meet the needs of the US Army, Air Force, Navy and Marines for a VTOL transport capable of fast horizontal flight; current

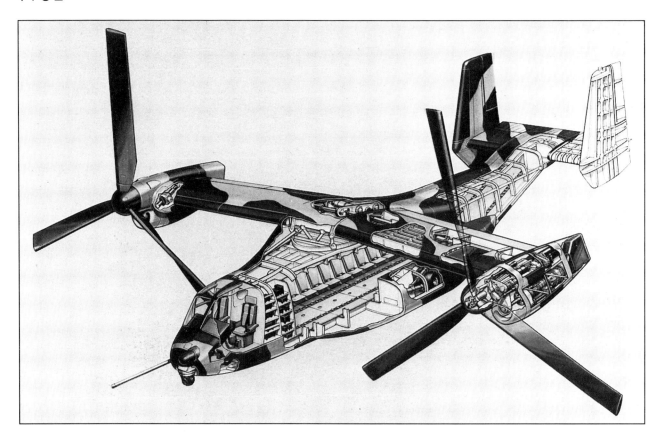

production requirements call for 900 to 1200 machines.

The V-22 is very much a scaled-up XV-15, and is of the same general configuration, though having a greatly increased gross weight of 40,000 pounds, a length of 57 feet, wingspan 45 feet and rotors of 38 feet in diameter. The fuselage of V-22 has interior dimensions 6ft by 6ft by 24ft, and can accommodate 24 combat-equipped troops or equivalent cargo loaded via a tail ramp. Sponsons on each side of the fuselage accommodate the main undercarriage, freeing the cabin of obstructions. The sponsons also carry part of the fuel load, and provide a measure of flotation in the event of ditching.

The wing is mounted above the fuselage on a seven foot diameter annular steel ring, or carousel. This permits the wing to be rotated parallel to the fuselage for shipboard storage. Prior to wing rotation, the rotor blades are folded and the engines are tilted from the vertical landing position back to the horizontal. Wing rotation is automatic and takes only 90 seconds.

The V-22 is powered by two Allison T406-AD-400 turboshaft engines. These will be rated initially at 6,000 shp, with future growth to 10,000 shp. As in the XV-15, a shaft through the wing will permit either engine to drive both rotors. An auxiliary

power unit, mounted at mid-wing, can be used to start the main engines, making the V-22 totally self-sufficient in the field.

The structure of the V-22 uses the latest composite material technology to obtain maximum strength with minimum weight. The 13,000 pounds of structure includes more than 6,000 pounds of graphite epoxy and only 1,000 pounds of metal.

The V-22 is designed for both VTOL and STOL operations. Its normal mission gross weight of 40,000 pounds can be increased to 47,000 pounds while retaining VTOL capability, and to 59,000 pounds as a STOL with 500 ft take-off run. External loads up to 15,000 pounds can be lifted.

In horizontal flight, the V-22 will be able to cruise at 275 knots and at altitudes up to 30,000 feet. This performance is comparable with that of the Gumman E-2C Hawkeye airborne-early-warning aircraft.

The Marine Corps version of the V-22 is the MV-22A, of which 552 are on order. Mission requirements include carriage of 24 fully-equipped troops 200 nautical miles, hover out of ground effect at 3,000ft altitude and 91.5°F, carriage of 10,000 pounds external load, operation from amphibious ships and world-wide self-deployment. The US Army will most likely take 231 of the Marines MV-22A Osprey to carry 24 troops, 12 litters, or 10,000 pounds of payload over

This view of the Bell-Boeing V-22 Osprey shows the internal structure and mechanism. The port nacelle is cut away to show the engine, the reducation gearbox and the rotor collective and cyclic pitch control mechanism. The wing is cut away to show the power transfer shaft connecting the two rotos. The tilt jack can be seen in the starboard nacelle. The circular carouselle permits the wing to be rotated to minimise under-deck stowage space. (Boeing)

The Osprey was rolled out in camouflage colours. These were applied in washable paint over the all-white colour scheme chosen for initial flight trials. (Boeing)

a 50 nautical mile mission radius at speeds up to 250 knots.

The US Navy has ordered 50 HV-22A Ospreys for combat search and rescue (SCAR), and 300 of a further V-22 variant to replace the Lockheed S-3 Viking anti-submarine warfare aircraft.

The US Air Force version is the CV-22A, and 80 have been ordered. These will replace the HH-53 fleet and will be able to carry 12 troops over a 540 nautical mile radius with the ability to hover at 4,000 feet and 95°F at mission midpoint.

Bell and Boeing will both make complete aircraft, and will supply sub-assemblies to each other for final production. They will then bid for contracts in competition with each other.

Pointer

Bell and Boeing are also working on another tiltrotor aircraft, the tiny Pointer Remotely Piloted Vehicle (RPV). This weighs only 500 pounds and is transportable by three people. Its fuselage is 12 ft long and it has a single fin and a rectangular tailplane. The high-mounted wing is of 11 ft span and the two tilting rotors are each 5ft in diameter. A 95 hp motor in the fuselage runs at 8000 rpm and is geared to drive the cross-shaft at 3000 rpm and the rotors at 1500 rpm. The tilt and control mechanisms at the wing tips are especially simple, with separate actuators for tilt, cyclic pitch, and (on one side only) differential collective pitch.

The Pointer carries a TV camera in its nose and can be radio-controlled at distances of up to 100 nautical miles with up to 5 hours loiter time over target. Vertical take-off and landing capabilities make launch and recovery much easier than with other RPVs. No launch ramp or catch net is needed. Missions include pure reconnaissance, target designation, night use with forward-looking infra-red (FLIR), electronic intelligence (ELINT), radar jamming, and communications relay.

The Pointer has flown and should be in production in the early nineties.

247